Publications of the
Center for Medieval
and Renaissance Studies,
UCLA

Jesus as Mother

In the twelfth century, a new awareness of differing social statuses or roles, each with religious significance, was reflected in literary and artistic images. In this illustration of the virtues and vices, the miniaturist has altered the conventional motif of a procession of monks toward the "crown of life" into a depiction of roles with their characteristic temptations: the lay woman and the knight, tempted by ornament and fornication; the cleric, tempted by luxury, including wealth, food and a friend (*amica clerici*); the nun, seduced by the gifts of priests, the pomp of the world, and the wealth of relatives; the monk, wooed by property and money; the recluse, longing for his bed; and the hermit, distracted by thoughts of his garden.

Jesus as Mother

Studies in the Spirituality
of the High Middle Ages

Caroline Walker Bynum

University
of California
Press
Berkeley
Los Angeles
London

The illustration facing title page is the
"Ladder of Virtues," from Hortus Deliciarum
(destroyed manuscript formerly in Strasbourg),
fol. 215v. Photograph by E. G. C. Menzies,
Princeton, N.J.; pl. IX of a hand-colored
copy of C. M. Engelhardt, *Herrad von Landsperg* . . .
(Stuttgart/Tübingen, 1818), in possession
of the Metropolitan Museum of Art, New York;
reproduced from R. Green *et al.*,
Herrad of Hohenbourg, Hortus Deliciarum
(London/Leiden, 1979), Pl. 124.

University of California Press
Berkeley and Los Angeles, California

University of California Press, Ltd.
London, England

© 1982 by
The Regents of the University of California

First Paperback Printing 1984

ISBN 0-520-05222-6

Printed in the United States of America

4   5   6   7   8   9

Library of Congress Cataloging in Publication Data

Bynum, Caroline Walker.
  Jesus as mother.

  Includes indexes.
    1. Spiritual life—Middle Ages, 600–1500—
Addresses, essays, lectures.   2. Monastic and
religious life—Middle Ages, 600–1500—Addresses,
essays, lectures.   3. God—Motherhood—History of
doctrines—Middle Ages, 600–1500—Addresses,
essays, lectures.   I. Title.
BV4490.B96   255   81-13137
                   AACR2

Contents

CONTENTS

Preface

A̲ᴜᴛʜᴏʀꜱ ᴏꜰ collections of essays often comment at the outset that nothing has been changed in their older work except obvious errors, either because resetting the originals was prohibitively expensive or because the author found it impossible or unnecessary to rethink the earlier formulations. My situation is different. For, in going back to work done during the 1970's, I found much that could be reformulated or clarified, much that needed to be put in a broader context—and the University of California Press has made it possible for me to do so. Thus, although the first four essays published here bear the titles of earlier articles and continue to address the historical problems and the historiography that gave rise to their namesakes, each has been substantially rewritten. I have revised these studies, not in order to link them artificially into an overview of the twelfth and thirteenth centuries (which they were never intended to be), but in an effort to make each a better and more broadly based case for the interpretation presented in the original article. I have also emphasized—in the introduction, in the revised essays, and in the new study that concludes the book—the methodological and substantive concerns that give unity to the work I have done over the past seven years. I am grateful to the publishers of *Medievalia et Humanistica*, the *Harvard Theological Review*, and the *Journal of Ecclesiastical History* for permission to publish new versions of earlier articles in a context that makes their interrelationship clearer and allows them to serve as background to a new study of thirteenth-century nuns.

I would also like to express my gratitude to the students in my seminar at the Harvard Divinity School (spring, 1976), who helped me to articulate my approach to religious imagery; to the members of the University of Washington Faculty Seminar on Religion (fall, 1978), who contributed to my understanding of religious authority; to the American Council of Learned Societies for a grant for fall and winter of 1978–79; to Emily L. D. Baker, Andrea Fahlenkamp, Sheryl Feldman, Margery A. Kepner, and Fred Paxton, who helped with the typing and copy editing; to my editor, Karen Reeds, for her perceptive suggestions; and to numerous friends and colleagues who read portions of these essays and gave advice. I have thanked below in the notes those who helped with individual articles, but I should mention here several mentors without whose encouragement and sometimes harsh criticism the whole collection would never have taken shape: Robert Benson, John Benton, Peter Brown, Giles Constable, C. Warren Hollister, Brian Stock, and Charles T. Wood. The book is dedicated, with deep appreciation and affection, to my fellow scholars in the field of religion, Guenther Roth and Judith Van Herik, whose values and insights have frequently provided the context within which I ask questions.

Seattle, Washington
September, 1980

Abbreviations

AASS   J. Bollandus and G. Henschenius, *Acta sancto-rum . . . editio novissima*, ed. J. Carnandet et al. (Paris, 1863–).

CCCM   Corpus christianorum: continuatio medievalis (Turnhout, 1966–).

COCR   *Collectanea ordinis Cisterciensium Reformatorum* (Rome, 1934–), superseded by *Collectanea Cisterciensia* (Rome, 1965–).

CSEL   Corpus scriptorum ecclesiasticorum latinorum (Vienna, 1866–).

DHGE   *Dictionnaire d'histoire et de géographie ecclésiastiques* (Paris, 1912–).

DS   *Dictionnaire de spiritualité, ascétique et mystique, doctrine et histoire* (Paris, 1932–).

DTC   *Dictionnaire de théologie catholique,* 15 vols. and *Tables générales* (Paris, 1909–1950).

OB   *Sancti Bernardi opera,* ed. J. Leclercq, C. H. Talbot, and H. M. Rochais (Rome, 1957–).

PL   *Patrologiae cursus completus: series latina,* ed. J.-P. Migne, 221 vols. (Paris, 1841–1864).

RAM   *Revue d'ascétique et de mystique* (Toulouse, 1920–1971), superseded by *Revue d'histoire de la spiritualité* (Paris, 1972–   ).

RB   *Benedicti Regula*, ed. R. Hanslik, CSEL 75 (Vienna, 1960).

RHE   *Revue d'histoire ecclésiastique* (Louvain, 1900–   ).

SC, Sér. mon.   Sources chrétiennes (Paris, 1941–   ), Série des textes monastiques d'Occident (Paris, 1958–   ).

Introduction

———✦

"Have women and priests pray for me."
—A SUFFERING SOUL
TO MECHTILD OF MAGDEBURG

THE OPPORTUNITY to rethink and republish several of my early articles in combination with a new essay on the thirteenth century has led me to consider the continuity—both of argument and of approach—that underlies them. In one sense, their interrelationship is obvious. The first two address a question that was more in the forefront of scholarship a dozen years ago than it is today: the question of differences among religious orders. These two essays set out a method of reading texts for imagery and borrowings as well as for spiritual teaching in order to determine whether individuals who live in different institutional settings hold differing assumptions about the significance of their lives. The essays apply the method to the broader question of differences between regular canons and monks and the narrower question of differences between one kind of monk—the Cistercians—and other religious groups, monastic and nonmonastic, of the twelfth century. The third essay draws on some of the themes of the first two, particularly the discussion of canonical and Cistercian conceptions of the individual brother as example, to suggest an interpretation of twelfth-century religious life as concerned with the nature of groups as well as with affective expression. The fourth essay, again on Cistercian monks, elaborates themes of the first three. Its subsidiary goals are to provide further evidence on distinctively Cistercian attitudes and to elaborate the Cistercian ambivalence about vocation that I delineate in the essay on conceptions of community. It also raises questions that have now become popular in non-academic as well as academic circles: what significance should we give to the increase of feminine imagery in twelfth-century religious writing by males? Can we learn anything about distinctively male or female spiritualities from this feminization of language? The fifth essay differs from the others in turning to the thirteenth century rather than the twelfth, to women rather than men, to detailed analysis of many themes in a few thinkers rather than one theme in many writers; it is nonetheless based on the conclusions of the earlier studies. The sense of monastic vocation and of the priesthood, of the authority of God and self, and of the significance of gender that I find in the three great mystics of late-thirteenth-century Helfta can be understood only against the background of the growing twelfth- and thirteenth-century concern for evangelism and for an approachable God, which are the basic themes of the first four essays.

Such connections between the essays will be clear to anyone who reads them. There are, however, deeper methodological and interpretive continuities among them that I wish to underline here. For these studies constitute a plea for an approach to medieval spirituality that is not now—and perhaps has never been—dominant in medieval scholarship. They also provide an interpretation of the religious life of the high Middle Ages that runs against the grain of recent emphases on the emergence of "lay spirituality." I therefore propose to give, as introduction, both a discussion of recent approaches to medieval piety and a short sketch of the religious history of the twelfth and thirteenth centuries, emphasizing those themes that are the context for my specific investigations. I do not want to be misunderstood. In providing here a discussion of approaches to and trends in medieval religion I am not claiming that the studies that follow constitute a general history nor that my method should *replace* that of social, institutional, and intellectual historians. A handful of Cistercians does not typ-ify the twelfth century, nor three nuns the thirteenth. Religious imagery, on which I concentrate, does not tell us how people lived. But because these essays approach texts in a way others have not done, focus on imagery others have not found important, and insist, as others have not insisted, on comparing groups to other groups (e.g., comparing what is peculiarly male to what is female as well as vice versa), I want to call attention to my approach to and my interpretation of the high Middle Ages in the hope of en-couraging others to ask similar questions.

Approaches to the History of Spirituality

"Spirituality," as André Vauchez has pointed out, is not a me-dieval word at all.[1] It was coined in the nineteenth century to des-ignate a field of study that might also be called ascetic or mystical theology. Thirty or forty years ago, books on the history of medi-eval spirituality were surveys of various theories of the stages of the soul's ascent to contemplation or union. Recently the history of spirituality has come to mean something quite different: the study of how basic religious attitudes and values are conditioned by the society within which they occur. This new definition brings spir-ituality very close to what the school of French historians known as *annalistes* call *mentalité*; the "history of spirituality" becomes al-most a branch of social history, deeply influenced by the work of structural-functionalist anthropologists and of phenomenologists of religion.

The new history of spirituality has increasingly been domi-nated by an interest in popular religion. This interest has involved, first, a determination to study those phenomena that might reveal the religious aspirations of the illiterate and, second, an interpreta-tion of the period from 1100 to 1517 as "the emergence of lay spirituality"—that is, the increasing diffusion outward into society from the monastery of religious practices and values and a new

---

1. André Vauchez, Introd., *La spiritualité du moyen âge occidental VIIIe–XIIe siècles*, Collection SUP (Paris, 1975), pp. 5–8.

willingness to define roles in the world as having religious significance. Reviving certain emphases of German scholarship in the first decades of this century, scholars are now also deeply interested in the class background of those who peopled the religious movements of the high Middle Ages.

In addition to the emphasis on social context, current work on Christianity in the twelfth and thirteenth centuries shows other common emphases. Continuing the interpretation of the French scholar, André Wilmart,[2] recent studies stress the new psychological subtlety and interiority of twelfth-century religion and tend to see the affective spirituality of the Cistercians and later the Franciscans as the dominant note in the religious writing of the period. Insofar as the spirituality of women has been treated—and it has been surprisingly neglected when we consider that the most important work on twelfth and thirteenth-century religion in the past fifty years has been Grundmann's study of the beguines[3]—it has been treated as an aspect of this new affective emphasis. Furthermore, in direct and intended contrast to earlier histories of spirituality, the new scholarship avoids the question of the particular characteristics of religious orders (e.g., Franciscans as opposed to Dominicans, Cistercians in contrast to old-style Benedictines), attempting instead to set out those features that characterize many groups, including the heterodox. Following the lead of Grundmann and M. D. Chenu,[4] recent work, while showing a keen interest in heresy, nonetheless sees dissident groups as basically reformist. It sees the most pressing issues of the period as matters not of doctrine but of practice or what we might call lifestyle, particularly the question of what "true poverty" is and of how "evangelism" (which comes increasingly to mean preaching) is to be carried out.

2. André Wilmart, *Auteurs spirituels et textes dévots du moyen âge latin: Études d'histoire littéraire* (Paris, 1932). See below, pp. 83–84 and 134.

3. Herbert Grundmann, *Religiöse Bewegungen im Mittelalter: Untersuchungen über die geschichtlichen Zusammenhänge zwischen der Ketzerei, den Bettelorden und der religiösen Frauenbewegung im 12. und. 13. Jahrhundert* . . . (1935; reprint ed. with additions, Hildesheim, 1961).

4. Marie-Dominique Chenu, *La théologie au douzième siècle*, Études de philosophie médiévale 45 (Paris, 1957).

Much current work on medieval religion has thus abandoned the sources that were so carefully studied by scholars half a century ago—mystical treatises, sermons, biblical commentaries, works of advice for novices, collections of visions, saints' lives—and turned instead to prosopographical work or to analysis of artifacts with which the laity had contact, documents the laity executed (mostly wills and charters), and rituals the laity attended. Use of these materials presents enormous methodological problems, however, if—having established what lay people did or which groups they joined—we then try to ascertain the religious meaning of these facts. For example, lay people frequently behave as they do because they have been told to do so by priests; priests are themselves, in the absence of hereditary succession, recruited from lay society; if lay people do not write, the question of what a "lay attitude" is becomes exceedingly difficult to establish in any way other than by arbitrary definition.[5] The new history of spirituality is therefore in a curious situation. It has abandoned detailed study of most of the material medieval people themselves produced on the subject of religion in favor of far more intractable sources. It has done this partly from the admirable desire to correct the concentration of earlier scholarship on mainline groups (i.e., those who succeeded in recruiting members and presenting their visions of the Christian life to others) but partly, I suspect, from boredom and frustration with the interminable discussions of the soul's approach to God, which is the major subject of medieval religious writing.[6]

5. This point is made by Marie-Humbert Vicaire, Introd., *Assistance et charité*, Cahiers de Fanjeaux: Collection d'histoire religieuse du Languedoc au XIIIe et au début de XIVe siècles 13 (Toulouse, 1978), p. 7.

6. A few examples of the new approach are Raoul Manselli, *La religion populaire au moyen âge: problèmes de méthode et d'histoire*, Conférence Albert-le-Grand 1973 (Montreal and Paris, 1975); Vauchez, *La spiritualité*; Patrick J. Geary, *Furta Sacra: Thefts of Relics in the Central Middle Ages* (Princeton, 1978); Lester K. Little, *Religious Poverty and the Profit Economy in Medieval Europe* (Ithaca, 1978); Alexander Murray, *Reason and Society in the Middle Ages* (Oxford, 1978), pp. 317–404. And see below, p. 24. Solid institutional and legal histories of specific houses and orders and their rules continue, of course, to appear and to add to our knowledge.

We cannot, however, afford to abandon what will always be the bulk of our information on medieval religion. Nor can we afford to abandon questions of how one group contrasts with another—whether these groups be differentiated by gender (men and women) or status (cleric and layperson) or vocation (Franciscan and Cistercian)—simply because these issues have often been raised polemically by members of the groups in question. We urgently need a middle ground between the older history of doctrine or mystical theology, which has exhaustively catalogued medieval theories of purgation and contemplation, and the newer stress on the changing social context of religious movements. In addition to new kinds of material, we need new ways of reading the material we have had all along, new ways of determining how the differences between people are reflected in their discussions of topics that tradition and convention required them to treat in ostensibly similar manners. If we are ever to know what gave significance to life for even some of the medieval population, which aspects of reality they were rejecting and which they were affirming when they "renounced the world," where they felt themselves able to make choices, and what they felt to be the important differences in the roles open to them or imposed upon them, we must find ways of answering these questions from the works they actually wrote.

In the essays that follow, I have tried to find new ways of using this conventional material by concentrating on the images in which religious people presented their theories of the soul's journey. Imagery has, of course, often been studied by medievalists, most commonly with a view to determining its sources in earlier writings or using it to test medieval theories of language but sometimes with the idea that it may supplement other information about medieval life. (For example, a metaphor in which a king or a plow figures just might include a detail about medieval kings or plows that we would otherwise not know.) None of these approaches is very helpful in determining basic religious attitudes, and the attempt to argue from the details of metaphors to social reality can be positively misleading if one assumes that people construct images from what they actually perceive without realizing that images may just as frequently reflect what people *wish* they perceived. But if we trace the networks of images built up by medieval authors and locate those networks in the psyches and social experiences of those who create or use them, we find that they reveal to us what the writers cared about most deeply themselves and what they felt it necessary to present or justify to others.

In each of my studies I have attempted to penetrate to the basic concerns of authors by analyzing very carefully a few images or phrases. For example, in the first two essays, a study of the verbs *love, teach, serve, re-form,* or *be a form (pattern) for* becomes a way of detecting which activities a certain kind of religious person feels most obligated to perform as part of his vocation; in the fourth article, a study of the metaphorical uses of *mother, nurse, womb, breast,* and *feed* leads into an exploration of concepts of leadership; in the fifth study, analysis of the full range of images used by three women to talk about their own authority and God's becomes a way of establishing what the women felt entitled to do and why. These essays are thus sometimes a kind of psycho-historical interpretation, sometimes a structural interpretation, without being linked closely to any current body of psychological or structuralist theory. I have simply assumed that the emotional significance of a word or image (even very common words) cannot be inferred from its modern meaning but must be established by a careful study of the other images and phrases among which it occurs in a text. I have also assumed that the more images or phrases depart in certain ways from traditions to which they otherwise belong or link aspects of reality not obviously linked by common sense, logic, or previous usage, the more they convey the needs, the anxieties, and the sources of repose in the hearts of men and women. I have then tried to place these needs, anxieties, and solutions in the context of the interpersonal experiences that formed personalities and the kinds of communities within which people lived.[7] For example, in the third essay, I show that mechanical metaphors of

7. I am in agreement with the methodological statement made by Jean Leclercq in *Monks and Love in Twelfth-Century France: Psycho-Historical Essays* (Oxford, 1979), pp. 1–7, although not with some of his conclusions; see my review in *Speculum* 55 (1980): 595–97. My understanding of how one ought to relate images to the social context of the authors

putting on garments, constructing buildings, or stamping out patterns appear in twelfth-century literature alongside organic images of burgeoning or flowering; that these metaphors express intense concern for conforming personal behavior and community life to prescribed patterns; and that such patterns are seen as the precondition for the flowering of souls toward God. Thus the affectivity or psychological subtlety so emphasized in recent interpretations of the twelfth-century is rooted in a new concern with external behavior, and the new concern with externals is in turn rooted in a proliferation of religious and social groups. In the fourth and fifth essays, I suggest that images taken from friendship, marriage, and family grow more common and more complex in the twelfth and thirteenth centuries, supplementing but not replacing older images of ruler and follower, and that these images reflect a need, felt especially by males, for a view of authority that balances discipline with love. In the fifth study, I argue that images of food and drink, of brimming fountains and streams of blood, which are used with special intensity by thirteenth-century women, express desire for direct, almost physical contact with Christ in the eucharist and for power to handle this Christ as only the priest is authorized to do.

However partial the picture of the twelfth and thirteenth centuries presented by the five topics treated here, these studies suggest that broadening the history of spirituality from a history of mystical theology to a history of religious attitudes need not involve abandoning the spiritual treatises, saints' lives, and collections of visions that medieval people produced in such relative abundance. In addition to study of rules and institutions, crowd movements and persecutions, social conditions, and the diffusion of texts, careful reading of spiritual treatises can reveal to us shifts in sensibility and values. For such treatises take us into the complexities of a few hearts, and in these complexities we find reflected, if we read with sensitivity, the ways in which larger groups of people were burdened or healed, oppressed or encouraged, by the structures of the church and by society.

---

who produce them is deeply indebted to Clifford Geertz's influential article: "Religion as a Cultural System," in Michael Banton, ed., *Anthropological Approaches to the Study of Religion*, Association of Social Anthropologists Monographs 3 (London, 1966), pp. 1–42.

The Religious Revival of the Twelfth and Thirteenth Centuries and the Clericalization of the Church

The essays that follow have been written in the context of the recent history of spirituality and assume many of its most persuasive and original insights. But they differ from that history, not only in turning back to the kind of source material treated by the old-style history of doctrine but also in seeing at the heart of twelfth- and thirteenth-century developments the problem of authority. In the post-Gregorian church the roles of clergy and laity were more carefully distinguished than they had been before. Although the separation did in the long run prepare the way for a positive valuation of the secular qua secular, the short-run effect was increased prominence and power to the clergy. Each of my studies finds at the core of high medieval spirituality not only the growth of affective response and the rise of the laity but also deep desire for and fear of the clergy's right to rule and to serve. Because each essay in certain ways assumes this latter trend and none describes it directly, it seems wise to conclude my introduction with a brief sketch of the clericalization of the church.

The first five hundred years of Christianity had established that a male clergy, whose authority was based on office, would serve as the fundamental channel of God's message and God's grace to the laity—that is, all men (including monks) who were not clergy and all women. But despite the continuing importance of ecclesiastical office, the early Middle Ages have frequently been seen as the period of "monastic spirituality," both in the sense that monks were the vicarious worshippers for all of society and in the sense that the monastic role was held up to all as the Christian ideal. To ordinary people in the ninth and tenth centuries contact with the clergy was often limited to baptism, burial, and paying tithes; bishops were far more visible for their control of large feudal properties than for their pastoral care; Rome was important not as an administrative center but as the residence of St. Peter, whose relics were charged with special power. Salvation, for oneself and one's relatives, came by making gifts to monks and nuns who said the prayers that assured a right relationship to God. More immediate needs, like the fertility of one's fields or one's cow or one's beehive, might as often be taken care of by "wise women and men" or "white magic" as by the blessing of priests or holy water. The most significant locations of holiness and supernatural power were the relics of saints. It was the Gregorian Reform movement of the mid-eleventh century that created a church headed by the clergy and began the process of locating supernatural power most centrally in the eucharist, which the priest controlled. Moreover, the great religious revival of the same period— usually known as the "search for the *vita apostolica*"—created so many new nonmonastic or quasi-monastic models for a specialized religious life that male monasticism never recovered from the challenge.[8]

Beginning with an attack on simony and clerical marriage, Gregorian reformers hoped to impose generally on the clergy what was in the mid-eleventh century called "the apostolic or full common life" (i.e., renunciation of private property) and to extricate the church from the control of feudal rulers by renouncing feudal relationships. Because, as G. Tellenbach has pointed out,[9] to a medieval person freedom meant "freedom to" as well as "freedom from," the reformers increasingly saw the extrication of church property and personnel from the control of secular rulers as a precondition for the church's exercise of its leadership role. Their work began the century and a half of development that made the church the most advanced bureaucracy in Europe.

8. To say this is to take the long view and see the friars (an institutional innovation and not a monastic reform) as the culmination of the twelfth-century religious revival. I do not mean to detract in any way from the Cistercians and other new monks, who were, in the twelfth century, more successful at recruiting members than regular canons, who were clerics by definition. See Jean Leclercq, François Vandenbroucke, and Louis Bouyer, *La spiritualité du moyen âge*, Histoire de la spiritualité chrétienne 2 (Paris, 1960), pp. 233–72 and 345–46; Marie-Humbert Vicaire, *L'imitation des apôtres: moines, chanoines, mendiants (IVᵉ–XIIIᵉ siècles)* (Paris, 1963); and Louis Bouyer, *The Cistercian Heritage*, trans. E. A. Livingstone (Westminster, Md., 1958). For general bibliography on the religious revival, see below, pp. 22–25.

9. Gerd Tellenbach, *Church, State and Christian Society at the Time of the Investiture Contest*, trans. R. F. Bennett (Oxford, 1948).

The post-Gregorian church is a break from the early Middle Ages in several senses. The reformers' successful campaign for clerical celibacy and their emphasis on the freedom of episcopal elections (which fairly rapidly became papal appointments) created a clergy that was set apart much more radically than before from ordinary Christians and was also welded into a hierarchy. In the course of the twelfth century, canon law was elaborated, the sacraments were defined, the penitential system and theory that functioned in the later Middle Ages were established, and higher education was brought firmly under the control of the church with the result that advanced theological training became by definition the preserve of the clergy and denied to women. The Gregorian reformers thus began a process that sharply expanded the clergy's service of and control over the laity. Clerical status—an amorphous concept in the early twelfth century when *clericus* often meant simply "ordained" or "literate"—was increasingly defined as the right to preach and practice the *cura animarum*; the role of the priest in consecrating the eucharist was more and more held in awe. "Oh revered dignity of priests, in whose hands the Son of God is incarnated as in the Virgin's womb . . ." reads an often cited twelfth-century text.[10] And the following lines have been attributed to the wandering preacher Norbert of Xanten, who founded an order of clerics:

> Priest, you are not you, because you are God.
> You are not yours, because you are Christ's servant
> and minister.
>
> You are not of yourself because you are nothing.
> What therefore are you, oh priest? Nothing and all
> things . . .[11]

As clerical direction of the laity increased, however, the clergy was removed further and further from the lifestyle of the laity and from certain kinds of contact with women and family. Although

10. Quoted in Yves Congar, "Modèle monastique et modèle sacerdotal en Occident de Grégoire VII (1073–1085) à Innocent III (1198)," *Études de civilisation médiévale (IXe–XIIe siècles): mélanges offerts à Edmond-René Labande* (Poitiers, 1973), p. 159.
11. Quoted in ibid.

twelfth-century theologians argued that marriage is a sacrament, these same theologians held the clergy to be "purer" once they renounced it. Moreover, the reformers, in their distinction between the bishop's sacramental authority and the property that was the economic base for his administration, and in their attacks on sacerdotal kingship, initiated that awareness of a sharp line between sacred and secular, spiritual and material, that is such a striking feature of more modern western Christianity. From the world of the early Middle Ages, in which the supernatural may break into everyday life at any moment and anything may be a sign or "sacrament" of the holy, we move in the twelfth century into a world in which what we today call the material or secular is increasingly seen as having its own laws and operations, as *other than* the spiritual and perhaps even corrupting to it. To ninth-century theologians, for example, the problem in dealing with the eucharist was really the problem of explaining how it could be of special import when in fact any object or event might suddenly reveal God; by the thirteenth century the problem was to explain how bread and wine, which looked like bread and wine, could be anything else.

But the later eleventh century saw other changes in Christianity as fundamental as the new Gregorian sense of the spiritual, the clergy, and the church as separate from and dominant over the secular world. The years between 1050 and 1216 saw a proliferation of new types of specialized religious vocations, all of which departed from the old model of the monk, withdrawn from the world by renunciation of family and marriage and private property but part of a wealthy collectivity that offered to God an elaborate and splendid cycle of public prayer. Some of these new groups withdrew to barren and threatening wilderness, receiving only uncleared areas free of feudal ties and living a "poverty" that meant hard manual labor, near starvation, and great personal isolation. Other groups—and this was increasingly true as the period wore on—interpreted the "apostolic life" not simply as personal poverty and hardship but also as preaching the gospel in imitation of Christ's disciples; they formed wandering bands that went from place to place whipping up religious fervor, often to the considerable discontent of local religious authorities. Although it has become standard in the scholarship to say that all these groups, including some who followed the dualist Cathars, represented shades of reform concern more than doctrinal aberration,[12] it is clear that some of these individuals were not merely clerics (like Norbert of Xanten) who wanted to provide for the growing urban population, or lay people (like some of the Patarenes) who wanted a purer clergy, or even lay people (like Francis of Assisi and Peter Valdes) who simply tried to follow Christ literally and spread the sense of joy they found in so doing. Some were indeed attacking the authority of the clergy so greatly expanded by the Gregorian reform. In any case, throughout the new types of religious life created in the twelfth century ran a tension, present also in the Gregorian ideology, between withdrawal from and service of the world. But with the founding of the friars in the early thirteenth century a new religious role was created, whose core was a combination of evangelical preaching and radical renunciation of material support. The old monastic goal of personal salvation through withdrawal and salvation of society through prayer was eclipsed; the male talent of Europe flocked to the friars. Monasteries, of course, continued to play an important role in intellectual and economic as well as religious life. But the major philosophical, theological, and spiritual leaders of Europe in the thirteenth century were Franciscans and Dominicans. Thus, by the mid-thirteenth century not only had the clerical hierarchy expanded its responsibility for and its authority over the world but the most visible

12. This emphasis in recent scholarship derives from the ground-breaking work of Grundmann (*Religiöse Bewegungen*), who was reacting against interpretations that stressed social and economic causes. For a fine recent synthesis in the Grundmann tradition, see Malcolm Lambert, *Medieval Heresy: Popular Movements from Bogomil to Hus* (New York, 1976). We are just beginning to see criticism of Grundmann, both from scholars who follow him but wish for a more precise exploration of the social setting of religious movements (e.g., John B. Freed, *The Friars and German Society in the Thirteenth Century*, Medieval Academy of America Publications 86 [Cambridge, Mass., 1977]) and from scholars who go further in opposing Grundmann's view of the twelfth century as a spectrum of reformist movements and see anticlericalism as fundamental (e.g., R. I. Moore, *The Origins of European Dissent* [New York, 1977], especially pp. 82–114; see also R. E. Lerner, review of Moore, *American Historical Review* 83 [1978]: 698–99, and Brian Stock, review of Lambert, *The Historian* 40 [1978]: 530–31).

and apparently attractive form of "Christ's poor" who renounced the world were also devoted to pastoral care and preaching. The basic male religious role therefore became that of preacher and administrator of the sacraments (chiefly penance and eucharist); authority in this role derived from both office (i.e., ordination) and lifestyle.

These fundamental changes in attitudes and institutions had important consequences for women. In contrast to the central Middle Ages, in which few female monasteries were founded, the twelfth- and thirteenth-century search for the *vita apostolica* attracted so many women to a specialized religious life that contemporary chroniclers themselves commented upon the phenomenon, sometimes with admiration and sometimes with trepidation. Women flocked to wandering preachers, like Norbert of Xanten and Robert of Arbrissel, and these preachers founded monasteries for them, never intending to establish bands of itinerant female evangelists. The number of Premonstratensian and Cistercian houses for women grew at a speed that alarmed the orders. The Premonstratensians were the first to curtail this growth, followed by the Cistercians. But recent research has shown that the Cistercian decree of 1228 forbidding the incorporation of any more convents remained a dead letter, and throughout the thirteenth century Cistercian nunneries proliferated in the Low Countries and lower Rhineland. In addition, among those known as the beguines (found especially in northern France, the Low Countries, Switzerland, and the Rhineland, but paralleled in some ways in the south by the mendicant third orders and heretical groups, like the Humiliati), we find what is probably the first "women's movement" in western history. These women chose to set themselves apart from the world by living austere, poor lives in which manual labor and service were joined to worship (which was not, however, rigidly prescribed as it was in convents). At least initially they contrasted sharply with traditional monasticism by taking no vows and having no complex organization and rules, no order linking the houses, no hierarchy of officials, and no wealthy founders or leaders.

Early in our own century, some historians argued that the beguines (like other new religious groups of the twelfth and thirteenth centuries) were an expression of protest by the urban poor. Other historians suggested demographic causes: these were the daughters for whom no husbands could be found. Still others suggested that they were simply a religious surplus, left on the fringes to attempt some kind of semireligious life after Cistercian and Premonstratensian doors closed and friars showed reluctance to expand their pastorate to large numbers of nuns. Although the first of these arguments has been disproved, there is plausibility in the second and third; there were certainly demographic factors behind all later medieval religious movements. The structure of the medieval family and of inheritance necessitated alternative roles to marriage and procreation for a large portion of the population. But we must not ignore the extent to which virginity—as a source of spiritual power—was a compelling religious ideal in its own right, not merely a second-best substitute for marriage. Nor were the beguines merely the result of pastoral negligence; their life was a new and attractive alternative because of its contrast to traditional monasticism.[13]

Thus thirteenth-century women created a new religious role, the beguine, that was opposed to complex institutional structures. They also continued to flock into the traditional monastic role (especially Cistercian and Dominican convents) at a time when it was losing some of its appeal for men. Women did exercise direct "clerical" authority in the thirteenth-century church (preaching, hearing confessions from nuns under them, and bestowing blessings), as Pope Innocent III noted in 1210 to his astonishment. But such things were increasingly criticized and suppressed.[14] The decretalist Bernard of Parma, in his commentary (ca. 1245), argued that, whatever might be found in earlier practice, women could not teach or preach, touch sacred vessels, veil or absolve nuns, or exercise judgment, and that "in general, the office of a man is for-

13. For bibliography on the "women's movement" see below, chapter 5, n. 33.
14. *Nova quaedam nuper*, PL 216: col. 356A–C; see August Potthast, ed., *Regesta pontificum . . .* , 2 vols. (1874; reprint ed., Graz, 1957), 1: 357, no. 4143. See also Ernest W. McDonnell, *The Beguines and Beghards in Medieval Culture with Special Emphasis on the Belgian Scene* (Rutgers, 1954, reprint ed., New York, 1969), p. 343.

bidden to women."[15] Double monasteries in which abbesses ruled
were mostly eliminated by the thirteenth century. At a time when
the preferred male religious role—whether as secular cleric or
friar—was that of evangelist, women were espousing religious
roles in which the exercise of authority by office was not part of
the definition.

As is well known, fundamental changes in piety (at least as
revealed in the writings of those in religious vocations) accompanied these basic changes in ideas about church, clergy, and the
apostolic life.[16] The God of early medieval writing and art is a
judge and king, to whom propitiation is offered by the hordes of
monks presenting correct and beautiful prayers before countless
altars; Christ is a prince, reigning from the throne of the cross after
defeating humankind's captor, and Mary is his queen. The fundamental dramas of religion are cosmic—wars between Christ and
the devil, saints or angels and demons. Hagiography in this period
concentrates on religious figures who have a remarkable impact
(e.g., bishops, itinerant missionaries, reformers, founders of great
monastic houses); their social background is usually noble, their
sanctity frequently proven by miracles that effect change in the
world (converting the heathen, etc.).[17] In contrast, eleventh- and
twelfth-century writers begin to stress Christ's humanity, both in
affective and sentimentalized responses to the gospel story (e.g.,
the devotion of Mary of Oignies to the Christmas crêche) and in a
new compulsion to build into the Christian life a literal imitation
of the details of Jesus' ministry. The fundamental religious drama
is now located within the self, and it is less a battle than a journey—a journey toward God. Hagiography, whose subjects more
and more frequently are women and laity,[18] focuses increasingly

15. Quoted in Francine Cardman, "The Medieval Question of Women
and Orders," *The Thomist* 42 (1978): 596. See also Ida Raming, *The
Exclusion of Women From the Priesthood: Divine Law or Sex Discrimina-
tion?*, trans. N. R. Adams (Metuchen, N.J., 1976), pp. 81–82.

16. See below, pp. 82–90 and 134.

17. Simone Roisin, *L'Hagiographie cistercienne dans le diocèse de Liège au
XIIIe siècle* (Louvain, 1947), especially pp. 81–91; and Joseph-Claude
Poulin, *L'idéal de sainteté dans l'Aquitaine carolingienne d'après les sources
hagiographiques (750–950)* (Quebec, 1975).

18. See below, chapter 4, nn. 92–94.

on inner virtues and experiences (often accompanied by external phenomena such as trances, levitation, and stigmata) rather than grand actions on the stage of history. Alongside the increase in efforts to stimulate affective responses, twelfth-century religious writing (most of which was produced by men) shows an outburst of mystical theology after hundreds of years of silence about it and a great increase in devotion to female figures, in use of feminine metaphors, and in admiration for characteristics (e.g., tears, weakness, and mercy or "ethical irrationality") that people of the period stereotyped as feminine.[19]

The new devotion to Christ's humanity was also at least implicitly a shift in theological emphasis from atonement-resurrection and last judgment to creation and incarnation. In twelfth-century religious writing, great stress is placed on God's creating of us "in his image and likeness" and on Christ's taking our humanity into himself.[20] Humankind is seen as assured of its capacity for God by its very creation and by Christ's incarnation; it needs not so much a captor slain or a rupture in the universe knit up as a nudge along a preordained journey. By the fourteenth century, theology, although not technically Pelagian, nonetheless concentrates not on Christ as propitiation but on the way in which the individual works his way toward God through the grace imparted by sacraments and through the practice of virtue.[21] Mysticism, whether it draws on the affective piety of the Cistercians and Franciscans or on philosophical roots in neo-Platonism, more and more emphasizes a core of "likeness" to God in our being. Thus some mystics find increasing difficulty in attributing evil to man or justice to God. Their concept of an image of God within us, which is at worst tarnished and never destroyed, and their personal experience of ecstasy as ultimate joy lead them to see moral evil as the opposite of union—that is, as an experience of aloneness, alienation, emptiness, a personal suffering or loss of what is good and meaningful, rather than as a chosen rebellion against good or a deliberately espoused corruption. Some fourteenth-century mys-

19. See below, pp. 129–46.
20. See below, pp. 101–2.
21. Heiko A. Obermann, *The Harvest of Medieval Theology: Gabriel Biel and Late Medieval Nominalism* (Cambridge, Mass., 1963).

tics even question the church's teaching about sin and damnation—for how can a soul choose alienation?[22]

We can detect specifically female influences on the development of thirteenth- and fourteenth-century piety. Although the new devotion to the Virgin can be shown to have been particularly prominent in male writing, certain aspects of the new interest in Christ's humanity, especially the emphasis on the infant Jesus, were characteristic of women.[23] It was clearly women who created, from suggestions in twelfth-century male writing, the thirteenth-century devotion to the sacred heart and to the wounds of Jesus.[24] Women elaborated nuptial mysticism much more fully than did the twelfth-century males with whom it originated.[25] Women mystics seem to have been more numerous than male mystics after 1200; their ecstasies were more frequent and more often accompanied by paramystical phenomena.[26] Moreover, the increasing centering of Christian devotional life on the eucharist, which is one of the major ways in which late medieval spirituality points toward modern Catholicism, was clearly inspired by women mystics, at whose insistence the feast of *Corpus Christi* was instituted. Saints' lives and legislation reveal that some nuns had to be forbidden from communicating constantly in an effort to consume as much of Christ as possible; others abstained from even communion for which they were properly prepared out of fear of the

22. See below, pp. 153, 234 and 247.

23. Roisin, *Hagiographie*, pp. 108 and 111–20; André Raÿez, "Humanité du Christ: La mystique féminine . . . ," DS 7.1 (Paris, 1969): cols. 1088–90.

24. Louis Gougaud, *Devotional and Ascetic Practices in the Middle Ages*, trans. G. C. Bateman (London, 1927), pp. 75–130; McDonnell, *Beguines*, pp. 299–330.

25. See Roisin, *Hagiographie*, pp. 113–23; Leclercq, Vandenbroucke, and Bouyer, *La spiritualité*, pp. 430–38, 448–54, 471–76 and the literature cited there; John Bugge, *Virginitas: An Essay in the History of a Medieval Ideal*, Archives internationales d'histoire des idées, series minor 17 (The Hague, 1975). I. M. Lewis, *Ecstatic Religion: An Anthropological Study of Spirit Possession and Shamanism* (Harmondsworth, Middlesex, England, 1971), p. 58, provides cross-cultural evidence that such metaphors are more common with female ecstatics.

26. Roisin, *Hagiographie*, pp. 106–22, 151, 155, 205–6, and 234–35.

awesome responsibility of receiving God.[27] But the prominence and influence of women in religious life should not cause us to forget that negative stereotypes of women as less rational than men and more lustful—stereotypes that had roots in the ancient scientific tradition as well as in the writings of the Fathers—continued in the thirteenth century and contributed both to efforts to prevent women from instructing others and to the condemnation of the beguines for heterodox ideas at the council of Vienne in 1311.[28]

Behind the many changes in twelfth- and thirteenth-century religion lies therefore a paradox: the period saw the increased power of the clergy as well as waves of antisacerdotal heresy and lay religiosity; it produced a new sense of God as father/mother/lover/friend as well as an increasing emphasis on the priest as *necessary* intermediary between the soul and God. As grace was more and more narrowly confined to moments in the priest's control, ordinary roles and actions (e.g., marriage, begging, weaving, etc.) were given religious significance. As the priest became more distant, God became more accessible; as the priest was "divinized," God became "human."

These developments provide the context for the topics treated below. For example, the polemic between monks and regular canons discussed in the first and third essays makes it clear that twelfth-century people cared passionately about what constituted the prerogatives of the clergy and about serving others through teaching. The metaphors explored in the second and fourth articles show that attraction toward and hesitation about evangelism—that is, direct service of the world through preaching—formed a creative tension at the heart of Cistercian monasticism. The visions explored in the final study show that women's lack of clerical authority, and especially of the priest's control over the eucharist, was a major factor in their self-conception and in the nature of the religious life available to them.

These five studies are concerned with the differences among

27. See below, chapter 5, nn. 300–303.
28. See below, pp. 131–46; especially nn. 84 and 117.

religious groups—which medieval people themselves saw as "diversity within unity"—and with the tensions at the heart of religious ideals. They cannot therefore be completely subsumed under a single theme, not even the paradoxical one of divine accessibility coupled with clerical power. But if I cannot summarize these studies in a single hypothesis or phrase, I can nevertheless suggest an epigraph. In one of her many visions, the beguine Mechtild of Magdeburg, whom I study below, saw the soul of a friar suffering in purgatory for the sin of disobedience. It implored: "Have women and priests pray for me."[29] Such a plea has a deceptively modern ring, for Catholics and Protestants alike in late twentieth-century America often assume that religion is the business of women and clergy.[30] Mechtild's vision has, of course, nothing to do with such ideas, although they may have distant roots in the later Middle Ages.[31] But in the words of the suffering

29. See below, chapter 5, n. 272.

30. On the prominence of women in present-day European Catholicism, see William A. Christian, Jr., *Person and God in a Spanish Valley* (New York, 1972); Carmelo Lison-Tolosana, *Belmonte de los Caballeros: A Sociological Study of a Spanish Town* (Oxford, 1966), especially p. 309; and John Davis, "The Sexual Division of Religious Labour in the Mediterranean," unpublished paper.

31. Clergy and women were also the two groups most commonly charged with witchcraft. They were therefore seen by contemporaries as especially in touch with demonic as well as with divine inspiration. See Norman Cohn, *Europe's Inner Demons: An Enquiry Inspired by the Great Witch-Hunt* (New York, 1975), pp. 154 n. 31 and 194ff. Most charges against clerics were for ritual magic, sorcery, or invocation of demons rather than for *maleficium*; see Richard Kieckhefer, *European Witch Trials: Their Foundations in Popular and Learned Culture, 1300–1500* (Berkeley and Los Angeles, 1976), pp. 10–26 and 69–71. According to Mary O'Neil of the University of Washington, who is working on the Modena trials, clerics frequently learned their *incanti* from women in confession or from female relatives.

For the theory that the romanticizing of women (in the cult of the Virgin and in courtly love) and the persecution of women may be causally linked, see Jeffrey B. Russell, *Witchcraft in the Middle Ages* (Ithaca, 1972), p. 284; but see also E. W. Monter, "The Pedestal and the Stake: Courtly Love and Witchcraft," *Becoming Visible: Women in European History*, eds. R. Bridenthal and C. Koonz (Boston, 1977), pp. 119–36.

soul in Mechtild's vision, we do find a paradigm of the two sources of religious authority in the high Middle Ages. Behind the priest lies the power of office; behind the woman, the inspiration of a Christ who makes wise the foolish and gives the earth to the meek. The essays presented here are about how cloistered men and women responded to these sources of religious authority.

1

The Spirituality
of Regular Canons
in the Twelfth Century

——✒

The State of the Question

*H*ISTORIANS OF medieval spirituality agree that the years between 1050 and 1215 saw a fundamental change in men's basic conceptions of the Christian life, a change perhaps as deep and as lasting as the Reformation of the sixteenth century or the spread of Christianity in the second to fourth centuries A.D. Central to this change was a new emphasis on the obligation to love and serve one's neighbor, a new sense that Christ wished his followers not merely to worship him and avoid wrongdoing but also to care for their brothers.[1] Scholars are fond of contrasting earlier monastic reforms, characterized by a concern for offering correct worship to God, with the activity and ideas of twelfth-century itinerant preachers, such as Vitalis of Savigny, Norbert of Xanten, Peter Valdes, or Francis of Assisi. But historians have not agreed about

---

This essay is an expanded version of "The Spirituality of Regular Canons in the Twelfth Century: A New Approach," *Medievalia et Humanistica: Studies in Medieval and Renaissance Culture*, n.s. 4 (1973): 3–24, reprinted by permission. The original published version of this essay was greatly improved as a result of suggestions made by Stephen D. White of Wesleyan University, Middletown, Connecticut.

1. See, for example, M.-D. Chenu, *La théologie au douzième siècle* (Paris, 1957), pp. 225–51; and Ernest W. McDonnell, "The *Vita Apostolica*: Diversity or Dissent?" *Church History* 24 (1955): 15–31.

exactly when or how this awareness of an obligation to care for one's fellow man emerged. At the moment, a particular stumbling block to the understanding of this development is the lack of a scholarly consensus on the place of the group known as regular canons in the history of twelfth-century spirituality.

Until the middle years of the twentieth century, regular canons (i.e., clergy who live a common life under a rule, renouncing all private property) were little studied. If they were treated at all, they were seen as a kind of monk, a result of the efforts of Gregorian reformers to "monasticize" the clergy.[2] In the 1940s and 1950s, above all as a result of the work of Charles Dereine, major scholarship on regular canons began to appear.[3] In part because it was the product of canons themselves, who were defensive about the tendency of monastic historians to equate twelfth-century spirituality with monastic spirituality, this scholarship often argued for a "canonical spirituality." Here, as elsewhere in twentieth-century writing on medieval religious movements, the methodological problems involved in establishing the spirituality of a given group were never fully sorted out. (Above all, the difference between establishing "the spirituality of such and such"—i.e., the characteristics shown by the group—and "the distinctive spirituality of such and such"—i.e., characteristics shown by the group and not by other groups—was often forgotten.)[4] This modern debate over monastic and canonical sensibilities reached a climax at the La Mendola Conference in 1959.[5] Since then it has faded somewhat from scholarly consciousness as a result of a general tendency to dismiss as unimportant the effort to correlate differences in ideas

2. See Jean Becquet, "Chanoines réguliers et érémitisme clérical," RAM 48 (1972): 361–70.

3. See below nn. 11, 15, and 18; for fuller bibliography, see my book *Docere Verbo et Exemplo: An Aspect of Twelfth-Century Spirituality*, Harvard Theological Studies 31 (Missoula, Montana, 1979), pp. 1–8.

4. On this point, see my review article, "Franciscan Spirituality: Two Approaches," *Medievalia et Humanistica*, n.s. 7 (1976): 195–97.

5. Papers published in *La vita comune del clero nei secoli XI e XII: Atti della Settimana di Studio: Mendola, settembre 1959*, Pubblicazioni dell'Università Cattolica del Sacro Cuore 3.2 and 3, Miscellanea del Centro di Studi Medioevali 3, 2 vols. (Milan, 1962). On the conference see Pierre Toubert, "La vie commune des clercs aux XIᵉ–XIIᵉ siècles: un questionnaire," *Revue historique* 231 (1964): 11–26.

with differences in religious institutions. This loss of interest in different spiritualities reflects very broad trends which have nothing specifically to do with research on regular canons: the ecumenism in Catholic circles following Vatican II;[6] the increasing impact of scholars like Grundmann and Chenu, who have provided new interpretations of twelfth-century religion based on themes that cut across movements;[7] the move of a new generation of scholars away from interest in the content of spiritual teaching toward questions of how certain general concerns of twelfth-century groups relate to and reflect social change.[8] Recent neglect of the question of the regular canons' spirituality does not, however, mean that the issue is either unimportant or solved.[9]

Where then do things stand with historians who study the question? General works on medieval spirituality, reflecting the research of Dereine, Schreiber, Petit, and others, continue to assume that regular canons formed a separate movement within the religious ferment of the twelfth century, a separate movement that wedded service of others to a life of monastic withdrawal and

6. For examples of ecumenism leading directly to distrust of an emphasis on spiritualities, see Louis Bouyer, Preface, *The Spirituality of the New Testament and the Fathers*, trans. M. P. Ryan (New York, 1963), pp. vi–xi; and A. Vauchez, *La spiritualité du moyen âge occidental VIIIe–XIIe* *siècles* (Paris, 1975), pp. 5–8.

7. H. Grundmann, *Religiöse Bewegungen im Mittelalter* (1935, reprint ed., Hildesheim, 1961); Chenu, *La théologie*.

8. See, for example, "Une enquête sur les 'spiritualités populaires,'" RAM 49 (1973): 493–504; and L. K. Little, *Religious Poverty and the Profit Economy in Medieval Europe* (Ithaca, 1978). The recent change in name of the *Revue d'ascétique et de mystique* to the *Revue d'histoire de la spiritualité* and its subsequent suspension of publication reflects a kind of crisis of identity in the field that at first seemed salutary.

9. The limited scholarship on regular canons as compared to the enormous amount on monks is also related to the small number of present-day groups of canons regular. There is no general bibliography of work on canons, despite plans at La Mendola to establish one. Aside from the *Analecta Praemonstratensia* and the *Revue des études augustiniennes*, which publishes material on Augustinian canons, there is no periodical devoted to canons regular. The periodical *Ordo canonicus*, which started in 1947, ceased to appear in 1960. This situation can be compared with the large number of periodicals presently devoted to the Cistercians alone. See Becquet, "Chanoines réguliers," pp. 361–70.

thereby foreshadowed the friars' concern with love of neighbor. This view sees monks and regular canons as clearly distinguishable because of the centrality granted to service in the canonical movement, and argues that the life led by regular canons was in some way a form of religious vocation that provides a transition from monk to mendicant.[10] More specialized studies on regular canons done between the 1940s and 1970s often assert or assume a similar view of the place of regular canons in the history of medieval religion.[11] But, ironically, the same specialized studies have, over the past forty years, provided material for questioning these generalizations. It was, in part, this material that led the historian of monastic spirituality, Jean Leclercq, to suggest in 1959 that, despite certain distinctive ideas in the writings of eleventh-century regular canons, there was in the twelfth century no difference between canonical and monastic conceptions of the cloistered life, no unique canonical spirituality.[12] Leclercq's assertion, which occasioned much debate, still figured centrally in Becquet's review of

10. See, for example, M.-H. Vicaire, *L'imitation des apôtres* (Paris, 1963), pp. 62–66; R. W. Southern, *Western Society and the Church in the Middle Ages*, The Pelican History of the Church 2 (Harmondsworth, Middlesex, England, 1970), pp. 240–50; Vauchez, *La spiritualité*, pp. 96–100; and Little, *Religious Poverty*, pp. 99–112.

11. Georg Schreiber, "Praemonstratenserkultur des 12. Jahrhunderts," *Analecta Praemonstratensia* 16 (1940): 41–107, and 17 (1941): 5–33; Charles Dereine, "Vie commune, règle de saint Augustin, et chanoines réguliers au XIᵉ siècle," RHE 41 (1946): 365; idem, "L'élaboration du statut canonique des chanoines réguliers spécialement sous Urbain II," RHE 46 (1951): 563–64; idem, "Chanoines," DHGE 12 (Paris, 1953): cols. 401–3; J. Chatillon, "La spiritualité canoniale," *Saint Chrodegang: communications présentées au colloque tenu à Metz à l'occasion du douzième centenaire de sa mort* (Metz, 1967), p. 120; François Petit, *La spiritualité des Prémontrés au XIIᵉ et XIIIᵉ siècles* (Paris, 1947), pp. 266–67; idem, *La réforme des prêtres au moyen-âge: pauvreté et vie commune: textes choisis . . .* (Paris, 1968), pp. 18–20, 157–59; Jakob Mois, *Das Stift Rottenbuch in der Kirchenreform des XI.–XII. Jahrhunderts: Ein Beitrag zur Ordensgeschichte der Augustiner-Chorherren*, Beiträge zur altbayerischen Kirchengeschichte: Beiträge zur Geschichte, Topographie und Statistik des Erzbistums München und Freising 3.19 (Munich, 1953); Cosimo Damiano Fonseca, *Medioevo canonicale*, Pubblicazione dell'Università Cattolica del Sacro Cuore (Milan, 1970).

12. J. Leclercq, "La spiritualité des chanoines réguliers," in *La vita comune* 1:134. Leclercq's interpretation is accepted by G. Oury, "L'idéal

research on regular canons published thirteen years later.[13] Despite the discomfort it has caused, it has not been refuted.

Most historians continue to feel that monks and regular canons differed in basic ways and to relate this difference to the fact that regular canons were clerics by definition, monks were not. In a recent survey of spirituality, for example, André Vauchez writes that the goal of the canonical reform was not the monasticization of the clergy but the elevation of sacerdotal office.

> The observances of Arrouaise or Prémontré can appear very close to those of contemporary monks; but they are to be distinguished from the latter by the fact that their goal is apostolic not eschatological. Thus study, which occupies a great role in the canonical life, prepares one not only for prayer but also for preaching.[14]

But it has become more and more difficult to adduce evidence of widespread and consistent contrasts between the two groups, to say exactly how regular canons are "apostolic" rather than "contemplative" or "monastic." Recent research does not support the argument that twelfth-century canons and monks differed generally in actual practices, nor has current scholarship established that monks and regular canons diverged widely in the prerogatives they claimed or in the conceptions of the spiritual life revealed in the noncontroversial writings of their orders.

Although historians have long known that the second half of the eleventh century saw a general effort to reform existing groups of secular clergy by enforcing on them a life in common and complete renunciation of private property, the research of Dereine has gradually revealed the great diversity of early canonical foundations, some of which were, in their first years, as austere and as isolated as the early Cîteaux.[15] In the years between 1050 and 1120,

---

monastique dans la vie canoniale: le bienheureux Hervé de Tours (†1022)," *Revue Mabillon* 52 (1962): 1–31.

13. Becquet, "Chanoines réguliers," pp. 361–70.

14. Vauchez, *La spiritualité*, p. 99. But cf. Guntram G. Bischoff, "Early Premonstratensian Eschatology: The Apocalyptic Myth," *The Spirituality of Western Christendom*, ed. Rozanne Elder, Cistercian Studies Series 30 (Kalamazoo, 1976), p. 68.

15. For what follows, see the works cited in n. 11 above and Charles Dereine, *Les chanoines réguliers au diocèse de Liège avant saint Norbert*, Aca-

groups of clerics living the common life included: existing foundations that underwent reform when clerics, either spontaneously or
under pressure from bishops or patrons, gave up prebends; groups
that split away from unreformed colleges of canons; new foundations that arose in a variety of situations, sometimes as hostels for
pilgrims, sometimes as eremitical groups of clergy and laity. In the
early years, such houses adopted a variety of rules: some wrote
their own; some followed the Rule of Aachen, modified as regards
poverty; some adopted the so-called Rule of St. Augustine, which
was available in both a strict and a moderate form. Where new
foundations appeared, they occurred sometimes at places with
parochial rights, sometimes at places without. Some houses of
regular canons held, without themselves staffing, parish churches.

No one would deny that some of the eleventh-century canonical houses in Italy differed from eleventh-century monastic movements in emphasizing the role of every brother as priest. But given
the great diversity of the actual life practiced in eleventh- and
early twelfth-century canonical foundations it is now questionable
whether all houses of clerics who renounced private property
should be grouped together by historians and distinguished from
monastic houses. Indeed the evidence presented by modern scholars suggests other characterizations. For example, an approach
that groups together the early Premonstratensians (regular canons)
and Cistercians (monks) on the one hand, and, on the other, the
Pataria of Milan (a partly lay movement that became heretical) and
the canons for whom the compilation found in MS Ottoboni
Lat. 175 was composed may be far more historically valid; for it
might well be argued that austerity of life was the central concern
to the former, reform of the clergy to the latter.[16] Even for the
period beginning in the second decade of the twelfth century,
when clerics living a full common life came increasingly to be
characterized by adoption of the Rule of St. Augustine, historians

démie royale de Belgique: classe des lettres . . . Mémoires in-8°, ser.
2, 47.1 (Brussels, 1952); idem, "Les origines de Prémontré," RHE 42
(1947): 352–78; idem, "Les coutumiers de saint-Quentin de Beauvais et
de Springiersbach," RHE 43 (1948): 411–42; idem, "La spiritualité
'apostolique' des premiers fondateurs d'Afflighem (1083–1100)," RHE
54 (1959): 41–65.
16. On the text found in MS Ottoboni Lat. 175, see below n. 46.

have found it difficult to identify "canonical characteristics." By the twelfth century, the number of monks in holy orders had increased to the point where some monastic houses had many priests and many brothers in orders.[17] The major historians of the canonical movement agree that pastoral work—that is, service of parish churches and preaching to those outside the cloister—was not an essential element in all canonical life,[18] whereas it was not uncommon in the same period for monks to exercise the *cura animarum*, including preaching.[19] Thus, despite repeated assertions by scholars that regular canons combined monastic practice with a new orientation toward the cure of souls, no evidence has as yet been presented to demonstrate that the actual life lived in most canonical houses in the twelfth century differed generally from the life in most monastic cloisters.[20]

If we turn from the realm of practice to the realm of ideas, we

17. Philibert Schmitz, *Histoire de l'ordre de saint Benoît*, 7 vols. (Maredsous, 1942–56) 1: 264–65.

18. See John Compton Dickinson, *The Origins of the Austin Canons and Their Introduction into England* (London, 1950), especially pp. 73 and 76; Dereine, "Chanoines," cols. 391–95; and idem, *Liège*, pp. 30–31, where he points out that he and Dickinson and Mois agree that "l'exercice de la *cura animarum* a souvent été présenté par les historiens comme un élément essentiel de la profession canoniale régulière, ce par quoi elle se distingue du monachisme. Mais l'étude attentive des origines de la réforme canoniale ne révèle chez ses promoteurs aucune préoccupation de ce genre ni, à fortiori, une orientation systematique vers la prédication ou le service des paroisses."

19. U. Berlière, "L'exercice du ministère paroissial par les moines du XIIᵉ au XVIIᵉ siècles," *Revue bénédictine* 39 (1927): 340–64; G. Constable, "The Second Crusade as Seen by Contemporaries," "Appendix A," *Traditio* 9 (1953): 276–78; P. Hofmeister, "Mönchtum und Seelsorge bis zum 13. Jahrhundert," *Studien und Mitteilungen zur Geschichte des Benediktiner-Ordens und seiner Zweige* 65 (1955): 209–73; F. J. Schmale, "Kanonie, Seelsorge, Eigenkirche," *Historisches Jahrbuch* 78 (1959): 38–63; M. Peuchmaurd, "Le prêtre ministre de la parole dans la théologie du XIIᵉ siècle (canonistes, moines et chanoines)," *Recherches de théologie ancienne et médiévale* 29 (1962): 52–76.

20. In "Discussione," *La vita comune* 1: 136–37, Dereine and Leclercq differed briefly over whether the establishment of hospitals might be a particular interest of canons. On this point see also Becquet, "Chanoines réguliers," pp. 361–70. The question has not been explored in depth.

find that, in the later eleventh and twelfth centuries, regular canons and monks engaged in various controversies over the nature and relative superiority of their respective movements, controversies that have sometimes been cited by historians as evidence of distinctive monastic and canonical spiritualities. The existence of such polemical writings certainly indicates that some canons and some monks felt that a distinction existed between their respective forms of the religious life. It also indicates that certain polemical writers desired to underline that difference. A careful consideration of the treatises themselves reveals, however, that in some cases the two groups were claiming the same prerogatives—both the right to the *cura animarum* and a state of spiritual superiority—and this fact suggests that the controversy may tell historians more about new spiritual ideals that touched both monastic and canonical traditions in the twelfth century than about differences between canons and monks.[21]

Regular canons tended to argue that their order was older, going back beyond Augustine to the apostles and prefigured by Aaron and the Levites; they also argued that they were superior to the monks, who were laity, and that the canonical vocation was more dangerous (because less withdrawn from the world) but more useful.[22] Anselm of Havelberg's letter of 1138 to a certain Egbert characterizes the conversion of a regular canon to monastic life as a "descent"; Arno of Reichersberg argues that canons are superior because of their "moderation."[23] It is canonical polemicists in the early twelfth century who tell monks that their task is (in St. Jerome's words) "to weep." It is regular canons who stress the penitential nature of monastic life and its incompatibility with

---

21. On this controversial literature, see Dereine, "L'élaboration," pp. 558–64; idem, "Chanoines," cols. 391–98; Peuchmaurd, "Le prêtre," p. 76; Dickinson, *Origins*, p. 121 and passim; and Giles Constable, *Monastic Tithes from Their Origins to the Twelfth Century*, Cambridge Studies in Medieval Life and Thought, n.s. 10 (Cambridge, 1964), pp. 136–85 passim.

22. Dereine, "Chanoines," cols. 396–97; and idem, "L'élaboration," pp. 534–65.

23. Anselm of Havelberg, *Epistola apologetica pro ordine canonicorum regularium*, PL 188: cols. 1119–40; Arno of Reichersberg, *Scutum canonicorum*, PL 194: cols. 1493–528.

preaching, although there were penitential elements in the early canonical movement.[24] Moreover, regular canons made collections of canon law to justify their status, including, among a wealth of patristic material, two crucial bulls of Urban II, which authorized regular canons to practice the cure of souls and gave equal value to the monastic and the canonical life. Even in nonpolemical works regular canons sometimes grouped themselves with clergy, not with monks.[25]

Monastic polemicists, however, argued against the distinctiveness of regular canons. The author of the *Dialogue Between Two Monks*, for example, tries to assimilate regular canons to monks.[26] Moreover, monastic authors did not agree about the incompatibility of the monastic life and the *cura animarum*; they argued for themselves as preachers. Rupert of Deutz, Hugh of Rouen, and Peter Damian, among others, actually argue that monks make better preachers because of their sanctity of life.[27] And Urban II, in canons 2–3 of the council of Nîmes (1096), seems to see both monks and regular canons as simultaneously contemplatives and evangelists.

> We find persons, basing themselves on foolish ideas, who, inflamed by bitter jealousy rather than charity, assert that monks who are dead to the world and live only for God are unworthy of the sacerdotal charge, that they cannot give penance or baptism or absolution. . . . This is a complete error. . . . Priests, both monks and canons, who announce the precepts of God are

24. Ivo of Chartres inserted into his *Decretum*, along with texts favorable to canons, extracts from Jerome on the penitential character of monasticism; see Dereine, "L'élaboration," p. 545, n. 1.

25. On these canon law collections see Dereine, "L'élaboration," pp. 534–65. Philip of Harvengt in his *De institutione clericorum*, PL 203, cols. 665–1206, groups regular canons with clerics, not monks.

26. [Idung of Prüfening], *Dialogus inter Cluniacensem monachum et Cisterciensem* in Edmond Martène and Ursin Durand, eds., *Thesaurus novus anecdotorum*, 5 vols. (Paris, 1717), 5: 1614. With reference to the Rule of St. Augustine, the author says: "Velint, nolint omnes qui illam regulam professi sunt, monachi sunt. Aut enim monachi sunt, aut de nullo ordine sunt." On the title of this work, see Grover A. Zinn, in *Speculum* 55 (1980): 364.

27. See Peuchmaurd, "Le prêtre," pp. 52–76; and Dereine, "Chanoines," col. 397.

called angels. For such an angelic hierarchy, the more it contemplates God, the more sublimely it is confirmed in dignity. . . . It is proper that those who have left the world have the major care to pray for the sins of the people and more power to absolve them than secular priests. Because these live according to the apostolic rule and following in the footsteps of [the apostles] live the common life. . . . Thus it seems to us that they who renounce their own things for God are permitted to baptize, to distribute communion, to give penance and absolve from sins. . . . That is why we decide that those who hold to the pattern [*figura*] of the apostles can preach, baptize, give communion, receive penitents and give absolution.[28]

Indeed it was only in the course of the twelfth century that preaching was closely attached to the office of priest, so that the right to preach came by the fact of ordination. This occurred in part as a result of the controversy between monks and regular canons; in part it was a response to the challenge of wandering lay preachers. We should not assume that people in the early twelfth century saw preaching as central to clerical status.[29] In fact, any monk who was also a priest might request permission to preach. Even nuns like Hildegard of Bingen occasionally preached, although canonists in the twelfth century were already objecting that women, however learned and holy, were disqualified from instructing men.[30] Some regular canons felt that members of their own order would be wise not to practice the right, even though they possessed it by definition.[31] Moreover, the apostolic life that regular canons claimed to practice meant "poverty" to them (as it did to monks) far more frequently than it meant baptizing or preaching. In short, the polemical claims of monks and canons regular do not give the impression either that contemporaries were very clear about the dif-

28. Joannes D. Mansi, ed., *Sacrorum conciliorum nova et amplissima collectio* 20 (Venice, 1775): cols. 934–35.

29. See Peuchmaurd, "La prêtre."

30. According to Gratian: "Mulier, quamvis docta et sancta, viros in conventu docere non praesumat." Aemilius Friedburg, ed., *Corpus iuris canonici* 1: *Decretum magistri Gratiani* (1879; reprint ed., Graz, 1959), Distinction 23, canon 19, col. 86. See also Southern, *Western Society and the Church*, pp. 310 and 315.

31. Ivo of Chartres urged prudence in taking on pastoral care; letters 69 and 213, PL 162: cols. 88–89 and 216–17.

ferences between them or that regular canons saw themselves as preachers and pastors whereas monks did not.

There is, furthermore, a fallacy in assuming that polemical claims reflect actual practice. Nor can we assume that a few polemical treatises represent the opinion of canons in general. Statements made in the heat of argument are not the best guide to men's ideas about themselves. Polemical defenses of the right to preach do not necessarily reflect a conception shared by canons (or monks) living together in the cloister that an obligation for one's brother is an integral aspect of the religious vocation.

Perhaps more telling than polemical claims to difference is the confusion about statuses and groups that we find in many writers. In the early years of the canonical movement individuals sometimes saw themselves as a mixture of categories. Several lives of regular canons in the early twelfth century describe them as clerics and hermits, or as "leading an eremitical life in a clerical habit." [32] And later we still find individuals who are confused about themselves. For example, a group that wrote to Hildegard of Bingen (scholars today debate whether it was a house of regular canons or monks) asked rather plaintively: What are we? We do not follow the Benedictine Rule; we have our own customs; we are being attacked. Can you please tell us what a monk is anyway? [33]

Contemporaries themselves sometimes felt other categories to be more important than the distinction between monk and regular canon. The anonymous author of the *Libellus de diversis ordinibus*, whose suggestion has been followed in a recent survey of twelfth-

---

32. Dereine, "Chanoines," col. 384.

33. *Congregatio Hunniensis coenobii Hildegardi petunt interpretationem regulae S. Benedicti*, PL 197: cols. 1053–54. According to M. Alfred Schroll, *Benedictine Monasticism as Reflected in the Warnefrid-Hildemar Commentaries on the Rule* (New York, 1941) p. 203, the petitioning house was a convent of Cluniac nuns at Huy near Liège. Jean Mabillon, *Annales ordinis s. Benedicti* . . . 6 (Lucca, 1745), bk. 80, sec. 14, p. 488, suggests a certain *Hunniensis*, founded by count Eunuchus and perhaps identical with *Heningense* in the diocese of Worms. Johannes Wirges, *Die Anfänge der Augustiner-Chorherren und die Gründung des Augustiner-Chorherrenstiftes Ravengiersburg (Hunsrück) Diözese Trier* (Betzdorf, 1928), pp. 153–54, says that the petitioners were members of the house of regular canons at Ravengiersburg (Hunsrück), the third oldest Augustinian house in Germany.

century religious life, himself felt that the relationship of religious houses to the new urban centers was a more pertinent principle of categorization.[34] And there were certainly authors, both monastic and canonical, who wrote for regular canons and monks without any sense of the two as being basically different. For example, Peter of Celle, a monk, and Hugh of Folieto, a canon, wrote general works on the cloistered life addressed to a common audience.[35]

Thus neither actual practice, polemical claims, or even non-polemical reflections on personal status reveal general and widespread differences between monks and regular canons. Historians, however, continue to claim that canons developed a new self-conception, a "new orientation,"[36] that "although all the elements of the apostolic life . . . are found in the monastic order, we must assert that the emphasis is not the same [as in the canonical order]."[37] Only a few specific pieces of evidence for a distinctive canonical orientation have, however, been cited. The first is the fact, noticed by several historians, that the Premonstratensian Anselm of Havelberg, changing the traditional exegesis of the story of Mary and Martha, clearly foreshadows the thirteenth-century notion of the "mixed life" of service and contemplation as higher than the life of contemplation alone.[38] The second and related piece of evidence, which has been pointed out most clearly perhaps by Chatillon, is a new emphasis on preaching found in some canonical writings, an emphasis that frequently exists alongside traditional interpretations of the active and contemplative lives.[39] A

34. *Libellus de diversis ordinibus et professionibus qui sunt in ecclesia*, ed. and trans. Giles Constable and Bernard Smith, Oxford Medieval Texts (Oxford, 1972). And see Little, *Religious Poverty*.

35. Peter of Celle, *Tractatus de disciplina claustrali*, *L'École du cloître*, ed. Gérard de Martel, SC 240, Sér. mon. 47 (Paris, 1977), pp. 96–324; Hugh of Folieto (or Fouilloy), *De claustro animae*, PL 176: cols. 1017–182.

36. Vicaire, *L'imitation*, p. 62.

37. Petit, *La spiritualité des Prémontrés*, p. 266.

38. See, for example, Kurt Fina, "Anselm von Havelberg," *Analecta Praemonstratensia* 33 (1957): 7–16; and F. Petit, "L'ordre de Prémontré de saint Norbert à Anselme de Havelberg," in *La vita comune* 1: 476–78. The passage in question is Anselm of Havelberg, *Epistola apologetica*, PL 188: cols. 1131–32.

39. J. Chatillon, "Contemplation, action et prédication d'après un sermon inédit de Richard de saint-Victor . . . ," *L'homme devant Dieu:*

third argument, which has been made in passing by some historians or can be deduced from their presentations, suggests that an interest in the sacraments or in history and ecclesiology characterizes canonical more than monastic theology.[40] But Anselm of Havelberg's new exegesis of the story of Mary and Martha does not seem to have been common among regular canons, or even among Premonstratensians,[41] and efforts to increase the importance of the active life are not unknown in monastic writings of the same period.[42] Anselm's exegesis differs markedly from interpretations of the passage (and conceptions of the religious life) from the early Middle Ages. It is not clear, however, that his concern is characteristically "canonical." Chatillon's suggestion that a new concern with preaching is evidence of a new canonical orientation has been documented only by reference to a single sermon of Richard of St. Victor and a few passages from Philip of Harvengt. The emphasis on the sacraments and on history that can be found in, for example, the canons Hugh of St. Victor and Gerhoh of Reichersberg can also be found in the monks Gratian and Otto of Freising. In general, as Leclercq has shown, monastic and canonical treatises agree in stressing the soul's obligation to worship and love its creator as the central aspect of the life of the cloister.[43] On the basis of the evidence presented by recent historians, there is

---

mélanges offerts au Père Henri de Lubac, 2 vols. (Paris, 1964), 2:89–98. Leclercq, "La spiritualité des chanoines réguliers," pp. 117–35, implies that this is true for the late eleventh century. The texts cited in Petit, *Réforme des prêtres*, pp. 77–109, would also suggest this, although Petit does not argue the point.

40. See P. Classen, "Discussione," in *La vita comune* 1: 140; Vauchez, *La spiritualité*, pp. 96–100; and Bischoff, "Premonstratensian Eschatology," pp. 41–71.

41. See, for example, Philip of Harvengt, *De obedientia*, chaps. 31–36, PL 203: cols. 905–21; Adam of Dryburgh [or Adam Scot], *De tripartito tabernaculo*, bk. 3, chaps. 13–15, PL 198: cols. 773–80; Richard of St. Victor, *De questionibus regule sancti Augustini solutis*, chap. 14, ed. in M. L. Colker, "Richard of St. Victor and the Anonymous of Bridlington," *Traditio* 18 (1962): 216; and Richard of St. Victor, *Liber exceptionum*, pt. 2, bk. 14, chap. 5, ed. J. Chatillon (Paris, 1958), pp. 503–4.

42. See, for example, Aelred of Rievaulx, sermon 17, PL 195: cols. 303–9.

43. Leclercq, "La spiritualité des chanoines réguliers," pp. 117–35.

then little reason to argue that twelfth-century monks and regular canons differed in their conceptions of the Christian life.

Current scholarship has adduced increasing amounts of evidence on the actual practices of monks and regular canons, has analyzed monastic and canonical polemic with some care, and has glanced, with less care, at nonpolemical writings. None of this evidence, as currently presented and analyzed, proves that there was a general difference between twelfth-century monks and regular canons either in practice or in ideas. And yet, the efforts of canonical authors to defend and define their order in polemic and the few texts cited by Petit and Chatillon do suggest that when a twelfth-century man joined a canonical house he saw in that house a religious ideal somewhat different from the ideals of contemporary monasticism. No historian has shown what that ideal was, and it seems unlikely that further investigation of practice or polemic will reveal a clear distinction between monks and canons. But a survey of recent scholarship leaves us with a nagging suspicion that, in the area of ideas and self-conceptions, the case is not closed. The nonpolemical writings of the canons have not been carefully studied. Present arguments about self-conception tend to be based on single texts, single themes, or single authors. More work is clearly needed. If we are to conclude with Leclercq that monastic and canonical attitudes are the same, we must show that, in an extensive body of nonpolemical literature, they agree on all aspects of the spiritual life. If we maintain with Petit that they are different, we must be able to show that, in works of similar form and purpose, virtually all canonical authors use language or voice concerns that virtually all monastic authors ignore.

In my effort to answer the question of the difference or similarity of monastic and canonical ideas, I have thus chosen for study the fairly large group of what we might call "works of practical spiritual advice"—that is, works about the soul's spiritual and moral progress within the cloistered life. Such works include treatises on the formation of novices, commentaries on the Benedictine and Augustinian Rules, and certain other works that are clearly parallel to these two genre in form and intention.[44] These

44. The discussion of canonical and monastic spirituality that occupies the remainder of this essay is based on a close analysis of the treatises

works reveal the assumptions of the cloistered about the purpose of their lives much more clearly than abstract treatises of mystical or biblical theology, works of polemic, or the practical details of custumals. Because each author writes for members of his own order, we need not worry that his attitudes toward the Christian life reflect his readers' vocation and status rather than his own. Because the treatises all have the same ostensible subject (to explain the cloistered life to those engaged in its practice) we need not worry that the assumptions of the authors differ because of different purposes in writing. Characteristics that appear in almost all canonical treatises and almost no monastic ones can therefore be related to the self-conception of the canonical authors qua canons.

The Canonical Concern with Edification *Verbo et Exemplo*

Commentaries on the Benedictine and Augustinian Rules and works of advice for novices have usually been studied for their information on actual monastic or canonical practices or for their theories about the soul's relationship to God. In neither of these areas do we find consistent differences between monastic and canonical writings. But if we look at the language, the emphasis, and the specific borrowings with which the two groups of treatises describe the obligations of ordinary cloistered brothers, a revealing contrast emerges: canonical authors see canons as teachers and learners, whereas monastic authors see monks only as learners. What distinguishes regular canons from monks is the canon's sense of a responsibility to edify his fellow men both by what he says and by what he does.

---

listed in the Appendix below. It is not possible here to give a full discussion of problems of dating, authenticity, etc., that pertain to individual treatises, nor is it possible to provide a lengthy justification for the decision to include certain texts as parallel. Many (but not all) of these texts are discussed at greater length in my book *Docere Verbo et Exemplo*. Several of the themes I explore in this essay are treated with great sensitivity in Darrell R. Reinke, "Authority and Community in Twelfth-Century Commentaries on the Rule of St. Augustine," unpublished paper.

The concern for edification is found in virtually all twelfth-century canonical commentaries and treatises for novices (with the possible exception of the *De questionibus* of Richard of St. Victor) and in virtually no monastic treatises (with the exception of Peter of Celle's *De disciplina claustrali*, Arnulf of Bohéries's *Speculum monachorum*, and Stephen of Salley's *Speculum novitii*).[45] The majority of twelfth-century canonical treatises express this concern in language that links the moral education offered by word to that offered by example and emphasizes both. In several canonical treatises the concern is expressed in descriptions of canons as teachers *verbo et exemplo*: the compilation in MS Ottoboni Lat. 175, the *Regula clericorum* of Peter of Porto, the *De institutione novitiorum* of Hugh of St. Victor, Odo of St. Victor's letters on the canonical life, and Philip of Harvengt's *De institutione clericorum* all use some form of the phrase *docere* (or *instruere*, etc.) *verbo et exemplo* (or *vita et doctrina*, etc.).[46] In addition, a concern with the effects of canonical action and words and a general tendency to

45. Peter of Celle's *Tractatus de disciplina* contains several suggestions that the monk should be concerned about the effect of his behavior or words (ibid., chaps. 3, 4, and 8, ed. de Martel, pp. 132–44 and 176); the most important of these are in chaps. 3–4, pp. 132–38. But Peter's occasional lapses from the monastic focus may be partly explained by the fact that he addresses canons as well as monks. Arnulf of Bohéries's *Speculum monachorum* contains one phrase that clearly departs from the monastic focus (Pl 184: col. 1176A). In Stephen of Salley's *Speculum novitii*, the basic perspective is definitely monastic: the author is concerned with virtue as an aspect of the soul's appearance before God; the only relationship discussed at any length is that between the soul and Christ. There are, however, a few references to avoiding the unedifying effects of behavior or enhancing the edifying effects: *Speculum novitii*, chaps. 1 and 18, ed. Edmond Mikkers, "Un 'Speculum novitii' inédit d'Étienne de Salley," COCR 8 (1946): 45–46 and 61.

46. Anonymous, Compilation of texts relating to regular canons taken from MS Ottoboni Lat. 175, in Jean Leclercq, "Un témoignage sur l'influence de Grégoire VII dans la réforme canoniale," *Studi Gregoriani* 6 (1959–61): 218–19 [hereafter Compilation, *Studi Gregoriani* 6]. Peter [of Porto] (?), *Regula clericorum*, bk. 1, chaps. 2 and 27, PL 163: cols. 708C–D, 709C, and 718B. Hugh of St. Victor, *De institutione novitiorum*, chap. 4, PL 176: col. 928A. Odo of St. Victor, *Epistolae de observantia canonicae professionis recte praestanda*, letter 2, PL 196: col. 1404; letter 4, PL 196: cols. 1406–8; letter 5, PL 196: cols. 1409–11. On Philip, see below n. 51.

link the exhortation to effective speech and the exhortation to edifying behavior appears in the anonymous *Expositio in regulam beati Augustini*, which has been attributed to Hugh of St. Victor and Letbert of St. Rufus; in the Vienna commentary; and in Adam of Dryburgh's *Liber de ordine, habitu et professione canonicorum ordinis praemonstratensis.*[47] In the Bridlington Dialogue and to a slight extent in Richard of St. Victor's *De questionibus* we find, if not the phrase *docere verbo et exemplo* or a linking of word and deed, at least treatments of conduct and speech that reveal an awareness of the obligation to edify.[48] Even in the *De claustro animae*, written by the regular canon Hugh of Folieto but addressed to all the cloistered (Hugh calls his audience *monachi*, not *clerici* or *canonici*), we find the idea that ordinary brothers should teach their neighbors and the idea that brothers should be examples.[49]

In a few canonical treatises, the concern for edification is closely and explicitly linked to a conception of the canon as preacher either to those outside or to those within the cloister. When the prologue of the anonymous compilation found in MS Ottoboni Lat. 175 refers to the task of canons, it is clearly describing preaching.

> Since the order of canons seems to have been established especially for this . . . —that is, to found the life of men in the

47. [Anonymous, attributed to Hugh of St. Victor and Letbert of St. Rufus], *Expositio in regulam beati Augustini*, chaps. 6, 7, and 9, PL 176: cols. 897C–8C, 901D, 902A–C, 909, 910D, and 912B. Anonymous, Preface *In regulam beati Augustini*, MS Vienna Nationalbibliothek 2207, fols. 11ᵛ and 13 bisᵛ–14ʳ. Adam of Dryburgh [or Adam Scot], *Liber de ordine, habitu et professione canonicorum ordinis praemonstratensis*, sermons 2 and 6, PL 198: cols. 457–60 and 489–94.

48. [Bridlington Anonymous or Robert of Bridlington], *The Bridlington Dialogue: An Exposition of the Rule of St. Augustine . . .* , ed. A Religious of C.S.V.M. [Sister Penelope] (London, 1960), pp. 39, 112, 130, 141, 173–74, and 187. Richard of St. Victor, *De questionibus*, chap. 1, ed. Colker, pp. 203–4, chap. 13, pp. 214–15, and chap. 20, p. 223. Whatever emphasis on verbal or nonverbal teaching there is in Richard's commentary is very faint. It should be noted however that Richard's treatise is not really a work of moral and spiritual advice that ranges over the entire Augustinian Rule but rather a discussion of twenty questions of a practical nature concerning the daily life of regular canons.

49. Hugh, *De claustro animae*, PL 176: cols. 1106D and 1125C.

catholic faith, to instruct according to the laws and morals of the Fathers, to correct, comfort and rebuke disciples by the words of holy doctrine, [and] to establish and nourish [them] for the purpose of guarding it—it is right that they should be moved by fear, broadened by hope, inflamed by charity, adorned with knowledge, outstanding in the light of the faith and in purity of life. And it is fitting that they have in themselves what they preach to others, lest they displease God or become reprobate to men.[50]

Philip of Harvengt's descriptions of clerics, which are directed toward and primarily about regular canons, use the phrase *docere verbo et exemplo* (or the idea behind it) repeatedly in referring to an obligation to preach.[51] Moreover, it is true that canonical commentaries are more likely than monastic ones to include discussions of preaching.[52] But the crucial distinction in focus between monastic and canonical works does not lie in the fact that canons claim for canons the right to preach. Indeed, Rupert of Deutz's monastic commentary claims the right for monks, the commentary in MS Vienna 2207 claims the right for both monks and canons, and Joachim of Flora in his commentary on the Benedictine Rule claims the prerogative for Cistercians.[53] Nor does the crucial dif-

50. Compilation, *Studi Gregoriani* 6: 181–82.
51. For example, Philip of Harvengt, *De scientia*, chaps. 23, 27, and 29, PL 203: cols. 695B–C, 699C–700C, and 702A–D; idem, *De justitia*, chap. 42, PL 203: col. 719A–B; and idem, *De silentio*, chaps. 76 and 88, PL 203: cols. 1102C and 1123B–24A.
52. The compilation in MS Ottoboni Lat. 175 (*Studi Gregoriani* 6:181–82 and 218), the commentary in MS Vienna 2207 (Preface, MS Vienna 2207, fols. 13 bis ᵛ–14ʳ), the Bridlington commentary (*Bridlington Dialogue*, pp. 99 and 134–35), Philip of Harvengt's *De institutione clericorum* (*De scientia*, PL 203: cols. 693–708), and Richard of St. Victor's sermon on Gregory the Great (see excerpts in Chatillon, "Contemplation, action et prédication . . . ," pp. 89–98) all devote attention to preaching. The only Benedictine commentaries to consider preaching are the commentary of Stephen of Paris, which was written not by a monk but by a secular cleric (see n. 103 below) and Peter the Deacon's odd and derivative compilation, the *Exortatorium*, in *Bibliotheca Casinensis*, ed. the monks of Monte Cassino, 5 (Monte Cassino, 1894), *Florilegium*: 66b–67b.
53. Rupert of Deutz, *Super quaedam capitula regulae divi Benedicti abbatis*, PL 170: cols. 515–17, 532, and 534. Preface, MS Vienna 2207, fol. 14ʳ.

ference between monastic and canonical authors lie in the fact that canons discuss preaching more frequently than monks; for many canonical commentaries and treatises do not discuss preaching. Rather the basic distinction is that canons advise canons about the religious life as if an obligation to educate by word and example is a crucial component. More important than the Vienna commentary's reference to preaching is the fact that it refers to canons as responsible for the effect of their words and behavior on others. More important than the fact that Rupert of Deutz and Philip of Harvengt both claim for their constituencies the right to preach is the fact that the monk Rupert generally ignores the educational effects of words and actions, whereas the canon Philip sees the words and deeds of ordinary cloistered brothers as educational. Anselm of Havelberg, in a work that, unlike the others considered here, has a polemical purpose, sums up the self-conception of regular canons when he says: ". . . being generally sought out by rude people, [the regular canon] is chosen and accepted and, like a lantern lighting a dark place, teaching by word and example, is loved and honored."[54]

Canonical and Monastic Views of Conduct

Behind the explicit exhortations to educate *verbo et exemplo* found in many canonical commentaries lies the assumption that an individual living the cloistered life is responsible in whatever he says or does not only for the state of his own soul but also for the progress of his neighbor. This assumption is frequently reflected in

---

Joachim of Flora (or Fiore), *Tractatus de vita sancti Benedicti et de officio secundum eius doctrinam*, chaps. 1, 12–14, and 37, ed. C. Baraut, "Un tratado inédito de Joaquín de Fiore: *De vita sancti Benedicti . . .* ," *Analecta sacra tarraconensia* 24 (1951): 42, 61, 63–70, and 105.

54. Anselm of Havelberg, *Epistola apologetica*, PL 188: col. 1129A. In the eleventh century, we occasionally find polemical works by monks that claim an edifying role. These works, however, tend to oppose word and example. Peter Damian writes: "Tu quoque valentius provocas videntes te properare post Christum, quam promovere potueras audientes qualibet multiplicitate verborum," *Opusculum* 45, *De sancta simplicitate scientiae inflanti antepoenenda*, chap. 3, PL 145: col. 697.

canonical discussions of behavior and in canonical discussions of speech or silence even where these discussions are not linked to each other and where words such as *docere* or *instruere* are not used. If we compare passages from canonical works that deal with behavior with similar passages from monastic works, we see clearly the difference in focus of the two groups.

When canonical authors treat conduct, they tend to emphasize its impact on the reader's fellows and to urge him to take care that the impact be a useful and wise one. Monastic authors, however, although they are sometimes aware of reciprocal relationships within the cloister, tend to see these relationships as affecting the reader and to see the reader's behavior as displayed before God. Occasionally they warn their readers to avoid causing scandal, but almost never do they urge them to bring others to good by their behavior. Thus the canon Hugh of St. Victor suggests that behavior may be even more important where it can be seen by men than where it will be seen only by God: "And, although a man ought in no place to desert his discipline, it ought however to be preserved more diligently and more solicitously there where being neglected it will cause scandal to many and being kept will cause an example of good imitation."[55] And Philip of Harvengt informs clerics, among whom he includes regular canons, that the life of the clergy is the pattern (*forma*) of the laity.[56] In contrast, when the monastic author of the Canterbury *Instructio* discusses behavior, he focuses entirely on personal virtue. In warning his reader against causing a disturbance in the dormitory, for example, he is concerned less with the novice's conduct before his brother than with his conduct before God:

> Therefore we must take care that nothing be done at night that will be shameful to hear in the morning. And if one takes care because of the brethren, what should be done because of God, whom naught can escape and to whom not even the thoughts of the heart are hidden? . . . Let all therefore within and without be done fittingly so that nothing appear that could offend the eyes of our Judge.[57]

55. Hugh, *De institutione*, chap. 3, PL 176: col. 927C.
56. See Philip, *De dignitate*, chap. 2, PL 203: cols. 669D–70B.
57. Anonymous, *Instructio novitiorum secundum consuetudinem ecclesiae cantuariensis*, MS Corpus Christi College, Cambridge, 441, portions

Even Bernard of Clairvaux, whose *De gradibus humilitatis* stresses the importance of the cloistered community, nevertheless ignores the individual monk's responsibility for edifying his neighbor. Bernard sees the *cenobium* as providing an opportunity for the individual monk to acquire discipline and to grow in love through identification with his neighbor's joys and sorrows.[58] The monk is urged to love his neighbor, but love here means an emotional response, not service and particularly not educational responsibility. The monk is to love *in order to learn*. Concern for the impression that one's words or deeds make on others is condemned as an element in conceit.[59] Moreover, in Aelred of Rievaulx's *Speculum caritatis*, where Bernard's conception of the community as teacher of charity is joined to an awareness of conduct as example, we still find a focus on the monk as learner. Although Aelred speaks of other monks as moving or shaping his reader by their example, he does not mention his reader's obligation to teach virtue or love to his fellows.[60]

The concern for appearance before God and union with him that is found in these monastic texts is not, of course, lacking in canonical writings. The new canonical focus on behavior as edification does not replace or shatter older traditions; rather it creeps in unobtrusively alongside them. Aelred's *Speculum* and Hugh of St. Victor's *De institutione novitiorum*, for example, are both studies of the "re-formation" of the image of God in man.[61] To both Hugh and Aelred, the novice is a learner progressing toward God and the novice's fellows are aids to his learning. In both authors, behavior is often seen as revealed before God. Hugh's emphasis on the novice as educator as well as learner, his emphasis on the novice's

---

published in David Knowles, ed. and trans., *The Monastic Constitutions of Lanfranc* (London, 1951), translation on p. 143ʳ, text on p. 143ᵛ.

58. Bernard, *De gradibus humilitatis*, chap. 3, OB 3, ed. Jean Leclercq and H. M. Rochais (Rome, 1963): 20–21.

59. Ibid., chap. 14, pp. 48–49.

60. Aelred, *Speculum caritatis*, bk. 2, chap. 24, in Aelred, *Opera omnia* 1: *Opera ascetica*, ed. A. Hoste and C. H. Talbot, CCCM 1 (Turnhout, 1971): 100–1; and bk. 3, chaps. 4–6, 12, and 24, pp. 108–14, 120–21, and 131–32. And see below, pp. 64–71.

61. See ibid., bk. 1, chaps. 3–5, pp. 16–19; and Hugh, *De institutione*, prologue, PL 176: cols. 925–26.

behavior as revealed before men, slips quietly into this treatise without any apparent tension or disharmony. Hugh simply pauses, while discussing man's relationship to God, to point out the effects of that relationship on man's fellows.

Canonical authors thus combine the canonical view of conduct with a concern for progress toward God. They are not unaware that offering behavior *coram hominibus* and offering behavior *coram Deo* imply two different intentions in the person behaving.[62] But they show little worry about the possibility of conflict between these two intentions. Indeed, because they move back and forth so naturally between edification of others through virtuous behavior and the offering of that same behavior to God as evidence of love for him, it is sometimes difficult to tell in a given passage exactly what the author's focus is. A description of good behavior that leads to God and a description of good behavior that educates men may, of course, be descriptions of the same behavior and therefore may, on occasion, be the same description, if the question of audience is ignored. An isolated phrase about conduct from Adam of Dryburgh's commentary on the Augustinian Rule and an isolated phrase about conduct from John of Fruttuaria's work for monastic novices may, when compared, seem identical. But the overall impact of the canonical treatises is different from that of monastic ones. Canonical authors assume that canons are not only learners who grow toward God but also pattern (*forma*) and example (*exemplum*) to those who encounter them.[63] Regular canons do not point out that their interest in the educational effects of their own behavior differs from the interests of their monastic contemporaries; the interest is different nonetheless.

Canonical and Monastic Views of Silence and Speech

Just as canonical and monastic treatises differ in their conceptions of conduct, so the two groups of works differ generally in

---

62. See, for example, *Bridlington Dialogue*, pp. 135–36.
63. This conception of life as example points toward the ideas of the friars. See below, pp. 105–6. The canons' conception of teaching *exemplo operis* and *documento sermonis* is found among the earliest Domin-

their treatment of words. With two or three exceptions, monastic authors do not exhort monks to teach each other by word, or even refer to monastic conversation as educational.[64] Moreover, monastic and canonical authors also differ in their treatment of the opposite of words—silence. Whereas canonical authors see silence as preparation for fruitful discourse between men, monastic authors tend to see silence as a good in itself or as a preparation for discourse with God.

The late twelfth-century *De novitiis instruendis*, for example, emphasizes monastic silence as an aspect of self-discipline. The author is concerned, not with the harm that words may do to listeners, but with the temptation that words may arouse for the speaker.[65] Similarly, the anonymous author of the sermons on the Benedictine Rule found in MS Auxerre 50 focuses on silence as a goal and fears speech as an opportunity for sin. In his discussion of chapter 6 of the Rule, the author warns monks to guard their mouths, avoid sin, and keep silence so that they may hear God; he interprets Isa. 6:5 "Woe is me because I have held my peace" in such a way that "holding one's peace" means "suppressing confession of faults."[66] Even Peter of Celle, whose treatment of behavior (and very occasionally of words) is an exception to the monas-

---

icans. The controversy among modern scholars over the extent to which Dominican poverty is means rather than end is therefore a little off the point. See Ralph F. Bennett, *The Early Dominicans* (Cambridge, 1937), pp. 31–51; William A. Hinnebusch, "Poverty in the Order of Preachers," *Catholic Historical Review* 45 (1959): 436–53; and Berthold Altaner, "Der Armutsgedanke beim hl. Dominikus," *Theologie und Glaube* 11 (1969): 404–17. To an early Dominican as to a regular canon, an *exemplum* was both the practice of the holy life for oneself and a pattern available for one's neighbor.

64. See above, n. 22. The only exception to the monastic approach to silence is Peter the Deacon, who borrows from Smaragdus (*Diadema monachorum*, chap. 38, PL 102: cols. 633C–34A) a passage that states that monks must sometimes speak for the sake of the spiritual health of others and omits the second portion of the same chapter that concludes that keeping silence is safest: see Peter, *Expositio super regulam sancti Benedicti*, in *Bibliotheca Casinensis*, ed. the monks of Monte Cassino, 5 (Monte Cassino, 1894), *Florilegium*: 129.

65. Anonymous, *De novitiis instruendis*, MS Douai 827, fols. 77ʳ–78ʳ.

66. [Commentary on the Benedictine Rule from Pontigny], MS Auxerre 50, fols. 20ᵛ·ᵇ–22ʳ·ᵃ, especially fols. 21ᵛ·ᵇ–22ʳ·ᵃ. On this work see Julian

tic focus, is entirely monastic in his treatment of silence. There are, writes Peter, seven seals with which the book of silence is sealed, seven reasons for keeping silence: tranquillity, profession, keeping the peace, quieting the movement and affection of the heart, withdrawing from secular business, scrutinizing the law of God, and contemplation. None of these reasons considers the effect of silence (or of words) on the monk's fellows.[67]

In contrast, when canonical authors set out to treat silence, the discussion frequently evolves into a discussion of useful speech. Philip of Harvengt's *De silentio* begins with the statement that silence is necessary for the cloistered so that they may talk with God but concludes by concentrating on the dangers of harmful silence and the wisdom of effective speech. And Hugh of St. Victor urges edifying speech as a cure for too much silence.[68] It is not surprising that the Vienna commentary on the Augustinian Rule, which sees regular canons as preachers, should see silence as preparation for didactic speech: ". . . they [the early canons] were silent thus in secret so that they might scatter the word of God in public; they appeared thus free from the acts of the world so that they, being careful, might rule the flock of the people committed to them."[69] It is, however, remarkable that, despite the wide diversity in actual canonical observance, those canonical authors who treat silence all imply that it is preparation for speech. Even Peter of Porto, whose rule allows room for the eremitical vocation and argues for periods of absolute silence in the cloister, betrays a concern for edifying words. Not only does Peter exhort canons to season their words with eloquence; he also states that one practices absolute silence at some periods in order to learn to abstain from lazy or useless words.[70] Peter sees silence less as an ascetic exercise of denial of the

---

G. Plante, "The Auxerre Commentary on the Regula S. Benedicti: The Prologue to the Regula: The Commentator's Main Concerns," *Regulae Benedicti Studia: Annuarium Internationale* 5 (1976): 171–82.

67. Peter of Celle, *Tractatus de disciplina*, chap. 18, ed. de Martel, pp. 224–32. See n. 45 above.

68. Cf. Philip, *De silentio*, chap. 1, PL 203: cols. 945C–46A, with chap. 14, cols. 969A–70C, and chap. 22, col. 981D. Hugh, *De institutione*, chap. 14, PL 176: col. 945B–D.

69. Preface, MS Vienna 2207, fols. 13 bis^v–14^r.

70. Peter, *Regula clericorum*, bk. 1, chaps. 32–36, PL 163: cols. 720–22. See also ibid., bk. 1, chaps. 2, 22, and 23, cols. 709B–C, 716, and 717A.

will than as a means of assuring that whatever talk takes place between brothers will be useful.

Canonical and Monastic Use of Sources

Monastic and canonical treatises of spiritual advice thus differ in their approaches to both behavior and words. The difference is subtle; often we feel, in reading these treatises, that it is more implicit than explicit. Regular canons and monks seem to be interested in slightly different things about themselves. Although ostensibly discussing the same topic—the life of the cloister—they shift the focus in different directions. We can see this difference in perspective in the use that certain authors make of traditional texts. When monastic authors borrow texts that describe clerics or preaching, they tend to alter or excerpt those texts so as to remove any emphasis on edifying behavior or speech. When canonical authors draw on earlier texts concerning the cloistered life they tend to add a concern for the educational responsibility of the individual brother.

The monk John of Fruttuaria, for example, borrows extensively from Ambrose's *De officiis ministrorum* in composing his treatise for novices. But his borrowings from Ambrose are taken, not from Ambrose's discussions of clerical functions or of clerical responsibility for the souls of others, but chiefly from chapters on the duties of the young and on modesty, which simply describe the appropriate virtues, and from Ambrose's opening discussion of silence. In almost every case where Ambrose moves from a consideration of silence to a consideration of the useful speech appropriate to clerics, John omits the latter emphasis and adds his own transitional sentences, treating silence as a goal, not as a means toward speech.[71] We can see the same process of selection and ad-

---

71. For example, chap. 2 of John of Fruttuaria, *Liber de vitae ordine et morum institutione*, PL 184: cols. 562D–65C is borrowed from Ambrose's *De officiis ministrorum*, PL 16: cols. 43–49, with omissions; chap. 3, PL 184: cols. 567D–68A, is from *De officiis*, PL 16: col. 49; chap. 3, PL 184: cols. 568A–B, is from *De officiis*, PL 16: col. 54; chap. 4, PL 184, the last sentence in col. 568 and the next few sentences could be

aptation at work in Peter the Deacon's *Exortatorium*. When Peter borrows from a sermon of Hildebert of Lavardin about the priesthood, he interpolates the words *et monachus* after *sacerdos* where the text refers to individual virtue; where the text refers to service of the altar and preaching Peter does not add *et monachus*.[72]

Canonical authors also tend to borrow from earlier texts what they wish to find, to add to earlier texts what they find lacking, and to emphasize in earlier texts what they see as important. The author of the Ottoboni compilation, for example, goes out of his way to select patristic passages that link life and reputation to effective service of one's neighbor by preaching. In a section entitled *Incipiunt capitula excerpta ex libris sanctorum de edificatione et correctione uite clericorum*, we find among the chapter headings: "(11) *Augustinus*. Ut clerici seruent bonam famam non solum coram Deo, sed etiam coram hominibus"; "(47) *Gregorius*. De his qui uerba legis meditantur et leuiter docent alios, male uerba uiuendo destruunt auditores"; "(201) *Augustinus*. Ut serui dei studeant non solum bonam uitam, sed etiam bonam famam seruare."[73]

Even more interesting than general canonical borrowing is the canonical reaction to the two major rules of the twelfth century: the Rule of St. Benedict and the canons' own Augustinian Rule. The Benedictine Rule itself is almost completely lacking in any suggestion that monks should, or could, offer moral education to one another. It sees in the *cenobium* primarily an opportunity for brothers to defer to, bear with, obey, and love each other in their

---

derived either from Ambrose's *Exhortatio virginitatis*, bk. 1, chap. 13, par. 87, PL 16: cols. 361D–62A, or from *De officiis*, PL 16: col. 43 and col. 26B. Much of chap. 4, par. 12, PL 184: col. 569B is from *De officiis*, PL 16: col. 33A–D; the first few sentences in chap. 4, par. 13, are from *De officiis*, PL 16: col. 28A; other sentences in chap. 4, par. 13, are from *De officiis*, PL 16: col. 27A.

72. Peter's text in *Bibliotheca Casinensis* 5, *Florilegium*: 68a–71a, is borrowed from a sermon of Hildebert which is numbered 97 in the Migne ed. (PL 171: cols. 786–90) and 9 in André Wilmart, "Les sermons d'Hildebert," *Revue bénédictine* 47 (1935): 33. See Paul Meyvaert, "The Exegetical Treatises of Peter the Deacon and Eriugena's Latin Rendering of the *Ad Thalassium* of Maximus the Confessor," *Sacris erudiri: Jaarboek voor Godsdienstwetenschappen* 14 (1963): 145.

73. Compilation, *Studi Gregoriani* 6: 190, 191, and 197.

search for individual salvation.[74] The Rule includes no exhortations to verbal teaching by ordinary monks and contains no references to the helpful effects of the good conduct of ordinary brothers.[75] It treats outward behavior entirely as an aspect of personal virtue. When twelfth-century monastic authors comment upon the Rule, they retain this focus. But when the canon Peter of Porto draws upon the Rule in composing his own rule for the canons of Santa Maria in Porto of Ravenna, he supplements the text with several telling additions. For example, much of book 1, chapter 2, of Peter's *Regula clericorum* is borrowed from chapter 4 of the Rule of St. Benedict. But in two separate places Peter specifically adds to Benedict's instruments of good works the obligation to bring others to virtue by word and example.[76] It is quite natural that the early twelfth-century *Regula clericorum*, composed before the widespread adoption of some form of the Augustinian Rule by regular canons, draws on the most respected rule for the cloistered life available, the Rule of St. Benedict. But Peter obviously feels a need to add an emphasis that is lacking in Benedict's text, an emphasis on the *cenobium* as a setting within which brothers not only love and obey but also edify each other *vita et doctrina*.

In contrast to the Benedictine Rule, the Rule of St. Augustine does contain a few traces of concern with edification. Ordinary brothers are not described as teaching by word and example, but the Rule stresses the responsibility of members of the community for each other, implying that brothers ought to aid their fellows by word and that an individual is responsible for the effect of his behavior on the spiritual growth of his neighbors.[77] Furthermore, Augustine's sermon 355 on the life of clerics, which was in the

---

74. See especially RB, chap. 72, pp. 162–63; see also RB, chap. 71, pp. 161–62. See below, pp. 75–77.

75. The only references to any kind of verbal aid are the vague references to the consoling of the sorrowful in the instruments of good works (RB, chap. 4, p. 30, par. 19) and the references to encouraging each other upon rising in chap. 22 (RB, p. 78, par. 8). There is a reference to evil conduct as a scandal in RB, chap. 31, p. 89, par. 16.

76. *Regula clericorum*, bk. 1, chap. 2, PL 163: cols. 708C–D and 709B–C.

77. *Praeceptum*, ed. [Melchior] Luc Verheijen, *La règle de saint Augustin*, 2 vols. (Paris, 1967), 1: 426–28, lines 106–33, especially pp. 426–27, lines 115–19: "Si enim frater tuus uulnus haberet in corpore, quod uellet

48

eleventh and early twelfth centuries treated almost as part of the *regula beati Augustini*, contains a very important passage that implies that behavior teaches:

> And indeed I do not wish that anyone acquire from you a pretext for evil living. *For we provide good things. the . . . apostle says, not only before God, but also before men* [2 Cor. 8:21; see also Rom. 12:17]. For our sake, our conscience is sufficient to us: for your sake, our reputation ought not to be soiled but it ought to have influence on you. . . . Two things are conscience and reputation. Conscience [is] for you, reputation for your neighbor. He who trusting in his conscience neglects reputation is cruel. . . . Before all *show yourself an example of good works* [Titus 2:7].[78]

But in commenting on the Rule of St. Augustine and in advising their fellows about the spiritual life, twelfth-century canonical authors do not merely reproduce these vague suggestions of responsibility for edification. Rather they again and again lay special emphasis on sermon 355 and on the sections of their rule that imply educational responsibility. Odo of St. Victor builds his advice about canonical reputation around borrowings from sermon 355.[79] The author of the *Expositio* uses sermon 355 to gloss the portion of the Rule that discusses the impact of gait and bearing.[80] Hugh of Folieto echoes the theme of conscience and reputation found in Augustine's sermon.[81] In the *Expositio*, the Bridlington Dialogue, and even in Richard of St. Victor's *De questionibus*, the portion of

---

occultare, cum timet sanari, nonne crudeliter abs te sileretur et misericorditer indicaretur? Quanto ergo potius eum debes manifestare ne perniciosius putrescat in corde?"

Ibid., 1: 423, lines 78–83: "Non sit nótabilis habitus uester, nec affectetis uestibus placere sed moribus. Quando proceditis, simul ambulate; cum ueneritis quo itis, simul state. In incessu, in statu, in omnibus motibus uestris nihil fiat quod cuiusquam offendat aspectum, sed quod uestram decet sanctitatem."

78. Augustine, sermon 355, in *Sermones selecti duodeviginti*, ed. C. Lambot, Stromata patristica et mediaevalia 1 (Utrecht, 1950), p. 124.

79. Odo quotes from Augustine's sermon 355 in letter 5, PL 196: col. 1411; all of letter 5 (ibid., cols. 1409–411) is strikingly similar to sermon 355.

80. *Expositio in regulam beati Augustini*, chap. 6, PL 176: cols. 897C–98C.

81. *De claustro animae*, PL 176: cols. 1070B–C and 1091B.

the Rule that discusses clothing, the gaze of others, and bearing is expounded in such a way as to emphasize the canon's responsibility for his effect.[82] Moreover, Adam of Dryburgh not only glosses this passage in a similar way,[83] he also deliberately returns to the passage several times in the course of his commentary, using it to emphasize the canon's impact on others.[84] It is the only passage from the Rule that he quotes out of order and more than once. The quotation from 2 Corinthians or Romans that Augustine used in sermon 355 becomes a major theme in Adam's treatment of behavior,[85] and he himself frequently joins the phrase *coram Deo, coram hominibus* to the Rule's injunction: ". . . let nothing be done that will offend the gaze of anyone. . . ."[86] Just as Peter of Porto chooses to add to the Benedictine Rule a concern for edification, so Adam of Dryburgh chooses to find in the Rule of St. Augustine a similar concern.

Monks and regular canons differ also, in subtle ways, in their use of biblical texts and figures (Mary and Martha; Rachel and Leah; Abraham, Sarah, and Hagar) traditionally taken to refer to "the two lives, active and contemplative." Having probed the nature of canonical concern for edification, we are now in a better position to understand what this difference is. The difference is not that canons alone develop a new conception of the "mixed life" of contemplation and service. Such an idea can be found in several twelfth-century monks, among them Aelred and Bernard of Clair-

---

82. See n. 80 above. Also *Bridlington Dialogue*, p. 130, and Richard of St. Victor, *De questionibus*, chap. 13, ed. Colker, pp. 214–15.

83. Adam of Dryburgh, *Liber de ordine*, sermon 2, PL 198: cols. 457C–60D.

84. Ibid., col. 459A; sermon 6, PL 198: cols. 489C and 492B; sermon 10, PL 198: col. 534A. The latter quotation occurs in the normal course of commenting on the Rule. Sermon 14, PL 198: col. 605A–B, is strongly reminiscent of the same phrases.

85. The words from Paul are quoted in ibid., sermon 2, PL 198: col. 459A; sermon 3, PL 198: col. 463C; sermon 4, PL 198: col. 489B; sermon 10, PL 198: col. 534B. The contrast *coram Deo, coram hominibus* is echoed throughout the sermons. See, for example, sermon 3, PL 198: col. 461D; and sermon 14, PL 198: col. 605B.

86. See ibid., sermon 10, PL 198: col. 534; and sermon 2, PL 198: cols. 457C–60D.

vaux,[87] and regular canons differ greatly in what they mean by the two lives. Adam of Dryburgh, who later left the Premonstratensians for the contemplative life of a Carthusian, speaks of alternation between action and contemplation, including both preaching and service in the active life.[88] Philip of Harvengt and Richard of St. Victor, both of whom were personally more interested in preaching, sometimes speak in the more conventional vein of "action" as good works and discipline that prepare the soul for contemplation.[89] The difference is one of emphasis, of how the author relates the various definitions to his own group or status. Where monastic authors speak of what we would call a mixed life as admirable, it is usually the role of someone else. Joachim of Flora concludes that preaching is not truly "monastic"; Bernard warns his monks that beginners should not be tempted by the high calling of sharing wisdom with others; Aelred sees such service as a decline or descent from Christ.[90] Guigo the Carthusian speaks of the "good works of the active life" as an obstacle to be "tolerated."[91] Regular canons, on the other hand, frequently find a way of attaching one of the variety of definitions of a mixed life to themselves. Adam of Dryburgh says that "we," along with Moses, should enter the tabernacle to talk with God and come out to talk with the people; the life outside is the *vita activa*, "which consists in . . . the preaching of truth and the works of virtue."[92]

---

87. See n. 42 above and below chapter 2, nn. 33–35.
88. Adam, *De tripartito tabernaculo*, PL 198: cols. 773–74. On Adam's life, see James Bulloch, *Adam of Dryburgh* (London, 1958).
89. Philip, *De obedientia*, chaps. 31–36, PL 203: cols. 905–21; Richard, *De questionibus*, chap. 14, ed. Colker, p. 216; idem, *Liber exceptionum*, pt. 2, bk. 14, chap. 5, ed. Chatillon, pp. 503–4; Chatillon on Richard, "Contemplation, action et prédication," pp. 96–7.
90. See below, pp. 69–71.
91. Guigo II, *Epistola de vita contemplativa (scala claustralium)*, chap. 15, in *Lettre sur la vie contemplative . . . Douze méditations*, ed. Edmund Colledge and James Walsh, SC 163, Sér. mon. 29 (Paris, 1970), p. 116. Cf. introd. to Guigo II, *The Ladder of Monks and Twelve Meditations*, ed. E. Colledge and J. Walsh (New York, 1978), pp. 37–8, where the editors try to assimilate Guigo's ideas to those of Hugh of St. Victor; the emphasis is, however, clearly different.
92. See passage cited in n. 88 above.

And Hugh of St. Victor, who, like Aelred and Guigo, speaks of churchly office as "deserting the secret places of the heart," says that those who do this, "not out of ambition but in obedience, are like Noah," a figure with whom canons identified.[93] Anselm of Havelberg's embracing of a dual life of contemplation and service of others as higher than a life of either service or contemplation alone is not typical of canons.[94] Canons are not alone in producing new definitions, new interpretations of traditional texts. But regular canons are more likely to see *as theirs* a dual responsibility for edification and personal growth.

The monastic focus on the individual's responsibility for his own salvation appears to have come down to twelfth-century authors from the early Middle Ages.[95] Throughout the century, it proved so powerful that no monastic author broke away. Twelfth-century monastic texts differ greatly in their descriptions of this search for salvation. Some authors see the virtue of the individual monk in completely static terms;[96] others see the monk's search for God as a dynamic process.[97] Some monastic authors feel entirely at home with the focus on the individual.[98] Others seem to feel a tension between love of neighbor and the rise to God. They struggle to retain an emphasis on individual salvation while allowing

93. *De arca Noe morali*, bk. 2, chap. 3, PL 176: cols. 637B–C: "Qui vero ecclesiastici regiminis curam, quae videlicet actio spiritualis est, agendam suscipiunt, et a secreto internae quietis, non ex ambitione, sed ex praecepto obedientiae ad publicum prodeunt; similes sunt Noe, qui exiens de arca sacrificium obtulit, quia saepe tales eos magis per abstinentiam omnes in se carnis motus occidunt, quo graviora internae quietis damna per occupationem se pertulisse cognoscunt." There is a suggestion here that the taking on of clerical office may be spiritually valuable exactly because it provides temptation and therefore discipline.
94. See above n. 38.
95. Jean Leclercq, *Initiation aux auteurs monastiques du moyen âge: l'amour des lettres et le désir de Dieu*, 2nd ed. (Paris, 1963).
96. For example, the commentary on the Rule from Pontigny, MS Auxerre 50, fols. 1ʳ–125ʳ. And see below, pp. 62–63.
97. Bernard, *De gradibus*, OB 3: 12–59.
98. For example, John of Fruttuaria, *Liber de vitae ordine*, PL 184: cols. 559–84; and Peter the Deacon, *Expositio*, in *Biliotheca Casinensis* 5, *Florilegium*: 82–165.

some room for man's awareness of his brother.[99] But, regardless of these differences and regardless of some monastic uneasiness over the appeal of love of neighbor as an emotional commitment, no monastic author breaks completely out of the monastic focus to voice unambiguously the idea that a cloistered individual ought to educate his fellow man. In contrast, canonical authors of the twelfth century, although they share with monastic authors the goal of individual salvation, formulate a new understanding of their obligation toward their neighbor. An analysis of works of practical spiritual advice clearly reveals that canonical authors employed distinctive language, emphasized new elements in the life of the cloister, and chose texts that would enhance their sense of moral responsibility.

The Canonical Focus: Revival or New Concern?

At first glance the sources on which canonical authors relied and the fact of the canons' clerical status might appear to explain the canonical perspective, to explain why canons broke away in part from a focus to which monks continued to adhere. Among the sources cited by twelfth-century canons, we can distinguish two groups that suggest the canonical emphasis: the patristic description of the preacher, and the treatment of reputation in the Augustinian Rule and sermon 355. The first of these traditions, the cliché "teaching by word and example," was a conventional description of the preacher that went back to Gregory the Great's *Pastoral Care* (and before that to the gospels) and appeared regularly in twelfth-century sermons of advice for preachers.[100] Some twelfth-century canonical writings are clearly drawing on this tradition when they connect the phrase *docere verbo et exemplo* to preaching. The second of these groups of sources, Augustine's sermon 355 and the section of the Augustinian Rule that treats the effects of behavior, was part of a larger body of material that was

---

99. Particularly Aelred, *Speculum caritatis, Opera omnia* 1: 3–161.
100. Jean Leclercq, "Le magistère du prédicateur au XIIIe siècle," *Archives d'histoire doctrinale et littéraire du moyen âge* 15 (1946): 105.

especially emphasized by reformers of the clerical life in the late eleventh and twelfth centuries.[101] Quotations from this material are common in twelfth-century canonical writing. These two groups of texts, one might argue, contain in germ the focus that characterizes twelfth-century canonical thought. One might further argue that canons drew on these traditions because they were clerics by definition, whereas monks, who were not always in orders, ignored the "clerical" texts.

Although twelfth-century authors disagreed about what constituted clerical status, there is no question that canonical authors saw regular canons as clerics.[102] Moreover, twelfth-century canons certainly saw the Augustinian Rule and Augustine's sermons on the life of clerics as "clerical" texts and as peculiarly their own. The tradition of advice to preachers undoubtedly also seemed, to some authors, to be a "clerical" tradition. Although clerical status in the twelfth century did not necessarily involve pastoral care or preaching, it is clear that some canonical (and indeed some monastic) authors saw clerical status as including the right to preach. It is therefore likely that some canonical writers felt comfortable borrowing the language of this tradition of advice to preachers exactly because they felt that canons were clerics and, as clerics, preachers. The fact that the secular cleric Stephen of Paris is the only commentator on the Benedictine Rule to emphasize the obligation to teach *verbo et exemplo* or to use the phrase to describe ordinary monks supports the idea that authors who thought of themselves as clerics tended to feel close to traditional descriptions of the preacher in a way that authors who were monks did not.[103] Thus it seems possible to argue that regular canons, because they consid-

101. Verheijen, *La règle*, 2: 215; Dereine, "Vie commune," pp. 385–401; and idem, *Liège*, pp. 23–27.

102. On changing ideas of clerical status in the twelfth century, see above p. 11, and A. Murray, *Reason and Society in the Middle Ages* (Oxford, 1978), pp. 263–65. Murray has been criticized for overstating the imprecision in the matter of who is clergy; review by J. W. Baldwin, *Speculum* 55 (1980): 604–6.

103. Stephen reveals a nonmonastic focus in two ways. First, he wanders away from his ostensible subject to explicit discussions of clerics and preaching: *Expositio super regulam beati Benedicti*, MS. Clm. 3029,

ered themselves clerics, drew on certain "clerical" traditions that suggested both the idea of behavior as a support to effective verbal teaching and the idea of behavior as an agent of moral education in its own right.

This argument implies that canons merely revived, in the context of the older monastic emphasis on individual salvation, a readily available, clerical emphasis on preaching and on reputation. But such an argument is unsatisfactory as an explanation of the canonical concern with edification. The canonical perspective goes beyond anything suggested in the traditions on which regular canons drew. The phrase *verbo et exemplo, vita et doctrina*, takes on in twelfth-century canonical authors a broader meaning than its earlier identification with preaching or with leadership. Several of the twelfth-century authors who explicitly use the phrase have in mind not preaching but rather ordinary human intercourse either inside or outside the cloister. They have transferred a sense of responsibility for edification from one role, that of preacher, to another role, that of the canon living a cloistered life (a role that might or might not include the role of preacher). The canonical concern for edification thus does not seem to be simply a union of traditional ideas of the preacher and traditional ideas of the monastic life. Some regular canons, such as Philip of Harvengt and the author of the Ottoboni compilation, borrow the phrase *verbo et exemplo* to describe preaching. But Peter of Porto and Hugh of St. Victor use the phrase to describe other human relationships. And Adam of Dryburgh, who does not use the phrase at all, treats words and actions as if they are agents of edification. The mere existence of a tradition for describing preaching does not explain

---

fols. [63$^{v.b}$–64$^{r.a}$], and [116$^{r.a}$–118$^{v.b}$]. Second, he suggests that *monks* have a responsibility to teach by word and example: MS Clm. 3029, fols. [46$^{r.a–b}$], [80$^{v.a}$–81$^{v.b}$], [82$^{v.a}$–83$^{v.a}$], and [106$^{v.a}$–107$^{r.a}$]. On Stephen see my article "Stephen of Paris and His Commentary on the Benedictine Rule," *Revue bénédictine* 81 (1971): 67–91; and Jean Leclercq, " Le commentaire d'Étienne de Paris sur la règle de s. Benoît," RAM 47 (1971): 129–44. Hugh of Folieto, like Stephen of Paris whom he influenced, displays great interest in the role of the prelate and in preaching; see *De claustro animae*, PL 176: cols. 1059–64, 1114–15, 1121C–D, 1122C–23D, and 1146A–C.

why regular canons used that tradition to describe almost all human intercourse.

Moreover, the mere existence of certain phrases and ideas in a body of material that canons used for regulating their lives and for meditation does not explain why those phrases took on an importance in canonical writing. The fact that Adam of Dryburgh quotes a passage from the Augustinian Rule is explained by the fact that he is commenting on the Rule; the fact that he emphasizes certain implications of that passage, and the fact that he returns repeatedly to cite the passage as a vehicle for conveying to others the ideas he sees there, is not explained simply by the commentary form or by the existence of the Rule itself. Twelfth-century canonical authors do not merely voice again a concern present in their sources since the early Middle Ages. Rather they make the Rule's vague references to reputation into explicit statements of an obligation to edify. What in the Rule is basically a concern with avoiding the negative effects of bad reputation becomes in many canonical writers a concern with offering to others the positive effects of good reputation.

The traditional monastic emphasis on individual salvation, the traditional description of the preacher, a few phrases in the Augustinian Rule and sermon 355—we cannot add these three elements together and come up with the conception of obligation that we find in twelfth-century canonical treatises. What canons were voicing was something new: a sense of the individual's responsibility for his fellows, both within and outside the cloister. Because of this new concern, canons turned to traditions that provided language for speaking of the concern, traditions that pointed beyond the monastic focus. Because of their clerical status, they found it easy to borrow from these particularly useful traditions. But the source of the new concern did not lie in the traditions that were borrowed or in the clerical status of the borrowers.[104]

---

104. This is not, of course, to argue that regular canons invented the new concern for neighbor that lies behind their concern for edification. As other historians have pointed out, such a concern seems to underlie many of the characteristics of eleventh- and twelfth-century religious movements. See n. 1 above.

Like most genuinely new concerns in a conservative and traditional society, the shift in focus that we find in canonical (but not monastic) texts is subtle. Canonical authors did not call attention to this change: they spoke in a new way without any clear sense that it was something new.[105] They felt a commitment to educate others that was no longer attached to the role of the preacher or leader, a commitment that gave a new importance to example as well as speech. But the new commitment rested easily alongside the search for individual salvation. The new focus did not replace the old. It did not have to. If speech and action of themselves communicated, then each could be offered *coram hominibus* as well as *coram Deo*. The ordinary brother in the cloister could serve his fellow man and his God by what he was, what he said, and what he did.[106]

The basic distinction between monks and regular canons, which historians have sought in actual practices, in polemical stance, and in articulated conceptions of the spiritual life, thus seems to lie in the area of attitudes and assumptions. Although frequently living similar lives, regular canons and monks understood in very different ways the significance of what they did and the responsibilities entrusted to them. Once we understand correctly the nature of the difference between canonical and monastic spirituality, we realize that the traditional view of the place of canons in twelfth-century history must be revised. Throughout the century, isolated individuals, who sometimes were (or became) both monks and canons, engaged in wandering preaching, in pastoral work, and in the care of pilgrims, the sick, and the poor. There were many such individuals, but we cannot identify them, as a group, as either canons or monks. These actions were new, wherever they appeared; they were not, however, "monastic" or "canonical." The majority of canons, like the majority of monks, only rarely joined actual service of men in the world to the discipline of cloistered withdrawal. What is new and distinctive about the canons as a group is not their actions or the rights they

105. Indeed, in their use of models from the past they frequently tried to make their concerns look traditional. See below pp. 103–4.
106. See above n. 63.

claimed. It is simply the quality of their awareness, their sense of responsibility for the edification of their fellow men. In this awareness we find a note not heard in the older traditions to which twelfth-century monks clung. And it is in this new sense of responsibility for moral education that the writings and thought of the regular canons point toward the appearance of the friars in the early thirteenth century.

II

The Cistercian Conception of Community

——————/

In 1919, Cuthbert Butler, abbot of Downside abbey and one of the major figures in Roman Catholic intellectual life in England in the early years of this century, published an interpretation of Benedictine history that stressed the cenobitical spirit of the Benedictine Rule.[1] Butler felt that Benedict avoided the excesses of physical asceticism and lonely competition found in earlier, more eremitical forms of monasticism and emphasized instead a life of obedience and stability within the monastic family. This interpretation has so dominated more recent scholarship on medieval monasticism that few students of the Benedictine Rule have noticed how little discussion of community it actually contains.[2]

This essay is an expanded version of "The Cistercian Conception of Community: An Aspect of Twelfth-Century Spirituality," *Harvard Theological Review*, 68 (1975): 273–86, copyright 1977 by the President and Fellows of Harvard University, reprinted by permission. Earlier versions were read at the American Academy of Religion meeting in 1973 and the Fifth Annual Cistercian Conference at Western Michigan University in 1974.

1. Cuthbert Butler, *Benedictine Monachism: Studies in Benedictine Life and Rule*, 2nd ed. (London, 1924). On Butler, see David Knowles, *The Historian and Character and Other Essays* (Cambridge, 1963), pp. 264–362.
2. Butler's emphases have been continued by the most influential English historian of monasticism, David Knowles. See *The Monastic Order*

The assumption that the monasticism of the "Benedictine centuries" (600–1100) was essentially cenobitical has led recent monastic historians to see the religious upheaval of the later eleventh and twelfth centuries as a "crisis of cenobitism"—a reform movement within monasticism that turned away from communal life and liturgy towards eremiticism.[3] Although the most imaginative recent scholarship on medieval religion suggests that some of the new religious groups of the eleventh and twelfth centuries joined an emphasis on service of others with an emphasis on physical and spiritual withdrawal,[4] most scholars have not located the monastic reforms of the twelfth century against the background of the new concern for service. Thus, because of the current state of monastic

---

in England: A History of Its Development from the Time of Dunstan to the Fourth Lateran Council: 940–1216 (1940; reprint ed. with corrections, Cambridge, 1963) and Christian Monasticism, World University Library (New York, 1969). For an interpretation of the Rule closer to my own, see Adalbert de Vogüé, La communauté et l'abbé dans la règle de saint Benoît (Paris, 1961). See also Giles Constable, "The Study of Monastic History Today," Essays on the Reconstruction of Medieval History, ed. Vaclav Mudroch and G. S. Couse (Montreal, 1974), pp. 21–51.

3. See G. Morin, "Rainaud l'Ermite et Ives de Chartres: Un épisode de la crise du cénobitisme au XIᵉ–XIIᵉ siècle," Revue bénédictine 40 (1928): 99–115; C. Dereine, "Odon de Tournai et la crise du cénobitisme au XIᵉ siècle," Revue du moyen âge latin 4 (1948): 137–54; Jean Leclercq, "La crise du monachisme aux XIᵉ et XIIᵉ siècles," Bullettino dell'Istituto Storico Italiano per il Medioevo 70 (1958): 19–41; Norman Cantor, "The Crisis of Western Monasticism," American Historical Review 66 (1960): 47–67; and the works by Knowles cited in n. 2 above. See also the essays in The Cistercian Spirit: A Symposium in Memory of Thomas Merton, ed. M. B. Pennington, Cistercian Studies Series 3 (Spencer, Mass., 1970), especially pp. 23–24 and 43. There were, of course, real hermits throughout the early Middle Ages; see Jean Leclercq, "L'érémitisme en Occident jusqu'à l'an mil," L'eremitismo in Occidente nei secoli XI e XII: Atti della seconda Settimana Internazionale di Studio: Mendola, 30 agosto–6 settembre 1962, Pubblicazioni dell'Università Cattolica del Sacro Cuore 3.4, Miscellanea del Centro di Studi Medioevali 4 (Milan, 1965), pp. 31–35.

4. See H. Grundmann, Religiöse Bewegungen im Mittelalter (1935, reprint ed., Hildesheim, 1961); E. W. McDonnell, "The Vita Apostolica: Diversity or Dissent?" Church History 24 (1955): 15–31; M.-D. Chenu, La théologie au douzième siècle (Paris, 1957); M.-H. Vicaire, L'imitation des

historiography, scholars have not fully understood a phenomenon that could not escape their attention: the interest in community and love of neighbor that characterizes Cistercian writings of the twelfth century.

Although the monastic *cenobium* of the early Middle Ages undoubtedly did in fact provide for the individual brother the kind of monastic family Butler has stressed, the black monks of the twelfth century, who continue the traditions of the great tenth-century houses, show little interest in interpersonal relations. It is the Cistercians—products of the so-called crisis of cenobitism—who work out an articulated awareness of the rich possibilities of communal life. Many monographs have been written describing the conception of love in individual Cistercian thinkers, and these monographs usually note that Cistercians made room for brotherly love in their accounts of growth toward God.[5] But monastic historians do not seem to have wondered why these Cistercians emphasized love of neighbor or what exactly they meant by the community of the cloister. In this essay I will explain the Cistercian sense of community and brotherly love by seeing in it a fruitful tension between the new twelfth-century interest in service of neighbor and the traditional conception of the monastic vocation, which was less "cenobitical" than Butler supposed.

---

apôtres (Paris, 1963); and L. K. Little, *Religious Poverty and the Profit Economy in Medieval Europe* (Ithaca, 1978). These works suggest that the religious revival of the eleventh and twelfth centuries was not merely a reform within monasticism but rather an outburst of religious feeling that touched clergy and laity as well as monks and resulted in a plethora of new groups, heterodox and orthodox.

5. See, for example, Étienne Gilson, *La théologie mystique de saint Bernard* (Paris, 1934); Pacifique Delfgaauw, "La nature et les degrés de l'amour selon saint Bernard," *Saint Bernard théologien: Actes du congrès de Dijon 15–19 septembre 1953, Analecta sacri ordinis cisterciensis* 11 (1953): 234–52; idem, "La lumière de la charité chez saint Bernard," COCR 18 (1956): 42–69, 306–20; Amédée Hallier, *Un éducateur monastique: Aelred de Rievaulx* (Paris, 1959); the essays by Pennington, Leclercq, and Ryan in *The Cistercian Spirit*, ed. Pennington, pp. 1–26, 88–133, 224–53; Charles Dumont, "Seeking God in Community According to St. Aelred," *Cistercian Studies* 6 (1971): 289–317; and the bibliography in Francis Wenner, "Charité: Le XIIe siècle," DS 2 (Paris, 1953): cols. 570–72.

Examples of Cistercian Treatment of Community

If we look at treatises on the cloistered life written by eleventh- and twelfth-century monastic authors for members of their own orders,[6] we find that treatises by black monks tend to discuss specific observances[7] or to describe, in rather static language, virtuous behavior.[8] Such treatises contain few references to the interior psychological development of the individual or to the emotions; they are inclined to stress obedience to the rule or to one's superiors more than love;[9] they show relatively little awareness of relationships between ordinary brothers within the cloister and do not stress these relationships as either a setting for or an incentive to personal spiritual growth. On the other hand, Cistercian authors, such as Bernard of Clairvaux, William of St. Thierry, Aelred of Rievaulx, Guerric of Igny, Isaac of Stella, Adam of Perseigne, and Stephen of Salley (Sawley), discuss change as well as describe virtue; refer frequently to emotion (particularly "love") as well as to external behavior; show an awareness of relationships among equals as well as between abbots and monks, seniors and juniors;[10]

6. The conclusions in this essay are based on a close comparison of the works of spiritual advice listed in the Appendix below. I have also drawn on Cistercian sermons.

7. See Rupert of Deutz, *Super quaedam capitula*, PL 170: cols. 477–538; Hildegard of Bingen, *Explanatio regulae sancti Benedicti*, PL 197: cols. 1055–66; Peter Abelard, letter 8, ed. T. P. McLaughlin, "Abelard's Rule for Religious Women," *Mediaeval Studies* 18:241–92; and the anonymous *Instructio*, portions in D. Knowles ed., *The Monastic Constitutions of Lanfranc* (London, 1951), pp. 135–49.

8. See John of Fruttuaria, *Liber de vitae ordine*, PL 184: cols. 559–84, portions of which have been reedited in A. Wilmart, *Auteurs spirituels et textes dévots du moyen âge latin* (Paris, 1932), pp. 94–98; Peter the Deacon, *Expositio* and *Exortatorium . . . ad monachos . . .* in *Bibliotheca Casinensis* 5, *Florilegium*: 61–72 and 82–165; Peter of Celle, *Tractatus de disciplina claustrali*, ed. G. de Martel, SC 240, Sér. mon. 47 (Paris, 1977), pp. 96–324; and the anonymous *De novitiis instruendis*, MS Douai 827, cols. 60ᵛ–80, portions of which are published in RAM 33:388–93.

9. This is especially true of Peter the Deacon and Abelard; see nn. 7 and 8 above.

10. The Cistercian Bernard of Clairvaux pays a great deal of attention to the role of the abbot and to particular regulations; see his *De praecepto*

and see interpersonal relationships as an incentive to compassion and a setting for learning humility.[11] Indeed both Bernard and Aelred distrusted eremitical life, arguing that Cistercian practice was preferable because it combined solitude with community.[12]

In the theoretical discussion of the soul's rise to contemplation that opens his famous *Steps of Humility*, Bernard of Clairvaux discusses the growth in love that comes from identification with the joys and sorrows of one's neighbor.

For we seek truth in ourselves, in our neighbors, and in its own nature: in ourselves, judging ourselves; in our neighbors, sympathizing with their ills; in its own nature, contemplating with pure heart. Observe . . . the order. First let Truth itself teach you that you should seek it in your neighbors before seeking it in its

---

et dispensatione in OB 3, ed. Jean Leclercq and H. M. Rochais (Rome, 1963): 253–94. But he combines this with an emphasis on love and community; see below, nn. 13, 14, 39, and 42.

11. In addition to the works cited in nn. 13–20 below, there are three other Cistercian works that do not as clearly reflect the conception of community I outline here. Arnulf of Bohéries's *Speculum monachorum*, PL 184: cols. 1175–78, is a very short discussion of the monastic day and the monastic virtues—so short that its failure to outline a conception of spiritual progress within the cloistered community is not significant. Furthermore we should note that it contains some suggestion that the monk learns from the example of his brother; see n. 29 below. Joachim of Flora's *Tractatus*, ed. C. Baraut, *Analecta sacra tarraconensia* 24 (1951): 33–122, is a statement of Joachim's theory of history and of the place of the Cistercians in it, not a discussion of the cloistered life. The anonymous commentary on the Rule from Pontigny, MS Auxerre 50, cols. 1ʳ–125ʳ, portions of which have been published in C. H. Talbot, "A Cistercian Commentary on the Benedictine Rule," *Studia Anselmiana* 43, *Analecta monastica* 5 (1958): 102–59, and idem, "The Commentary on the Rule from Pontigny," *Studia monastica* 3 (1961): 77–122, is probably but not certainly Cistercian. It contains many unelaborated references to community, but is more like works of the older monasticism in lacking a sense of the individual's emotional development within the communal framework and in stressing abbot and superiors more than brothers.

12. Bernard of Clairvaux, letter *Contra vitam heremiticam*, in *Études sur saint Bernard et le texte de ses écrits*, ed. Jean Leclercq, *Analecta sacri ordinis cisterciensis* 9 (1953): 138–39; Aelred of Rievaulx, sermon 5 *In natali sancti Benedicti*, PL 195: cols. 241–43. And see Jean Leclercq, "Problèmes de l'érémitisme," *Studia monastica* 5 (1963): 208–12.

own nature. . . . For in the list of Beatitudes that [Christ] distinguished in his sermon, he placed the merciful before the pure in heart [Matt. 5:7–8]. The merciful quickly grasp truth in their neighbors, extending their own feelings to them and conforming themselves to them through love, so that they feel *their* joys or troubles as their own. They are weak with the weak; they burn with the offended. They *rejoice with them that do rejoice, and weep with them that weep* [Rom. 12:15]. After the spiritual vision has been purified by this brotherly love, they enjoy the contemplation of truth in its own nature, and then bear others' ills for the love of it. But those who do not unite themselves with their brethren in this way, but on the contrary either revile those who weep or disparage those who do rejoice, not feeling in themselves that which is in others, because they are not similarly affected—how can they grasp truth in their neighbors? . . . But in order to have a miserable heart because of another's misery, you must first know your own; so that you may find your neighbor's mind in your own and know from yourself how to help him, by the example of our Savior, who willed his passion in order to learn compassion. . . .[13]

Later in the same treatise Bernard describes the monastic community as providing an opportunity for growth in humility through abasing oneself before others, comparing oneself unfavorably to others, concealing one's own virtue, and rejoicing in the virtue of one's neighbor.[14] Aelred of Rievaulx's *Mirror of Charity* elaborates the idea of growing toward love of God through a love of neighbor that means actual identification with the neighbor's emotions and sufferings.[15] It describes the example of one's neighbor as a major incentive to growth in virtue.[16]

13. Bernard of Clairvaux, *De gradibus humilitatis*, chap. 3, OB 3:20–21. Translation by George B. Burch, *The Steps of Humility* (Cambridge, Mass., 1950), pp. 133–35.
14. Bernard's analyses of the descent into pride, which makes up the second part of the treatise, assumes a communal setting. See *De gradibus*, chaps. 11–15, OB 3:46–50.
15. Aelred of Rievaulx, *Speculum caritatis*, bk. 3, chaps. 4 and 6, in *Opera omnia,* ed. A. Hoste and C. H. Talbot, CCCM 1 (Turnhout, 1971) 1:108–9 and 113–14.
16. Ibid., bk. 2, chap. 24, and bk. 3, chap. 12, *Opera omnia* 1:99 and 120. The themes mentioned here are also found in Aelred's *De spirituali*

Therefore it is known that rational affection, which arises from contemplation of the virtue of another, is more perfect than other feelings by which we are aroused to love of neighbor. For this love of virtue is no small indication of virtue. . . . I do not think our desire to be either pernicious or guilty, if it is directed according to this feeling; for it hinders nothing and indeed it is very profitable, if we desire his presence by whose example we are corrected if we are evil, by which we are pushed forward if we are good. . . .[17]

Guerric of Igny, Adam of Perseigne and Stephen of Salley see the *cenobium* as providing not only an opportunity for the practice of obedience but also an opportunity to imitate the virtuous conduct of the brothers and to grow emotionally through the stimulation of the good example of others.[18] Elaborating the idea, found also in Geoffrey of Auxerre, that the *cenobium* is the best hermitage, Guerric writes:

It is provided by the marvelous grace of God's providence that in these deserts of ours we have the quiet of solitude without lacking the consolation of sweet and holy companionship. It is possible for each of us to sit alone and be silent, for no one interrupts us; and yet it cannot be said of us: *Woe to him who is alone*, for he has no one to comfort him or *lift him up if he falls* [Eccles. 4:10]. We are in the company of men but without a crowd.[19]

amicitia, *Opera omnia* 1:287–350. For two very different interpretations of Aelred's doctrine of friendship, see C. Dumont, "Seeking God in Community," pp. 312–16, and John C. Moore, "Love in Twelfth-Century France: A Failure of Synthesis," *Traditio* 24 (1968): 429–43, especially 440.

17. Aelred, *Speculum caritatis*, bk. 3, chap. 24, *Opera omnia* 1:131.

18. Adam of Perseigne, Letter to Osmond, in Adam, *Lettres*, ed. J. Bouvet, 1, SC 66, Sér. mon. 4 (Paris, 1960): 7–29; and Letter to G. of Pontigny, PL 211: cols. 614–23. Stephen of Salley, *Speculum novitii*, ed. E. Mikkers, COCR 8 (1946): 45–68; see especially p. 67. Guerric of Igny, second sermon for Saints Peter and Paul, PL 185: col. 182C–D, and idem, fourth sermon for Advent, in Guerric of Igny, *Sermons*, 2 vols., ed. J. Morson and H. Costello, SC 166 and 202, Sér. mon. 31 and 43 (Paris, 1970 and 1973) 1:134–40.

19. Guerric, fourth sermon for Advent, *Sermons* 1, ed. Morson and Costello: 136–38, and see Jean Leclercq, "Le témoignage de Geoffroy d'Auxerre sur la vie cistercienne," *Studia Anselmiana* 31, *Analecta monastica* 2 (1953): 179–80.

William of St. Thierry, in a treatise for Carthusians, describes even these hermit monks as learning from the example of their comrades in the cloistered life.

> This is the holy intercourse that goes on between well regulated cells, their venerable pursuits, their busy leisure, their active repose, their ordered charity, to hold converse with one another in silence and to enjoy one another more while remaining apart from one another, to be an occasion of progress to one another, and although they do not see one another, to find matter for imitation each in the other, but in themselves only grounds for weeping.[20]

In contrast, black monks such as John of Fruttuaria in the eleventh century, Rupert of Deutz, Peter the Deacon, Abelard, and Peter of Celle in the twelfth, may have some sense that the monk learns from others, particularly his superiors, but they do not stress relationships among brothers as contributing to emotional change within the advancing soul.[21]

Cistercian Ideas Compared to Those of Regular Canons

Cistercians were not the only twelfth-century authors to develop a new conception of the cloistered community. Regular canons also tended to emphasize relationships between ordinary brothers more than did black monks, and a comparison of the canonical conception of community with the Cistercian one helps us not only to understand the nature of Cistercian ideas but also to suggest reasons why they took the form they did. Regular canons in general pay less attention to cloistered superiors than do monastic authors. Like Cistercians, they frequently mention relation-

20. William of St. Thierry, *Epistola ad fratres de Monte Dei*, pt. 2, chap. 1, *Lettre aux frères du Mont-Dieu*, ed. Jean Déchanet, SC 223, Sér. mon. 45 (Paris, 1975), p. 300; trans. Theodore Berkeley, *The Golden Epistle: A Letter to the Brethren at Mont Dieu*, The Works of William of St. Thierry 4, Cistercian Fathers Series 12 (Spencer, Mass., 1971), p. 77. Even Isaac of Stella, who felt great enthusiasm for the eremitical life, had a sense of community; see below chapter 3, n. 31.

21. See nn. 7 and 8 above. John of Fruttuaria's *Liber de vitae ordine* sees novices as learning from seniors.

ships between ordinary brothers. But, in addition, regular canons see the ordinary brother not only as learner but also as teacher.[22] They exhort those they address to edify others within and outside the cloister both "by word" and "by example." Like Cistercian authors, they see interpersonal relations as an incentive to and a setting for the practice of virtue; unlike Cistercians, however, they tell their readers to speak and act in order to edify their brothers. Hugh of St. Victor in his work for novices urges the canon to speak in order to teach virtue to his neighbor and states that virtuous conduct is even more necessary where it may be seen by men than where it will be seen by God alone.[23] Even the Premonstratensian Adam of Dryburg, who later joined an eremitical order, includes in his discussion of virtuous conduct references to the impact of the canon's example on his fellows.[24] Regular canons, of course, see the individual brother as responsible for his own growth toward salvation, but they feel no conflict between the individual's obligation for himself and his obligation to edify others. Their conception of the cloistered vocation thus integrates a particular kind of service of neighbor into a life of withdrawal from the world for the purpose of seeking and serving God.

The religious revival of the later eleventh and twelfth centuries included many activities and concerns that appear to express a new sense of man's obligation to love and serve his fellow man: the founding of hospitals for the care of travelers, the poor, and the sick; the appearance all over Europe of wandering preachers, sometimes themselves laymen, determined to bring the gospel to the laity; quarrels among the more established orders over the right to preach and practice the cure of souls.[25] The conception of edification found in treatises by regular canons is clearly a reflection of this new concern. In articulating the concern, canons drew on the traditional conception of the preacher's obligation to teach *verbo et exemplo*, which was a commonplace by the twelfth cen-

---

22. On the regular canons' concern for edification see above, chapter 2.
23. Hugh of St. Victor, *De institutione*, chaps. 3, 4, and 14, PL 176: cols. 927C, 928A, and 945A–B.
24. Adam of Dryburgh, *Liber de ordine*, sermons 2 and 6, PL 198: cols. 457–60 and 489–94.
25. See the works cited in n. 4 above.

tury, but was most often borrowed from Gregory the Great's *Pastoral Care*, and on the treatment of virtuous reputation found in the Augustinian Rule and in Augustine's sermon 355 "on the life and morals of clerics." Because of their clerical status, regular canons had a body of "clerical" material to draw on in addition to the wealth of patristic and medieval material on the cloistered life.

Cistercian authors were also drawn toward the concern for neighbor that regular canons incorporate as a concern for edification. Although eleventh- and twelfth-century monastic authors in general avoid the regular canons' focus on teaching *verbo et exemplo*, the few exceptions to this occur almost exclusively in Cistercian works.[26] Aelred of Rievaulx refers three times to the brother's obligation to correct his fellows;[27] Adam of Perseigne remarks that the monk should offer to his brothers an example of edification, not an example of corruption;[28] Arnulf of Boheries's *Mirror for Monks* admonishes: "In all things, let [the monk] edify those who see him . . .";[29] Stephen of Salley warns the novice to confess his failures to edify others;[30] and William of St. Thierry discusses the Carthusian order as example.[31] Moreover, both Bernard and Aelred move away from the early medieval idea that the "active life" consists of ascetic discipline and provides merely a first stage toward the higher goal of contemplation. Although neither author goes as far as the regular canon Anselm of Havelberg in working out a new conception of the "two lives"[32] and neither author is consistent in his treatment of the question, Bernard in at least one passage moves toward a view that places preaching

26. The one non-Cistercian exception is Peter of Celle's *Tractatus de disciplina*, which is addressed to regular canons as well as monks. Thus the fact that Peter departs from the monastic focus does not necessarily indicate that he sees an obligation to edify as part of the *monastic* vocation.
27. Aelred, *Speculum caritatis*, bk. 3, chap. 37, *Opera omnia* 1: 153–54; chap. 38, p. 157; and chap. 40, pp. 160–61.
28. Adam, Letter to G. of Pontigny, PL 211: col. 622C.
29. Arnulf, *Speculum monachorum*, PL 184: col. 1176A.
30. Stephen, *Speculum novitii*, chap. 1, ed. Mikkers, p. 46.
31. William, *Epistola ad fratres de Monte Dei*, preliminary sect., chaps. 1 and 3, ed. Déchanet, pp. 148 and 160–62.
32. See above, p. 33.

alongside self-discipline.[33] And Aelred in at least one passage assigns to monks the role of Martha (feeding the hungry and comforting the tempted) as well as the role of Mary (contemplation).[34] Both Bernard of Clairvaux and Joachim of Flora in his early, Cistercian phase show an admiration for the role of the preacher, and Bernard goes so far as to advise monks that preaching and saving others is a higher role—although he and Joachim agree that it is not a *monastic* one.[35]

The Basic Conception
of Monastic Vocation in
Cistercians and Other Monks

Despite the fact that Cistercian authors are personally drawn toward an ideal of service, they consciously reject the incorporation of this ideal into their conception of the monastic vocation. Aelred of Rievaulx is usually quite careful to locate his references to comforting others in a discussion of individual progress toward God that sees contemplation as the goal.[36] He states explicitly that

33. Bernard of Clairvaux, sermon 50 on the Song of Songs, OB 2, ed. J. Leclercq, C. H. Talbot, and H. M. Rochais (Rome, 1958): 78–83. See also Cuthbert Butler, *Western Mysticism: The Teaching of SS. Augustine, Gregory and Bernard on Contemplation and the Contemplative Life: Neglected Chapters in the History of Religion*, 2nd ed. (London, 1927), pp. 277–87; and Jean-Marie Déchanet, "La contemplation au XIIᵉ siècle," DS 2: cols. 1948–66.
34. Aelred, sermon 17, PL 195: cols. 303–9. See also Charles Dumont, "L'equilibre humain de la vie cistercienne d'après le bienheureux Aelred de Rievaulx," COCR 18 (1956): 177–89; A. Squire, "Aelred of Rievaulx and the Monastic Tradition Concerning Action and Contemplation," *Downside Review* 72 (1954): 289–303; and Hallier, *Un éducateur monastique*, pp. 92–97.
35. Bernard, sermon 12, OB 1, ed. J. Leclercq, C. H. Talbot, and H. M. Rochais (Rome, 1957): 66; and see n. 38 below. Joachim, *Tractatus*, ed. Baraut, pp. 42, 61, 63, and passim.
36. See Aelred, *Speculum caritatis*, bk. 3, chap. 38, *Opera omnia* 1: 156–57, where references to action for men (praying for them, giving aid, and offering encouragement and correction) are encompassed in a

turning to the needs of one's neighbor is a painful (although sometimes necessary) departure from Christ.[37] In his treatise *When Jesus was Twelve Years Old*, he distinguishes superiors, who must "descend" to care for their flocks, from brothers, who rest hidden under Christ's wings.[38] Similarly, Bernard sees the preaching to which he is so attracted as a falling away from contemplation.[39] In the portion of the sermons on the Song of Songs in which he praises service of neighbor and says that it is a sin to retain what has been given to one to be expended for others, he appears far more comfortable when he discusses the sin of giving forth what should be retained.

> But certainly [two things are] to be avoided: giving forth what we have received for ourselves, or retaining what we have received for bequeathing [to others]. Truly you retain for yourself the possession of your neighbor if . . . when you are full of virtues and also outwardly adorned with gifts of knowledge and eloquence, you bind in useless and indeed destructive silence, because of fear or laziness or . . . humility, . . . the good word that would be useful to many. . . . On the other hand, you scatter abroad and squander what is yours if before you are filled you hasten to give forth. . . .
>
> Therefore, if you are wise, show yourself a vessel and not a conduit. . . .
>
> You, brother, whose own salvation is not yet secure enough, whose love is nothing yet . . . why do you go around seeking or accepting the care of others? . . . But hear now, what and how many things are necessary for one's own salvation, what and how many things must be poured in, before we presume to give forth anything. . . .[40]

---

discussion of love as an emotion. Indeed the subject of book 3 of the *Speculum* is the emotion, love, which leads to God; so all of the remarks listed in n. 27 above occur in that context.

37. Aelred, *Speculum caritatis*, bk. 3, chap. 37, *Opera omnia* 1:154–56.
38. Aelred, *De Jesu puero duodenni*, sect. 3, pars. 30–31, *Opera omnia* 1: 276–78.
39. Bernard, sermon 12, OB 1: 63–65, and sermon 57, ibid., pp. 124–25.
40. Bernard, sermon 18, ibid., pp. 103–8.

Bernard states explicitly that the vocation of the monk is to cultivate his own virtue, not to serve others.[41] And his famous description of himself as the "chimaera of his age" reflects not only his feeling of being neither cleric nor layman but also his agony at being torn between withdrawal from and service of the world.[42] Moreover, Aelred's casual references to serving one's neighbor usually mean "praying for," "weeping over," and so forth, and not more active service,[43] and both Aelred and Bernard seldom have in mind an activity when they refer to "love of neighbor." Although Bernard draws a theoretical distinction between "effective charity" and "affective charity,"[44] his own references to love are almost always in fact references to affective charity.[45] Furthermore, when Bernard, Aelred, Stephen, and Adam discuss love, they tend to be interested in the implications of that emotion for the one who experiences it, not for the neighbor to whom it is directed.

Thus, in spite of their attraction toward the new interest in service of neighbor, Cistercians are uncomfortable with at least some of the possible manifestations of the new concern. They do not therefore ever really make their interest in preaching, in love, in the active life, into a clear exhortation to monks to edify others. Rather they focus these concerns back on the individual brother by seeing his speech, silence, or conduct as signs of his own ethical and spiritual condition. They seem to hold themselves within a conception of the monastic vocation that derives from the Benedictine Rule itself and is found in all monastic writing of the twelfth century. I shall be able to make the nuances of the Cistercian conception of community clearer if I describe this traditional monastic focus more fully and give some illustrations.

Both white monks and black monks agree in focusing their

---

41. Bernard, sermon 12, ibid., p. 66.

42. Bernard, letter 250, *Ad Bernardum priorem Portarum*, PL 182: col. 451A. See M. André Fracheboud, "Je suis la chimère de mon siècle: le problème action-contemplation au coeur de saint Bernard," COCR 16 (1954): 45–52, 128–36, 183–91.

43. See, for example, Aelred, *Speculum caritatis*, bk. 3, chaps. 4 and 5, *Opera omnia* 1:108–13.

44. Bernard, sermon 50, OB 2:78–83.

45. See, for example, the passage cited in n. 13 above.

works of spiritual advice on the progress of the individual brother. Indeed this concentration on the salvation of the individual rather than on his obligation for his fellows is the unifying factor that underlies the widely disparate conceptions of the cloistered life found in twelfth-century monastic treatises. Black monks are more inclined to see monks as learning from obedience to the abbot or the cloistered superiors; white monks are more inclined to stress relations among equals. Black monks are more inclined to discuss the brother's external behavior or to give an abstract disquisition on the nature of virtue. In contrast, Cistercians emphasize emotional development. But all monastic authors write as if their monastic reader's fundamental concern is his own virtue. They discuss external behavior as displayed before God rather than men and insist that it must truly portray one's interior state because God reads hearts as well as manners. Although they warn the monk to avoid scandalizing others, they also warn against paying attention to how one's behavior appears to the brothers, because such attention can lead to pride. And they distrust speech. Whatever the particular regulations of their order concerning silence may be, they see it as the safest condition. Unlike regular canons, who see silence as preparation for teaching, monks—black and white—see silence as a goal in itself and as a preparation for discourse with God.[46]

Monastic authors, whether Cistercians, Carthusians, or black Benedictines, turn even discussions of word and of example into discussions of the individual's own condition. For example, in a Christmas sermon, Guerric of Igny makes God's almighty Word into an argument for silence:

> Truly it is a trustworthy word and deserving of every welcome, your almighty Word, Lord, which in such deep silence making its way down from the Father's royal throne into the manger of animals, speaks to us better by its silence. . . . [Christ] speaks peace for the holy people upon whom reverence for him and his example impose a religious silence. And most rightly was it imposed. For what recommends the discipline of silence with such weight and such authority . . . as the Word of God silent in the midst of men? There is no word on my tongue, the almighty

46. See above, pp. 43–46.

Word seems to confess while he is subject to his mother. What madness then will prompt us to say: *With our tongues we can do great things . . .* [Ps. 11:5]. If I were allowed I would gladly be dumb and be brought low, and be silent even from good things, that I might be able the more attentively and diligently to apply my ear to the secret utterances and sacred meaning of this divine silence, learning in silence in the school of the Word for as long as the Word himself was silent under the discipline of his mother.[47]

The compiler of the late twelfth-century *De novitiis instruendis* warns against *multiloquium* and sees speech as a river overflowing its banks and gathering mud.[48] Guigo II uses as a recommendation of silence the words of Ecclesiastes, which in the writings of regular canons serve as exhortation to edifying speech:

> . . . no one can be at peace until he has become humble. . . . Then indeed will he sit alone and be silent. And he who is not silent cannot hear you when you speak to him. The Scripture says: *The words of the wise are as a goad* [Eccles. 12:11] to those who listen to them in silence. Let all my world be silent in your presence, Lord, so that I may hear what the Lord God may say in my heart.[49]

A collection of sermons on the Benedictine Rule from Pontigny comments similarly that the wise man is known by few words and goes on to warn that monks should not be known; they should lie hidden; few among them have the wisdom for even *pauca verba*. But "truly there is one Word to whom I wish you to be known not in few words but in varied tongues and many words as the Holy Spirit will give to you to speak." Before men one should speak little; before God one should be known by prayer, but even before God tears and desire are preferable to words. Some men say to

47. Guerric of Igny, fifth season for Christmas, *Sermons*, ed. Morson and Costello 1:226–28; trans. the monks of Mount St. Bernard abbey, in Guerric of Igny, *Liturgical Sermons* 1, Cistercian Fathers Series 8 (Shannon, Ireland, 1971): 63–64, with minor changes.
48. *De novitiis instruendis*, MS Douai 827, fols. 77–78.
49. Guigo II, *Meditationes*, chap. 1, in *Lettre sur la vie contemplative . . . Douze méditations*, ed. E. Colledge and J. Walsh, SC 163, Sér. mon. 29 (Paris, 1970), p. 128, lines 36–44; trans. Colledge and Walsh, *The Ladder of Monks and Twelve Meditations* (New York, 1978), pp. 104–5.

monks "You are the light of the world" (Matt. 5:14); in fact, however, secular men frequently outshine monks and monks should be humble before them, learning from the example of those who have not renounced the world.[50] Abelard (an odd advocate of silence and humility) warns nuns against speech, quoting the phrase from the Benedictine Rule "Monks ought to study silence."

> Words indeed send out the understanding of the soul, so that it tends toward that which it understands and clings [to it] through thought. For by thinking we talk to God, just as by words to men. And while here [on earth] we tend toward the words of men, it is necessary that we be led from thence. . . . Not only idle words but even those that appear to have some utility are to be avoided for this reason, that one goes easily from necessary to idle, and from idle to harmful.[51]

This monastic tendency to emphasize the spiritual condition of the individual rather than its implications for other men is the frame within which the Cistercian sense of community appears.

Once we understand the ways in which twelfth-century monks—white and black—agreed about what lay at the heart of the monastic vocation, we see that even the occasional references to edification found in Cistercian treatises usually occur within broader discussions that see the community as a setting for individual growth, not as an opportunity for service. When Adam of Perseigne and Stephen of Salley refer to the possibility that external behavior can be a good example to others, their discussions are couched in the negative. Rather than urging the novice to show virtue to others in order to instruct them, they urge the novice to confess that his wickedness has been to others an example of corruption. Listing the failings of the novice, Adam writes:

> Often from the good things that we have or do through the grace of God, we seek not the glory of God but our own glory. . . . Often we pretend that we are other than we are. Often we are confounded less than we should be by evils recognized in ourselves. . . . Often when we ought to edify our brothers instead we show to them examples of corruption.[52]

50. Pontigny commentary, MS Auxerre 50, fols. 36ʳᵃ⁻ᵛᵇ and 88ʳᵃ.
51. Abelard, letter 8, ed. McLaughlin, pp. 244–46.
52. See n. 28 above.

The context is an exhortation to confession that condemns both hypocritical attention to exterior behavior and overattention to the spiritual condition of others. Similarly, Stephen chides the novice for offering bad examples and failing to edify, but the context of his discussion is also a discussion of confession and contrition.[53] Both Stephen and Adam concentrate on change within the novice. Stephen, like Aelred of Rievaulx, sees the example of others as stimulating and aiding those he addresses. This conception of example as an agent of edification stresses not the individual's obligation to teach others but rather his own spiritual growth.[54] And Adam of Perseigne includes an explicit obligation to teach virtue among the steps of spiritual growth when he writes to a novice master, but carefully excludes this step from his discussion when he writes to a novice.[55] Moreover, William of St. Thierry's reference to the Carthusian order as an example of virtue to others—which seems at first glance identical to the conception of example found in treatises by regular canons—is in one crucial aspect different. Whereas regular canons urge other canons to act *in order to edify*, William deals with the reputation of the order, not the individual, and explicitly urges the brothers to concentrate on their own salvation. He merely comments that, if the brothers ignore others, the example of their concentration on their own growth in virtue will itself influence the world.[56]

The Benedictine Rule as Source

The focus on the individual monk as learner that characterizes all twelfth-century monastic treatises is the focus of the Benedictine Rule. Benedict's "instruments of good works" (chapter 4) are a static description of virtue; they contain very few references to

53. See n. 30 above.
54. See, above, nn. 16, 17, and 18.
55. Cf. Adam's letters to Osmond, a novice master, and to H., abbot of Tiron, with his letter to Nicolas, a young Cistercian. Second letter to Osmond, in Adam, *Letters*, ed. Bouvet 1:136; Letter to H., abbot of Tiron, in Adam, *Correspondance d'Adam, abbé de Perseigne (1188–1221)*, ed. J. Bouvet, *Archives historiques du Maine* 13 (1953): 52–53; and Letter to Nicolas, PL 211: col. 628C–D.
56. See n. 31 above.

service, and none of these references has anything to do with edification.[57] The famous "steps of humility" (chapter 7) treat the behavior and the words of the monk as symptoms of his own virtue, not as examples to his neighbor.[58] Even where external appearance is the ostensible topic, the monk is not urged to edify by example.

> The twelfth step of humility is that a monk not only in heart but also even in body should always show humility to those who see him; that is, in the work of God, in the oratory, in the monastery, in the garden, on the road, in the field, or wherever he sits, walks, or stands, he should always be with bowed head and glance cast down toward the ground; at every hour thinking himself guilty because of his sins, let him consider that he is soon to be brought before the dread judgment, and say always to himself in his heart that which the publican in the gospel said with downcast eyes: Lord, I a sinner am not worthy to raise my eyes to heaven. . . . [Luke 18: 13][59]

In chapter 6, silence is urged because of the dangers of speech for the one who speaks.[60] The focus is entirely on the monastic life as training for the individual.

Benedict's Rule places more emphasis on abbot than on community and sees the abbot both as teacher *verbo et exemplo* and as ruler to be obeyed. Like treatises by black monks in the twelfth century, it contains no sense of the community as a laboratory within which the individual learns to feel compassion and contrition by emotional identification with the experience of his fellows. And it sees even the learning of humility as due more to obedience to abbot or seniors than to self-abasement before equals. It does not explore in detail the opportunities for pride or humility provided by the communal life.[61] But, in so far as it treats community, it does so entirely from the point of view of the "beginner" in the "school for the service of God."[62] It does not even mention a mo-

57. RB, chap. 4, pp. 29–30, par. 1–2, 14–19.
58. Ibid., chap. 7, pp. 39–52.
59. Ibid., pp. 50–51, par. 62–65.
60. Ibid., chap. 6, pp. 38–39; see also chap. 4, p. 32, par. 51–56.
61. See de Vogüé, *La communauté et l'abbé.*
62. The longest discussion of relations among equals (RB, chap. 72, pp. 162–63) focuses entirely on relations between brothers as an aspect of the discipline of the individual monk; see also chap. 71, pp. 161–62.

nastic responsibility to edify others. The Benedictine Rule itself thus suggested to those who commented upon its words and lived its prescriptions a concentration on displaying conduct, speech, and silence before God rather than before one's cloistered brothers.

Affective Subtlety

Just as regular canons were aided in their efforts to incorporate service of neighbor into the cloistered vocation by the availability of a clerical tradition, so monks, new and old, were held by their own rule to a definition of themselves as learners and beginners. It was apparently impossible for any monastic author in the twelfth century to develop a conception of community that included the obligation to edify. No matter how attracted Cistercians may have been to the new concern for service that permeated twelfth-century religious life, they continued to feel that the monk qua monk was responsible for his own salvation. But there are many aspects to relationships between human beings, and it is possible to incorporate an awareness of certain aspects of community into a concentration on individual spiritual growth. Indeed a conception of community that focuses on the individual makes possible certain kinds of depth that are not enhanced by a stress on service.

Many historians have noted the deep psychological sensitivity that characterizes Cistercian treatises. In their inwardness and interest in the emotions, Cistercians contrast not only with black monks but also with regular canons.[63] The canons' conception of community, which emphasizes reciprocity in relations, leads to a concentration on the external effects of speech and behavior. We can see this clearly in references by regular canons to the impact of example, which tend to focus on literal imitation.[64] In contrast, when an individual feels that an obligation to serve others cannot

63. There were, of course, regular canons, notably Richard of St. Victor, who wrote abstract treatises on love (see Wenner, "Charité," cols. 570–72). But these discussions occur in the context of allegorical exegesis, not of practical spiritual advice. A comparison of canons' works of advice for the cloistered with those by Cistercians shows that regular canons stress emotional change as a result of community life less than do Cistercians.

64. Hugh of St. Victor, *De institutione*, chap. 7, PL 176: cols. 923D–33C.

be an integral part of his vocation, an interest in human relationships has to become an arena for self-exploration. Thus Cistercians see human love as an opportunity for personal emotional expansion, as "affective" more than "effective" charity. When they deal at length with the impact of example, they tend not only to refer to it as changing conduct but also to explore the way in which it stimulates desire in the learner. Thus Aelred speaks of the example of others that "corrects" conduct as something "desired," something that "impels us forward," something that "floods our mind with a certain sweetness of joy." Bernard says that the merciful "extend their feelings" to their neighbors, "conforming" to them "through love." [65]

Connected to the emotional heightening that Cistercians give to learning from example is the emotional heightening they give to another traditional monastic theme, that of learning from experience rather than from schools or books. [66] Used by most cloistered writers in the twelfth century, the word *experientia* retains its older Augustinian meaning when it is used by regular canons and black monks: man learns from all that befalls him and particularly from his temptations and his mistakes. [67] For example, Odo of St. Victor says:

> . . . the cell indeed is said to instruct when he who remains in it, being enlightened by the Holy Spirit, is instructed. . . . We see that many who are unlettered, living in little cells, dispute subtly concerning conduct, understand with marvelous quickness the hidden temptations of the devil and fear [them] when they have been discovered, and moreover seek and love God above all

Philip of Harvengt, *De institutione*, PL 203: cols. 689-94, 719A–B, 738B–C, 748–50, 766B, 933C–D, 1035D, and 1202C.

65. See above nn. 13, 17, 18, and Aelred, *Speculum caritatis*, bk. 3, chaps. 12 and 19, *Opera omnia* 1:120–21 and 125–28.

66. See J. Leclercq, *Initiation aux auteurs monastiques du moyen âge: l'amour des lettres et le désir de Dieu*, 2nd ed. (Paris, 1963); A. Murray, *Reason and Society in the Middle Ages* (Oxford, 1978), pp. 250, 318, 393–94 and passim.

67. On this point see Aelred Squire, "The Composition of the *Speculum caritatis*," *Cîteaux: commentarii cistercienses* 14 (1963): 230; and Hallier, *Un éducateur monastique*, pp. 129–45.

things. Who, I ask, taught them? Not the eloquence of masters, but the grace of the Holy Spirit and the experience of temptations. . . .[68]

But to Cistercians, learning by experience becomes deeply affective and sensual: experience means "tasting," "embracing"—an almost tactile meeting with God. Aelred writes lyrically in this mode:

. . . the soul gradually becomes accustomed to so much consolation that it is eventually drawn into the further phase . . . in which it experiences some foretaste of the future reward, moving, as it were, into the house of God's holiness, into His very dwelling place. . . . Thus fear and love alternate in the soul, teaching us necessary lessons in this life until such time as the whole soul is thoroughly penetrated by love and longs for the embrace of Christ. . . .[69]

And in a similar vein he writes: "It seems to me that only experience teaches."[70] Guigo the Carthusian echoes this aspect of Cistercian thought:

O Lord Jesus, if these tears, provoked by thinking of you and longing for you, are so sweet, how sweet will be the joy that we shall have to see you face to face? . . . Those who have not known such things do not understand them, for they could learn more clearly of them only from the book of experience where God's grace itself is the teacher. Otherwise, it is no use for the reader to search in earthly books.[71]

Using the traditional cloistered theme of opposing the monastery to the secular school, grace and humility to intellectual quest and

68. Odo, letter 2, PL 196: cols. 1403–4. For another statement of the educational value of experience (chiefly the experience of temptation), see Hugh of St. Victor, *De institutione*, chaps. 7–8, PL 176: cols. 933D–34A.
69. Aelred, *Speculum caritatis*, bk. 2, chaps. 11–12, *Opera omnia* 1: 77–80; trans. Geoffrey Webb and Adrian Walker, *The Mirror of Charity* (London, 1962), pp. 52–53.
70. Aelred, *Sermones inediti b. Aelred abbatis Rievallensis*, ed. C. H. Talbot, Series scriptorum s. ordinis cisterciensis 1 (Rome, 1952), p. 106.
71. Guigo II, *Scala*, chap. 8, in *Lettre*, ed. Colledge and Walsh, pp.

academic wrangling, Cistercians express in deeply affective language the learning that comes from God and from the community of beginners in the service of God.

Thus, a comparison of Cistercian sermons and works of advice with treatises by their cloistered contemporaries underlines the Cistercians' affective intensity by showing its context. In contrast to black monks of the eleventh and twelfth centuries, Cistercians expand the attention paid to interpersonal relations. In contrast to black monks and regular canons, they introduce a passionate concern for emotional change. Like black monks, they retain a focus on the monk as learner. The Cistercian conception of community channels the general twelfth-century concern for love of neighbor into a deeper and more sophisticated version of Benedict's concentration on the individual's own salvation. The "crisis of cenobitism" produced a more intense awareness of the importance of community. But, among twelfth-century Cistercians, this emphasis never departed from Benedict's understanding of the monastic vocation as the search for and service of God.

Recent historiography has agreed that the affective spirituality of twelfth-century Cistercians is something new, whatever precursors and roots it has in the writings of Anselm and other eleventh-century figures. My comparison of Cistercian treatises and sermons with those of contemporary black Benedictines and regular canons suggests that the particular nature of this new affectivity arises from the acute need Cistercians felt both to turn their lives toward concern for neighbor, as did so many of the new orders, and yet to heed the clear warning of the Benedictine Rule that beginners in God's service should devote themselves to rooting out their own sins. The strength of the traditional monastic self-definition pulled the new conception of the "apostolic life" or "evangelism" as service of neighbor back into a concern for the monk's own cloistered community. Because of the Rule's definition of the brother as beginner—a beginner whose triumph is the attainment of humility—attention to community became attention to the ways in which community served as setting for the individual's spiritual journey. Yet awareness of the complexity of

---

98–100, lines 198–209; trans. Colledge and Walsh, *Ladder*, p. 89. See also chap. 5, in *Lettre*, pp. 90–92, lines 105–33.

that journey was enhanced by the ambivalence many Cistercians felt about their vocation. Bernard's cry, "I am the chimaera of my age," is only the sharpest expression of a desire to serve combined with guilt arising from a suspicion that the desire is in some way inappropriate, a subtle temptation to pride and self-aggrandizement. Indeed the very success of twelfth-century Cistercians in recruiting followers (and we must not forget that they were more successful than the regular canons, for all the canons' clerical status and articulated goal of edification) undoubtedly owes something to the particular way in which their spirituality drew on a new sense of both neighbor and self. Ambivalence, tension, paradox are not necessarily unattractive to those seeking a religious life, especially in a society changing as rapidly as twelfth-century society appeared to its members to be changing.

The Cistercian conception of community epitomizes the tension between denial and affirmation of the world that ran throughout the twelfth-century religious revival and the Gregorian reform movement that preceded it. In the essays that follow, we shall see the Cistercian ambivalence about service reflected in their conception of authority, even the authority of God. We shall also see that, despite their differences from more traditional monks and from regular canons, they shared with them a concern for external behavior and details of lifestyle, which is also part of the context for their new affectivity.

III

Did the
Twelfth Century
Discover
the Individual?

D̲ID THE twelfth century discover the individual? For a number
of years now medievalists have claimed that it did. Indeed, over
the past fifty years, in what Wallace Ferguson calls "the revolt of
the medievalists," scholars have claimed for the twelfth century
many of the characteristics once given to the fifteenth century by
Michelet and Burckhardt.[1] As a result, standard textbook accounts

This essay is an expanded version of "Did the Twelfth Century Discover the Individual?"
Journal of Ecclesiastical History 31 (1980): 1–17, reprinted by permission of the Cambridge
University Press. It was first delivered as a lecture at the University of Utah in April, 1978.
I am grateful to my host there, Glenn Olsen, for his interest and suggestions. I am also
grateful to Jere Bacharach, Gordon Griffiths, and Thomas Hankins of the University of
Washington, who read an early draft of the article; to John Benton of the California Institute
of Technology and Giles Constable of Dumbarton Oaks and Harvard, who have graciously
permitted me to draw upon their forthcoming work; and to Brian Stock of the Pontifical
Institute of Medieval Studies in Toronto, who has given me so many ideas over the past
four years that parts of this essay seem to me merely one side of a continuing conversation
with him. My essay was rewritten before I had an opportunity to see and profit from the
reply by Colin Morris, "Individualism in Twelfth-Century Religion: Some Further Reflections," *Journal of Ecclesiastical History* 31 (1980): 195–206. Morris adds some interesting
examples to support both his position and mine; our interpretations of the twelfth century
continue, however, to differ.
    1. Wallace K. Ferguson, *The Renaissance in Historical Thought: Five Cen-
turies of Interpretation* (Boston, 1948), pp. 329–85.

now attribute to the twelfth century some or all of the following: "humanism," both in the narrow sense of study of the Latin literary classics and in the broader sense of an emphasis on human dignity, virtue, and efficacy; "renaissance," both in the sense of a revival of forms and ideas from the past (classical and patristic) and in the sense of a consciousness of rebirth and historical perspective; and "the discovery of nature and man," both in the sense of an emphasis on the cosmos and human nature as entities with laws governing their behavior and in the sense of a new interest in the particular, seen especially in the "naturalism" of the visual arts around the year 1200. In the past fifteen years, however, claims for the twelfth century have increasingly been claims for the discovery of "the individual," who crops up—with his attendant characteristic "individuality"—in many recent titles. In the area of political theory, Walter Ullmann has seen the individual emerging in the shift from subject to citizen.[2] Peter Dronke, Robert Hanning, and other literary critics have argued for the emergence of the individual both as author and as hero of twelfth-century poetry and romance.[3] And, in the area of religious thought, R. W. Southern, Colin Morris, and John Benton have called to our attention a new concern with self-discovery and psychological self-examination, an increased sensitivity to the boundary between self and other, and an optimism about the capacity of the individual for achievement.[4]

It is to the last of these arguments—the characterization of twelfth-century religious life and writing as "the discovery of the individual"—that I wish to turn in this essay, not in order to contradict recent analyses, but in order to place the development

2. Walter Ullmann, *The Individual and Society in the Middle Ages* (Baltimore, 1966).

3. Peter Dronke, *Poetic Individuality in the Middle Ages* (Oxford, 1970); Robert W. Hanning, *The Individual in Twelfth-Century Romance* (New Haven, 1977). See also Per Nykrog, "The Rise of Literary Fiction," paper delivered at The Renaissance of the Twelfth Century Conference, 26–29 November 1977, Cambridge, Mass. [hereafter Twelfth-Century Ren. Conference], to appear.

4. Richard W. Southern, *The Making of the Middle Ages* (New Haven, 1959), pp. 219–57; idem, "Medieval Humanism," *Medieval Humanism*

to which they refer in a wider context and thereby delineate it more precisely. The concentration of scholars on the discovery and intense scrutiny of self in twelfth-century religious thought has sometimes implied that this individualism meant a loss of community—both community support and community control.[5] The interpretation has also sometimes implied that typological thinking and a sense of modeling oneself on earlier examples is in twelfth-century literature a vestige of an earlier mentality that simply gets in the way of a sense of individual quest, experience, and self-

and Other Studies (New York, 1970), pp. 29–60; Colin Morris, *The Discovery of the Individual: 1050–1200* (1972; paperback reprint ed., New York, 1973); John Benton, "Individualism and Conformity in Medieval Western Europe," *Individualism and Conformity in Classical Islam,* ed. A. Banani and S. Vryonis, Jr. (Wiesbaden, 1977), pp. 145–58; idem, "Consciousness of Self and of 'Personality'," paper delivered at Twelfth-Century Ren. Conference, to appear. While Benton explicitly rejects the phrase "discovery of the individual" to describe the twelfth century (see n. 11 below), his description of the new self-consciousness of twelfth-century writers has clear affinities with the positions of Morris and Southern. A similar interpretation is suggested in Peter Brown, "Society and the Supernatural: A Medieval Change," *Daedalus* 104 (Spring, 1975): 135–51, and Lynn White, "Science and the Sense of Self," *Daedalus* 107 (Spring, 1978): 47–59, and was adumbrated almost half a century ago in the works of André Wilmart; see idem, *Auteurs spirituels et textes dévots du moyen âge latin* (Paris, 1932). Charles M. Radding, "Evolution of Medieval Mentalities: A Cognitive-Structural Approach," *American Historical Review* 83 (1978): 577–97, agrees in passing (p. 596) with some of the points I make here. Radding's essay seems to me to provide, not the causal explanation that he claims to give, but rather an interesting way of describing aspects of the twelfth century noted by all the authors cited above. See also idem, "Superstition to Science: Nature, Fortune, and the Passing of the Medieval Ordeal," *American Historical Review* 84 (1979): 945–69.

5. See Morris, *Discovery,* pp. 11–13, where he says that "the Church of the twelfth century thus saw a revival of personal piety . . . but it failed to recover a sense of community for the faithful as a whole." Burckhardt, of course, saw a similar stress on the individual at the expense of community in the fifteenth century: Jacob Burckhardt, *The Civilization of the Renaissance in Italy* (1860; reprint of English trans., New York, 1954), p. 100.

expression.[6] Yet current research on the twelfth-century religious revival in fact underlines nothing else so clearly as its institutional creativity. It depicts a burgeoning throughout Europe of new forms of communities, with new rules and custumals providing new self-definitions and articulating new values.[7] My purpose is therefore to place the often discussed discovery of the individual in the context of another equally new and important twelfth-century interest to which scholars have paid less attention: a quite self-conscious interest in the process of belonging to groups and filling roles. For twelfth-century religion did not emphasize the individual personality at the expense of corporate awareness. Nor did it develop a new sense of spiritual and psychological change, of intention, and of personal responsibility by escaping from an earlier concern with types, patterns, and examples. Rather twelfth-century religious writing and behavior show a great concern with how groups are formed and differentiated from each other, how roles are defined and evaluated, how behavior is conformed to models. If the religious writing, the religious practice, and the religious orders of the twelfth century are characterized by a new concern for the "inner man," it is *because* of a new concern for the group, for types and examples, for the "outer man."[8]

"Discovery of the Individual" or "Discovery of Self"?

Before placing the discovery of the individual in the context of roles and group affiliation, I should say something more about

6. Hanning, *Individual in Romance*, pp. 1–5 and 17–19; Norman F. Cantor, *The Meaning of the Middle Ages* (Boston, 1973), p. 203.
7. There is a great deal of recent literature on this twelfth-century religious revival. The best discussions are still H. Grundmann, *Religiöse Bewegungen im Mittelalter* (1935; reprint ed., Hildesheim, 1961); M.-D. Chenu, *La théologie au douzième siècle* (Paris, 1957); and M.-H. Vicaire, *L'imitation des apôtres* (Paris, 1963). L. K. Little, *Religious Poverty and the Profit Economy in Medieval Europe* (Ithaca, 1978), provides a lively survey and a controversial interpretation.
8. In suggesting that the twelfth century in fact saw an increased awareness of self stimulated by and stimulating an awareness of community, I

what this popular description of the period actually means. For Robert Hanning, Colin Morris, and other scholars who have given the phrase currency, it refers to the emphasis placed by thinkers of the late eleventh and twelfth centuries on inner motivation, on the emotions, on psychological development. To begin with perhaps the most frequently cited example, Abelard's *Ethics* locates the ethical value of an act in the actor's intention, not in the outward deed. And other twelfth-century thinkers who do not go as far (including Abelard's opponent Bernard) frequently couch their discussions of particular matters as if in agreement with this theory.[9] Twelfth-century theories of penance locate remission of sin in contrition, not oral confession, although the requirement of confession is not removed. Bernard of Clairvaux and other "new monks" stress discovery of self—and of self-love—as the first step in a long process of returning to love of and likeness to God, a love and likeness in which the individual is not dissolved into God but rather becomes God's partner and friend. And twelfth-century discussions of the problems of novices show that both counselors and beginners are able to consider themselves as subjects of discussion, to stand apart from themselves and watch their own defenses, emotions, and motives as they move toward God or help others to do so.[10] In these examples and many others, we find a keener awareness than in the immediately preceding centuries both of the complexity of the individual's inner life and of the boundary that separates that varied and fascinating inner being from other equally fascinating and complex selves.[11]

---

am not proposing a general model for or explanation of cultural change. Other factors unquestionably underlay both the attitudinal changes of which I speak here. An interesting recent effort at explanation is A. Murray, *Reason and Society in the Middle Ages* (Oxford, 1978).

9. Morris, *Discovery*, pp. 74–75. Abelard's point is more subtle than many of his critics have realized; see D. E. Luscombe, *The School of Peter Abelard* (Cambridge, 1969); and *Peter Abelard's Ethics: An Edition . . .* , ed. D. E. Luscombe (Oxford, 1971).

10. See Morris, *Discovery*, and Benton, "Consciousness of Self," for these examples and others. And see pp. 16–17 and 64–65 above and p. 157 below.

11. For the purposes of this essay the twelfth century must be taken to begin about 1050, as the title of Morris's book suggests. Scholars have also questioned whether the verb should be "discover" or "rediscover,"

It is possible to ask whether "the individual" is the best term for what is being discovered in these new emphases of twelfth-century religious writing. As John Benton has himself pointed out, the Middle Ages did not have our twentieth-century concepts of the "individual" or "the personality." Their word *individuum* (*individualis, singularis*) was a technical term in the study of dialectic; what they thought they were discovering when they turned within was what they called "the soul" (*anima*), or "self" (*seipsum*), or the "inner man" (*homo interior*). And this self, this inner landscape on which they laid fresh and creative emphasis, was not what we mean by "the individual." When we speak of "the individual," we mean not only an inner core, a self; we also mean a particular self, a self unique and unlike other selves. When we speak of "the development of the individual," we mean something open-ended. In contrast, as Benton has noted, the twelfth century regarded the discovery of *homo interior*, or *seipsum*, as the discovery within oneself of human nature made in the image of God—an *imago Dei* that is the same for all human beings.[12] Moreover, the twelfth-century thinker explored himself *in a direction* and *for a purpose*. The development of the self was toward God. One might say, to simplify a little, that to the ancients the goal of development is the adult human being, for which one finds a model in the great works of the past; to the twelfth century the goal of development is likeness to God, built on the image of God found in "the inner man"; to the twentieth century the goal is the process itself.

It thus seems advisable to replace "the discovery of the individual" by "the discovery of self" and to give to the latter phrase two precise meanings: first, the twelfth century "discovered the self" in the sense that interest in the inner landscape of the human being increases after 1050 in comparison to the immediately preceding period; second, the twelfth century "discovered the self" in the sense that knowing the inner core of human nature within

pointing most frequently to the case of Augustine in late antiquity; see Benton, "Consciousness of Self." Whether or not we see Augustine as more aware of inner process than twelfth-century writers, it is clear that his treatment of consciousness, which has some affinities to modern phenomenology, is not very much like twelfth-century analyses.

12. See Benton, "Consciousness of Self," and Morris, *Discovery*, especially pp. 64–65.

one's own self is an explicit theme and preoccupation in literature of the period.

But, even with this modification in the popular phrase, to characterize the religious life of Europe from 1050 to 1200 as the "discovery of self" is to tell only half the story. For, although twelfth-century authors stressed intention in ethics, they also stressed literal imitation of the details of the life of Christ. Although several thinkers, primarily Cistercians and Carthusians, wrote treatises on the progression from love of self to love of God, others, primarily regular canons, wrote treatises classifying forms of life in the church. And, while the theology and devotion of the period stress the stance of the individual worshipper before God, focusing in theories of the Atonement on man's responsibility rather than on the devil's power, and emphasizing personal conversion and solitary prayer, these thinkers also love to discuss relationships. Friendship, like discovery of self, is treated as a step toward God, and the Trinity itself is explained by reference to the relationship of friends (and not just, as Augustine had done, by analogy to the individual psyche or mind). A sense of models or types, a sense of proliferating groups and structures and of the necessity to choose among them, and a sense of relationship are characteristics of the twelfth century at least as salient as a new sense of self.

So far I may appear to have made an obvious point. A number of reviewers and critics have responded to Colin Morris's book by noting that the twelfth century discovered the group as well as the individual.[13] And clearly the period from 1050 to 1200 is characterized by communes, guilds, and schools as well as by hermits, rebels, and wandering scholars. But I am not arguing simply that the twelfth century saw a proliferation of forms of institutionalized religious life: monastic orders differentiated from each other by constitutions and customs, new kinds of hermit groups, communities of regular canons or canonesses.[14] It is true that men and women had new opportunities to choose among types of religious life; it is also true that some twelfth and thirteenth-century preach-

13. Radding, "Evolution," p. 596; Brian Tierney, review of Morris, *Journal of Ecclesiastical History* 24 (1973): 295–96.
14. See note 7 above.

ers came to see as religious certain groups or roles in society—for example, the married—that were not so designated before. My point here, however, is not merely the existence of these roles or groups, although their existence is the precondition for the new awareness of which I am speaking. My point is that people felt an urgency, unlike anything we see in the early Middle Ages, about defining, classifying, and evaluating what they termed "orders" or "lives" or "callings" (which includes what we would term both voluntary religious associations and social roles). Throughout the period there was both intense competitiveness (and sometimes virulent invective) between organized religious groups and a growing sense of the positive value to be given to "diversity within unity."[15] But the competition was not merely competition for resources and influence; it was also an effort by each of the competing groups to define itself. The pluralism was never merely an acceptance that there are "many mansions" in one house of God, many forms but one (Christian) essence; there was always a concomitant effort to underline and articulate differences. And both competition and acceptance of diversity were expressed through discussions of models and types. A quite particular sense of the relationship between inner and outer, between motive and model, characterizes twelfth-century discussions of belonging to groups.

Twelfth-century nuns or monks, canons or wandering preachers, defined themselves as imitators of Christ and the apostles. And Christ—although he might come in vision or meditation as one individual to another—was not, of course, a model of personal uniqueness. Christ was imitated not in that which makes him particular (e.g., his maleness) but in what is generalizable (al-

15. Giles Constable, "The Multiplicity of Religious Orders in the Twelfth Century: Pluralism and Competition," paper delivered at The York University Conference on Consciousness and Group Identification in High Medieval Religion, 7–9 April 1978 [hereafter Conference on Consciousness]. See also idem, Introd., *Libellus de diversis ordinibus et professionibus qui sunt in aecclesia*, ed. G. Constable and B. Smith (Oxford, 1972), pp. xi–xxvii; and Yves Congar, "Les laïcs et l'ecclésiologie des 'ordines' chez les théologiens des XIᵉ et XIIᵉ siècles," *I laici nella "societas christiana" dei secoli XI e XII: Atti della terza Settimana Internazionale di Studio: Mendola, 21–27 agosto 1965*, Pubblicazioni dell'Università cattolica del Sacro Cuore 3.5, Miscellanea del Centro di Studi Medioevali 5 (Milan, 1968), pp. 83–117.

though this may seem quite particular to us—e.g., his not carry-ing a moneybag). The twelfth-century person affiliated with a group, converted to a Christian life, by adopting a model that simultaneously shaped both "outer man" (behavior) and "inner man" (soul). A pattern of behavior that was the same for all in the group defined the Christian life; to evangelize was to offer that pattern to others. The twelfth-century discovery of self or as-sertion of the individual is therefore not our twentieth-century awareness of personality or our stress on uniqueness; the twelfth-century emphasis on models is not the modern sense of lifestyle as expression of personality nor the modern assumption of a great gulf between role or model or exterior behavior and an inner core of the individual. The twelfth-century person did not "find him-self" by casting off inhibiting patterns but by adopting appropriate ones. Moreover, because to convert was to find a stricter pattern and because Christians learned what it was to be Christian from models, an individual who put off the "old man" for "the new" became himself a model available to others. To begin to behave in the pattern of Christ (as did Norbert of Xanten, Peter Valdes, Francis of Assisi, Clare, and others) was therefore often to found a movement almost in spite of oneself.

Awareness of Groups

Perhaps the most obvious indication of the new interest in re-ligious groups and their relationships to each other is the appear-ance of works that analyze the various orders or callings in the church—a kind of work unknown in the early Middle Ages. When Gerhoh of Reichersberg writes his *De aedificio Dei*—which is really a treatise on the "city of God"—he is not discussing, as was Augustine, either the church or the elect; he is trying to cata-logue and categorize the full range of roles in human society and to say how each is religious.[16] Herrad of Hohenbourg (or Landsberg), who also discusses the orders within the church, expresses an anal-ogous interest in ways of life in her image of the ladder of virtues.

16. Gerhoh of Reichersberg, *Liber de aedificio Dei*, partial ed. by E. Sackur, *Monumenta Germaniae Historica, Libelli de lite* 3 (Hannover, 1897): 136–202; older ed. PL 194: cols. 1187–1336.

(Each rung represents a religious or lay profession and its characteristic temptation, ranging from the hermit seduced by love of his garden to the lay woman and the soldier—on the same rung of the ladder—tempted by love of ornament and fornication.)[17] Elisabeth of Schönau has a vision of a hill, up which lead different paths for the married, the celibate, prelates, widows, hermits, and children.[18] Moreover, twelfth-century efforts do not stop at accepting the self-description of a given group; they create new categories and reanalyze existing ones. Anselm of Havelberg in his *Dialogues* tries to categorize groups by their historical evolution and suggests that new groups emerge to meet new needs.[19] The anonymous author of the *Libellus de diversis ordinibus* does not just describe the varieties of monks, canons, and hermits he sees around him; he comes up with a new "sociological" principle for grouping and analyzing them—whether they live close to or far from towns.[20] The always controversial Abelard even attempts to move beyond Christian and non-Christian as categories and ask how far philosophers, Christians, and Jews might share or not share fundamental religious perceptions.[21] And the visionary Hildegard of Bingen, who uses the metaphor of a building to represent the history of salvation, not only writes of the different orders in both church and society but also gives an analysis of male and female differ-

17. Frontispiece. Herrad of Hohenbourg, *Hortus deliciarum*, ed. Rosalie Green, Michael Evans, Christine Bischoff, and Michael Curschmann, 2 vols. (London, 1979), Reconstruction, pp. 352–53, and Commentary, p. 201. See also Reconstruction, pp. 375–78. Herrad is drawing on a Byzantine motif. It is indicative of the twelfth-century attitudes I am here discussing that she changes the standard depiction of a ladder of monks, aided by virtues and attacked by vices, into a representation of social groups. See Adolf Katzenellenbogen, *Allegories of the Virtues and Vices in Medieval Art* (1939; reprint ed. with new bibliographical references, New York, 1964), p. 24, and Gérard Cames, *Allégories et symboles dans l'Hortus deliciarum* (Leiden, 1971), pp. 88–90.

18. Elisabeth of Schönau, *Liber viarum Dei*, in *Die Visionen der hl. Elisabeth und die Schriften der Aebte Ekbert und Emecho von Schönau*, ed. F. W. E. Roth (Brünn, 1884), pp. 88–122.

19. Anselm of Havelberg, *Dialogues*, ed. Gaston Salet, SC 118, Sér. mon. 18 (Paris, 1966).

20. On the *Libellus* see above n. 15.

21. Peter Abelard, *Dialogus inter philosophum, Judaeum et Christianum*, PL 178: cols. 1611–84.

ences that diverges noticeably from received theological opinion. (To Hildegard, women are less concupiscent than men.) Her analysis serves as the basis for attributing to women a distinct role, both socially (as mothers) and religiously (as nuns and mystics), while emphatically denying their suitability for the priesthood.[22]

The consciousness and self-consciousness of groups is reflected, as I said above, in an increase of competition. The opening years of the twelfth century in particular were filled with *invectiones, altercationes,* and *apologiae.* Conflict erupted between new monks and old and between monks and regular canons—conflict that was not just competition between groups for members and donations (although it was that) but also a reflection of changing ideas of the Christian life. When we see monks and regular canons quarreling over who has the right to preach and practice the cure of souls, whose life is more ascetic and withdrawn from the world, whose rule is older, it is hard not to feel that the strident attacks and defenses reflect the authors' confusion about what their own life ought to be. For example, nearly all attackers and defenders seem to have found service of neighbor through preaching simultaneously enticing and threatening. Monks, who were told by canons in self-righteous tones that the monastic role was "weeping not teaching," nonetheless claimed the right to preach because preaching was best done by the most holy; regular canons, who were described by monks as more involved with the world and the active life, themselves claimed that their life was stricter and more "apostolic" because they were subject to temptation in the world. More moderate monks accused new, stricter groups of hypocrisy and Phariseeism; new groups accused older ones of laxness and corruption but at the same time began to write in positive ways about the "active life."[23] And when canonists developed a solution

22. The image of the building is worked out in Hildegard, *Scivias,* pt. 3, ed. Adelgundis Führkötter and Angela Carlevaris, CCCM 43, 2 vols. (Turnhout, 1978), vol. 2 passim; on the different orders in the church see pt. 2, vision 5, 1:172–224, especially chaps. 26, 27, and 35, pp. 197–98 and 205; on male and female differences and on access to the priesthood see pt. 2, vision 3, chap. 22, 1:147–48; pt. 1, vision 2, chaps. 11 and 12, 1:19–21; and pt. 2, vision 6, chaps. 76 and 77, 1:290–91.
23. On this polemical literature see above chapter 1, n. 21.

to competition between groups, or at least to the technical problem of transfer (*transitus*) from one house to another, by suggesting that one was permitted to transfer without permission *ad arctiorem vitam*, the problem became even clearer.[24] For what *was* the "stricter" life? Which *was* the religiously "better" order? It is hard to avoid the conclusion that behind the question "Which is the better life?" lay the questions: "Which life shall *I* choose?" "Have *I* chosen well?".

Alongside this strident competition, however, appeared a new acceptance of variety. Frequently expressed in corporate metaphors, Pauline or classical in origin ("there are many members but one body"), or in paraphrases of John 14:2 ("there are many mansions but one house of God"), this acceptance of difference was not an argument that all roles are equal or a denial that there are groups altogether extraneous or dangerous to the Christian body. Nonetheless, it appears to be true, as Giles Constable has argued, that between the eleventh and thirteenth centuries, religious writers come increasingly to suggest that there are many different organized religious groups each with its own task, that there are many different social roles (merchant, mother, peasant, craftsman) to all of which religious significance can be given, and that within any religious community there are complementary roles and talents for various individuals.[25] On the individual level this sense of roles and gifts complementing each other is expressed by Hildegard of Bingen when she modifies 1 Cor. 11:9 ("For the man was not created for the woman but the woman for the man") and differs from other theologians of her day by saying:

24. Philipp Hofmeister, "Der Übertritt in eine andere religiöse Genossenschaft," *Archiv für Katholisches Kirchenrecht* 108 (1928): 419–81; Kurt Fina, "'Ovem suam requirere.' Eine Studie zur Geschichte des Ordenswechsels im 12. Jahrhundert," *Augustiniana* 7 (1957): 33–56; Douglass Roby, "*Stabilitas* and *Transitus*: Understanding Passage from One Religious Order to Another in Twelfth-Century Monastic Controversy" (Ph.D. dissertation, Yale, 1971).
25. Constable, "Multiplicity," and Congar, "Les laïcs et l'ecclésiologie des 'ordines.'" For an analysis of how secular society saw itself and its divisions see Jacques Le Goff, "Note sur société tripartie, idéologie monarchique et renouveau économique dans la chrétienté du XIᵉ au XIIᵉ siècle," *Pour un autre Moyen Age: Temps, travail, et culture en Occident: 18 essais* (Paris, 1977), pp. 80–90.

> Thus it is written: *Woman is created for the man* and man is made for woman, since as she is made from man and man from her, neither is separated from the other in the unity of producing offspring, because they produce one thing in a single work just as air and wind are each involved in the work of the other.[26]

The complementarity of roles is also underlined by the author of the *Libellus de diversis ordinibus* when he says: "Love in others what you yourself do not have, so that another shall love in you what he does not have, so that what either does shall be good for the other and those shall be joined in love who are separate in works. . . ."[27]

Such sentiments clearly draw on Pauline themes. What differentiates these corporate metaphors from earlier usage, however, is the increasing sense that the mansions in the house of God are organized religious groups with rules and institutions, and, in the minds of several authors, the identification of social functions with such religious groups. The author of the *Libellus* continues the remark quoted above by saying (of different kinds of hermits):

> Let no one be disturbed if a certain diversity shall appear in this order and each arranges his life differently. . . . If it still displeases you that all men of this calling do not live in the same way, look at the creation fashioned by the good Creator in various ways, and how a harmony has been achieved from different chords, so that the heavens are placed above, the earth below, water made heavier, air lighter, man wiser than the beasts, one above and another below, and you will not wonder if even in God's service different things are preferred, for according to the Gospel: *In my Father's house there are many mansions.* [John 14:2].[28]

In a thirteenth-century passage to which Constable has called attention, James of Vitry writes that clerics, priests, married people, widows, virgins, soldiers, merchants, peasants, craftsmen,

---

26. Hildegard, *Scivias*, pt. 1, vision 2, chap. 12, 1:21, lines 300–6. See also Marie-Thérèse d'Alverny, "Comment les théologiens et les philosophes voient la femme?" *La femme dans les civilisations des Xe–XIIIe siècles: Actes du colloque tenu à Poitiers les 23–25 septembre 1976, Cahiers de civilisation médiévale* 20 (1977): 105–29, especially pp. 122–24.

27. *Libellus de diversis ordinibus*, p. 15.

28. Ibid., pp. 15–17; and see Anselm of Havelberg, *Dialogues*, ed. Salet, especially bk. 1, chaps. 1–2, pp. 34–45.

and "other multiform types of men," each group having its own rules and institutions "according to the diverse types of talents," make up collectively the body of the church under the abbot Christ.[29] Twelfth- and thirteenth-century authors seem to reflect an increasing sense both of choosing a specific role different from other roles and of the necessity for that role to complement others and be of use to the whole. Even those who left the world in radical withdrawal felt it necessary to stress their union with and service of all Christians in prayer. Aelred of Rievaulx exhorts recluses: "Thus clasp the whole world to your breast of love, there at once contemplate and rejoice in those who are good, gaze upon and weep for those who are evil."[30] And Isaac of Stella, a member of a small and very austere group of Cistercians who withdrew to a remote island, developed a theology of the mystical body of Christ that, going further than earlier ideas, argues that our salvation is necessary for the "completion" of Christ.[31]

The Sense of Model

It is not enough to modify the emphasis of recent scholarship on inwardness and consciousness of self by pointing out the urgency with which twelfth-century people attempted to define and analyze the "multiform lives of men" or "mansions in the church." For the stress of twelfth-century piety on feelings was also complemented by a new emphasis on conforming behavior to types or models. The twelfth century discovered the outer as well as the inner man, the literal and external as well as the subjective and emotional, the model as well as the motive. And the models that are so emphasized are a way of talking about the newly apparent groups, a way in which these groups created group identification.

29. James of Vitry, *Historia occidentalis*, bk. 2, chap. 34, ed. Francis Moschus (Douai, 1597), pp. 357–58; cited by Constable, "Multiplicity."

30. Aelred of Rievaulx, *De institutione inclusarum*, chap. 28, *Opera omnia* 1: *Opera ascetica*, ed. A. Hoste and C. H. Talbot, CCCM 1 (Turnhout, 1971); 661.

31. Isaac of Stella, *Sermons*, ed. A. Hoste and Gaston Salet, 2 vols. to date, SC 130 and 207, Sér. mon. 20 and 44 (Paris, 1967 and 1974), sermons 29 and 34, 2: 166–80 and 232–54. And see below pp. 149, 150 and 164.

Twelfth-century people tended to write about themselves and about others as types. For example, Abelard's autobiography, which (whether or not it is a forgery) is usually taken as the quintessence of twelfth-century individualism, is really the story of the rise and fall of a type: the philosopher. Abelard shows himself attempting to become the perfect philosopher and tempted as only a philosopher would be tempted: by lust, because a philosopher is supposed to be chaste, and by pride, because a philosopher is supposed to be dedicated not to self but to truth. Even at the end of the autobiography Abelard is still trying to show himself conforming to a model: the adviser to holy women, St. Jerome. Indeed Abelard's sense of having choices is probably made sharper by his awareness of roles; he explicitly sees himself as choosing between "the knight" and "the philosopher." He tells his story as the story of a type and this enables him to define himself and to talk about the significance of this story.[32] Twelfth-century biographers also see their subjects as following models. In a fine example from a somewhat later period (probably late thirteenth century), the biographer of Gerald of Salles describes Gerald (†1120) as follows: "In all his deeds, he was redolent of Hilarion, resembled Anthony, Christ really lived in him. He was totally on fire and he put others on fire; he acted and spoke now [like] John in the desert, now [like] Paul in public. . . ."[33] And in Aelred of Rievaulx's famous lament for his dead friend Simon we notice not just the new

32. Peter Abelard, *Historia calamitatum*, ed. J. T. Muckle, "Abelard's Letter of Consolation to a Friend (*Historia calamitatum*)," *Mediaeval Studies* 7 (1950): 163–213. And see R. W. Southern, "The Letters of Abelard and Heloise," *Humanism*, pp. 86–104; D. W. Robertson, *Abelard and Heloise* (New York, 1972), pp. 119–35; John Benton, "Fraud, Fiction and Borrowing in the Correspondence of Abelard and Heloise," *Pierre Abélard-Pierre le Venerable: Les Courants philosophiques, littéraires et artistiques en Occident au milieu de XIIᵉ siècle* (Paris, 1975), pp. 469–512; Mary M. McLaughlin, "Abelard as Autobiographer: The Motives and Meaning of His 'Story of Calamities,'" *Speculum* 42 (1967): 463–88; and Hanning, *Individual in Romance*, pp. 17–34.

33. *De B. Giraldo de Salis*, bk. 2, chap. 18, AASS: October, vol. 10 (Paris, 1869): 258D; cited by Giles Constable in "Reform and Renewal in Religious Life," paper delivered at Twelfth-Century Ren. Conference, to appear. This paper also gives a number of other examples of the importance of models in twelfth-century thought.

emotionalism of the high Middle Ages but also a sense that people can and should be models to each other: "Where have you gone, o example by whom I lived, pattern of my morals [*o exemplar uitae meae, compositio morum meorum*]? . . . Where shall I turn? Whom shall I take for my guide? How are you torn from my embrace, snatched from my kisses, hidden from my eyes? . . ."[34]

We have not, however, captured the full significance and flavor of these ideas of conformity to models if we stop with the observation that twelfth-century people describe themselves in these terms. We must also note that writers voice explicit theories of the impact of one person on another as a shaping by or adoption of patterns that affect the outer as well as the inner person. "Teach by example as well as word" was one of their favorite exhortations to evangelism, and teaching by example meant being oneself an observable pattern that was available to others for the reshaping of their lives. Gerhoh of Reichersberg says a person can be healed by looking on a citizen of Jerusalem, from whose example he is refreshed as from a fountain.[35] Hugh of St. Victor writes that our imitation of the saints is the imprinting of their lives in us as a seal molds the wax on which it is pressed.

> Why do you think, brothers, that we are instructed to imitate the life and conduct of good men, unless so that through imitation of them we may be re-formed to the likeness of a new life? In fact in them the form of the likeness of God is clear and therefore when we are imprinted by these things through imitation, we are also shaped in the image of the same similitude. But it should be known that unless wax is first softened, it does not receive the form, so indeed a man is not bent to the form of virtue through the power of another's action unless first through humility he is softened away from the hardness of all pride and contradiction. . . . Moreover the shape of the seal presents to the present matter another consideration. . . . For the figure that is raised in the seal, when imprinted appears concave in the impression in the wax, and that which appears sculptured inward in the seal is shown to be shaped convexly in the wax. Therefore what else is indicated for us in this, except that we, who desire to be re-

---

34. Aelred of Rievaulx, *Speculum caritatis*, bk. 1, chap. 34, par. 109, *Opera omnia* 1:61.
35. Gerhoh, *De aedificio Dei*, chap. 44, PL 194: col. 1305C.

formed through the example of the good as if by a certain seal that is very well sculptured out, discover in them certain lofty vestiges of works like projections and certain humble ones like depressions. . . . Therefore what in them projects, in us ought to be impressed within; and what in them is depressed, is to be erected in us, because we when we take their deeds for imitation ought to make the lofty things hidden and the humble ones manifest.[36]

The author of the life of Bernard of Tiron, in a passage that is typical of saints' lives, says that Bernard enlightened the whole monastery by the radiance of his sanctity and "moved [it] to better things not so much by words as by deeds"; he taught the learned who had first instructed him "now not by the argument of speech or the brightness of word but by the virtue of works."[37]

Twelfth-century people were, of course, aware of the complex relationships and disjunctions that may exist between inner and outer. They were aware of the possibility of hypocrisy. Indeed, excessive attention to the outer without concomitant inner growth and virtue—which they called Phariseeism or literalism or judaizing—was a favorite charge leveled against new monks by older groups. People of the period were also capable of "spiritualizing" literal observances and were aware when they did so. Observances like silence, withdrawal, and fasting, which were literally followed in some orders, became more "metaphorical" in others. Some groups withdrew to actual wasteland; to others the desert was a condition of the heart. For example, when Philip of Harvengt, a moderate regular canon, advocates silence, he means abstinence from speech, but more importantly abstinence from

36. Hugh of St. Victor, *De institutione*, chap. 7, PL 176: cols. 932D–33C. For the seal metaphor used slightly more inwardly, see Anselm of Canterbury, letter 4, *Opera omnia*, ed. Francis S. Schmitt, 6 vols. (Edinburgh, 1940–1961), 3:104; see also Eadmer, *The Life of St. Anselm, Archbishop of Canterbury*, ed. R. W. Southern (London, 1962), pp. 20–21 and 37–38.

37. Geoffrey the Fat, *Vita beati Bernardi fundatoris congregationis de Tironio*, PL 172: col. 1376A–B. For a similar sentiment see *Vita s. Aderaldi* (†1004), AASS: October, vol. 8 (Paris, 1866): 991–92: "Non aliter vivebat quam docebat, sed opus ejus voci concordabat, quaeque docebat verbis, astruebat exemplis."

vice.[38] Writers sometimes argued that unity in the more spiritual meaning of a term underlay diversity in the more literal meanings. For example, an anonymous representative of the older monasticism claimed, writing against the new orders with their new habits: "Religion lies not in the clothing [i.e., the particular form of the habit] but in the heart [i.e., in the humility with which any habit is worn]."[39] But in general writers assumed that, in reform and moral improvement, exterior and interior will and should go together. When Philip of Harvengt speaks of reform of life as putting on a new garment, when Hugh of St. Victor writes of the imprint of the saints in the wax of our selves, they assume that our whole person, inner and outer, is remade by the pattern.[40] In an exegesis of Aggeus 1:8 ("Go up to the mountain, bring timber and build the house"), Philip writes:

> He *takes timber*, he *builds the house*, when he makes use of the examples from Scripture of saints who have gone before and thus by prudent artifice employs them diligently in such a way that he both removes from his behavior the unsuitable animal condition of nudity and builds within himself a spiritual house for God.[41]

In his treatise on the moral ark of Noah, Hugh explains how a pattern (in this case literally a design, a drawing) can be transferred within so that it shapes the heart:

> And now then, as we promised, we must put before you the pattern of our ark. Thus you may learn from an external form, which we have visibly depicted, what you ought to do interiorly, and when you have impressed the form of this pattern on your heart, you may rejoice that the house of God has been built in you.[42]

---

38. Philip of Harvengt, *De silentio*, PL 203: cols. 943–1206, especially chap. 1, cols. 945–46.

39. *Reprehensio libelli Abbatis Claravallensis*, chap. 33, ed. A. Wilmart, "Une riposte de l'ancien monachisme au manifeste de S. Bérnard," *Revue bénédictine* 46 (1934): 343.

40. See n. 36 above and Philip of Harvengt, *De dignitate*, chaps. 19 and 22, PL 203: cols. 690B, 692B and 694A.

41. Philip, *De obedientia*, chap. 42, PL 203: col. 937C.

42. Hugh of St. Victor, *De arca Noe morali*, bk. 4, chap. 21, in *Hugh of*

A passage from the *Miscellanea* attributed to the same Hugh puts succinctly the idea of concomitant inner and outer reformation:

> Until you have Christ, you shall not rest; you shall be in need until you come to Christ. Christ is truth and Christ is wisdom. If you have taken on, in your exterior, likeness [*similitudinem*] and the habit of virtue, you have begun. If you have truth within you, you have been perfected. . . . Christ is all your good; he is your virtue; he is your wisdom, your example, your help, your victory, your crown.[43]

Even the Carthusian Guigo II, whose favorite metaphors are of eating, drinking, and digesting (i.e., of taking into the inner man the "experience" of Christ), stresses that example also shapes deeds:

> For what is the use of spending one's time in continuous reading, turning the pages of the lives and sayings of holy men, unless we can extract nourishment from them by chewing and digesting this food so that its strength can pass into our inmost heart? It is only thus that we can from their example carefully consider our state of soul, and reflect in our own deeds the lives about which we read so often and so eagerly.[44]

In a passage that gives two layers of examples (i.e., the example of Christ and the example of those who took Christ as example),

---

St. Victor: Selected Spiritual Writings, trans. a Religious of C.S.M.V. (London, 1962), p. 153; the Latin text of this is not given in the ed. in PL 176, cols. 617–80, but may be found in C. C. Mierow, "A Description of Manuscript Garret Deposit 1450, Princeton University Library, Together with a Collation of the First Work Contained in It, the De Arca Noe of Hugo de Sancto Victore," *Transactions of the American Library Institute for 1917* (Chicago, 1918), pp. 27–55. See Grover A. Zinn, Jr., "Mandala Symbolism and Use in the Mysticism of Hugh of St. Victor," *History of Religions* 12 (1973): 317–41, especially 334–35.

43. Hugh of St. Victor, *Miscellanea*, bk. 1, chap. 114, PL 177: col. 542A–C. On the *Miscellanea*, see Roger Baron, *Études sur Hugues de saint-Victor* (Paris, 1963), p. 66 and references given there.

44. Guigo II, *Epistola de vita contemplativa (scala claustralium)*, chap. 13, in *Lettre sur la vie contemplative . . . Douze méditations*, ed. E. Colledge and J. Walsh, SC 163, Sér. mon. 29 (Paris, 1970), p. 108, lines 306–12; trans. Colledge and Walsh, *The Ladder of Monks and Twelve Meditations* (New York, 1978), p. 93. Cf. Aelred of Rievaulx's conception of example; see above, chapter 2, nn. 16 and 17.

Guigo spells out his understanding of imitation as the fullest possible joining of one's self and life to Christ:

> . . . imitation proceeds from love. . . . Unless you love Christ you will not imitate Him, that is, you will not follow Him. For He said to Simon Peter after He had tested his love: "Follow me," that is, "Imitate me." The feet of Judas may have followed Christ, but what his heart followed was avarice. . . . But Christ must be followed with the love of our whole heart. . . . Simon of Cyrene indeed carried the cross and followed Christ, but he did not share in the torments of the cross. We must follow Christ and we must cling to Him, and we must not desert Him until death. . . . At the time of His Passion Peter followed him, but from afar, because he was to deny Him. There was only the thief who followed Him to death upon the cross.[45]

Thus Christ and the saints are not merely inspiration; the change they bring in us is not simply a stirring of our contrition or our spiritual ambition. Christ and the saints actually re-form us. Indeed, as Robert Javelet and Karl Morrison have recently argued, "likeness" was a fundamental theological category in the twelfth century.[46] To be holy was to be "like" God—to return the *imago*

---

45. Guigo, *Meditationes*, chap. 10, *Lettre*, ed. Colledge and Walsh, pp. 184–88, lines 100–26; trans. Colledge and Walsh, *Ladder*, pp. 135–36. For yet another example of the idea that exterior discipline produces interior change, see Hugh of Folieto, *De claustro animae*, bk. 3, PL 176: col. 1094.

46. Robert Javelet, *Image et ressemblance au douzième siècle de saint Anselme à Alain de Lille*, 2 vols. (Paris, 1967); and Karl F. Morrison, "The Structure of Holiness in Othloh's *Vita Bonifatii* and Ebo's *Vita Ottonis*," *Law, Church and Society: Essays in Honor of Stephan Kuttner*, ed. K. Pennington and R. Somerville (Philadelphia, 1977), pp. 131–56. It is perhaps not totally farfetched to point out that the theme of likeness is extremely important in love literature and literature of friendship in the twelfth century. The influence of Cicero's *De amicitia* suggested that love must be between "likes;" see Étienne Gilson, *La théologie mystique de Bernard* (Paris, 1934), and Douglass Roby, Introd., in Aelred of Rievaulx, *Spiritual Friendship*, Cistercian Fathers Series 5 (Washington D.C., 1974). We find this idea reflected in the romance of *Amis and Amiloun*, ed. MacEdward Leach (London, 1937), where two knights who are devoted to each other resemble each other so much that one can stand in for the other at a tournament.
Steven Ozment has suggested that the loss of the category of like-

Dei to "likeness" with Him. And grace brings about not only the conformity of the individual to God but also the conformity of inner and outer man. That is what a saint *is*: one in whom extraordinary life (without) reflects extraordinary virtue and grace (within). So Hugh of St. Victor warns us that in the process of being remade by imitation of the saints we must first hide within ourselves their accomplishments lest we should be guilty of hypocrisy by trying to show outer gifts before we are reshaped within. But sanctity is finally reformation of the total man, and it can be gained by imitation of the sanctity of others, which is accessible to us exactly because it is outer as well as inner.

Groups Reformed by Models

The twelfth-century concept of reform by model was applied to groups as well as to individuals. In the early 1100s those who debated which form of religious life was best and how this religious life was to be described carried out the debate by arguing about which life best fit models from the past. A variety of models were used: the primitive church (*forma primitivae ecclesiae*), the apostolic life (*vita apostolica*), the desert fathers, the garden of Eden, Christ himself.[47] Groups that were condemned and groups that became the inspiration of the church used such models and slogans in exactly similar ways, although those persecuted as heretics were perhaps more likely to associate themselves with the martyrs of the early church. According to the Premonstratensian Everwin of Steinfeld the adherents of a heresy detected at Cologne

---

ness marks a radical break between the twelfth and sixteenth centuries; idem, "Luther and the Late Middle Ages: The Formation of Reformation Thought," *Transition and Revolution: Problems and Issues of European Renaissance and Reformation History*, ed. Robert Kingdon (Minneapolis, 1974), pp. 109–29.

47. A great deal has been written recently on these themes. See *inter alia* Chenu, *La théologie*; E. W. McDonnell, "*Vita Apostolica*: Diversity or Dissent?" *Church History* 24 (1955): 15–31; Vicaire, *L'imitation*; Glenn Olsen, "The Idea of the *Ecclesia Primitiva* in the Writings of the Twelfth-Century Canonists," *Traditio* 25 (1969): 61–86; Giovanni Miccoli, *Chiesa Gregoriana: ricerche sulla riforma del secolo XI* (Florence, 1966), pp. 225–99; and Constable, "Reform."

claimed that "theirs alone is the Church, inasmuch as only they follow in the footsteps of Christ," and said of themselves: "We, the poor of Christ, who have no fixed abode and flee from city to city like sheep amidst wolves, are persecuted as were the apostles and the martyrs. . . ."[48]

Moreover, groups sought founders who were really prototypes. When regular canons claimed Augustine or Gregory the Great or even Aaron and the Levites as their founders, they were not simply trying to find an origin earlier than the monks' St. Benedict; they were also trying to define what was distinctive about themselves. (In this case, they were arguing that they went back to the Old Testament priesthood—i.e., that their distinctiveness was their clerical status.)[49] Many of these models were themselves not new in the twelfth century. And, as is well known, the meaning of the models changed. For example, the *vita apostolica*, which in the early Middle Ages generally meant the common life of monks and nuns, came in the course of the twelfth century (historians debate exactly when) to mean preaching. I do not intend here to give an account of the changing meanings of the various models and prototypes. My point is rather that it is itself significant that all the basic concerns of early twelfth-century spirituality—poverty and preaching, withdrawal and community, love of neighbor and love of God—were expressed in terms of models. The fact that the writers of religious polemic almost invariably disputed the meaning of models, accepted some meanings and not others, and argued over whether their own group best fitted the model, suggests that twelfth-century groups were really using these models as tools to define and judge themselves. Furthermore, the groups not only aspired to conform to models. They saw themselves as *being* models. In their own terms, they taught by example. If being a regular canon or friar meant con-

48. *Everwini Steinfeldensis praepositi ad S. Bernardum*, PL 182: cols. 676–80; trans. in *Heresies of the High Middle Ages*, ed. Walter Wakefield and A. P. Evans (New York, 1969), pp. 127–32, and quoted in M. Lambert, *Medieval Heresy* (New York, 1976), pp. 60–61.

49. See *Libellus de diversis ordinibus*, p. 59. The author is clearly aware that arguments about what can be compared to what or what is model for what are frequently efforts to define a way of life; see ibid., p. 13.

forming oneself to the life of Christ, one became more available as an instrument of reform for others as one became a better canon or friar.[50] The anonymous author of a commentary on the Augustinian Rule expresses this idea in his description of the apostles, whom canons are urged to imitate:

> For that blessed multitude [the believers to whom the apostles preached] was instructed not only for believing but also for living in common by the first founders of the church, who judged it a worthy thing not only to observe themselves but also to teach others this rule of living imposed on them by their head himself. . . . Therefore they judged it worthy to imitate that very healthy discipline of living that they learned from him who is alone our master in heaven, Christ the Lord, so that they, living thus and bringing others to live thus with them, might merit to live forever.[51]

Philip of Harvengt put it more succinctly: *vita clericorum forma sit laicorum*; the words of Christ invite canons to so shape themselves that they offer an example to others.[52]

Thus we see how misleading it would be to place in the center of the twelfth-century religious stage the isolated individual, with his personal conversion, his inner motivation, his exuberant emotions. Indeed it is probably our modern sense that a person's exterior may be a screen that keeps us from getting to his true personality—our idea that each personality is unique and therefore seeking a unique expression—that has led us to concentrate in twelfth-century writing on quest and development, inwardness and sense of self.[53] In the twelfth century, turning inward to explore motivation went hand in hand with a sense of belonging to a group that not only defined its own life by means of a model but

50. On the importance of this idea in twelfth-century religious writing, see my book, *Docere Verbo et Exemplo* (Missoula, Montana, 1979).
51. Anonymous, Preface, MS Vienna 2207, fols. 11ᵛ–12ᵛ.
52. Philip, *De dignitate*, chap. 2, PL 203: col. 670A-B, and *De obedientia*, chap. 41, PL 203: col. 933C-D.
53. This concentration on the inwardness of twelfth-century religion is also due to a tendency in recent scholarship to emphasize the Cistercians. I have tried in this essay to modify that emphasis by citing from a wide selection of twelfth-century authors.

also was itself—as group and as pattern—a means of salvation and of evangelism. A certain "literalism" or "externality" seems therefore to characterize twelfth-century religion. By literalism I do not mean that twelfth-century groups tried to adhere slavishly to earlier monastic rules, although this charge has been leveled against some of them (particularly the Cistercians) both by contemporaries and by modern scholars. Nor do I mean simply that twelfth-century groups debated matters of what we in the twentieth century call "lifestyle." I mean that twelfth-century religion was characterized by a strong concern for conforming the behavior of members of a group to a very precise pattern, that the existence of such an articulated pattern for the group helped to make it a group, and that explicit theories of re-formation by imitation (in the outer as well as the inner man) bolstered the importance of models.

A concentration on the outer man is reflected in many aspects of twelfth-century thought. As J.-C. Schmitt has pointed out, the twelfth century rediscovered the word *gestus* ("behavior" in the sense of "gesture" or "bearing")—and not just the word but also the concept. The same Hugh who developed the metaphor of the seal wrote for novices of St. Victor the first theoretical treatment of the meaning to be attached to details of behavior.[54]

This emphasis on external behavior finds its fullest expression in the literalism of the friars. Both Innocent III and Dominic saw the life of the Dominicans as a kind of teaching offered to heretics: Dominican poverty shaped not only the brother who adopted it but also the audience who saw as well as heard Christ's humility preached.[55] Francis of Assisi sums up not only the twelfth-century emphasis on emotion and inner change in his mystical ravishment

54. Jean-Claude Schmitt, "Techniques du corps et conscience de groupe: à propos du *De institutione novitiorum* de Hugues de saint Victor," paper delivered at Conference on Consciousness.

55. See Christine Thouzellier, *Catharisme et Valdéisme en Languedoc à la fin du XIIe et au début du XIIIe siècle*, Publications de la faculté des lettres et sciences humaines de Paris: Recherches 27 (Paris, 1966), p. 187; and idem, *Hérésie et hérétiques: Vaudois, Cathares, Patarins, Albigeois*, Storia e letteratura raccolta di studi e testi 116 (Rome, 1969), pp. 189–302; see also *Docere*, p. 72, n. 134.

but also the stress on imitation in that ultimate *imitatio*, the reception of stigmata.[56] In the late twelfth or early thirteenth century, the anonymous author of a series of sermons on the Benedictine Rule said—emphasizing inner, emotional change—that after all we cannot literally die for Christ.[57] But at the same time, some of the early Franciscans, going out as missionaries to the heathen, were intending quite literally to perform the ultimate teaching by example: martyrdom. If living the life of Christ before other men was not enough to bring those men to salvation, then those heathen might themselves assure that the missionaries died before them the death of Christ as the supreme preaching of the gospel.[58] Francis preached before the sultan without knowing his language. He once responded to a command to preach to Clare's nuns by forming a circle of cinders and praying in its midst.[59] What he was (his example) and what he said (his word) perfectly coincided: his sermon *was* the penance he did. In Francis, as his biographers saw him and as he saw himself, the individual who rebels against the world becomes the pattern for the world.

Conclusions

If the twelfth century did not "discover the individual" in the modern meaning of expression of unique personality and isolation of the person from firm group membership, it did in some sense discover—or rediscover—the self, the inner mystery, the inner man, the inner landscape. But it also discovered the group, in two

---

56. Francis was not, of course, the first case of stigmata. See E. Amann, "Stigmatisation," DTC 14.2 (Paris, 1941): col. 2617; and E. W. McDonnell, *The Beguines and Beghards in Medieval Culture with Special Emphasis on the Belgian Scene* (1954; reprint ed., New York, 1969), p. 318. Mary of Oignies, whose stigmata were self-induced, is perhaps an even better example of what I am calling literalism.

57. Pontigny commentary, MS Auxerre 50, fol. 116ᵛ·ᵃ·

58. See E. Randolph Daniel, *The Franciscan Concept of Mission in the High Middle Ages* (Lexington, 1975), pp. 26–54.

59. Thomas of Celano, *Vita secunda*, pt. 2, chap. 157, par. 207, in *Analecta Franciscana* 10 (Quaracchi, 1941): 249; see Rosalind B. and Christopher N.L. Brooke, "St. Clare," *Medieval Women: dedicated and presented to Professor Rosalind M.T. Hill . . .* , ed. Derek Baker, Studies in Church History: Subsidia 1 (Oxford, 1978), p. 282.

very precise senses: it discovered that many separate "callings" or "lives" were possible in the church, and it elaborated a language for talking about how those groups defined themselves and how individuals became part of them (the language of "conforming to a model"). Moreover, these two aspects of the twelfth century go hand in hand—inner with outer, motive with model, self with community. A new sense of self, of inner change and inner choice, is precipitated by the necessity to choose among roles, among groups. A new sense of becoming part of a group by conforming one's behavior to an external standard is necessitated by a new awareness of a choosing and interior self. If twelfth-century authors were more aware of their motives for acting, of the process of making a choice, of interior change, it was not only because there were in fact a wider variety of social roles and a new diversity of religious groups that made choice necessary; it was also because people now had ways of talking about groups as groups, roles as roles, and about group formation. Therefore they could be conscious of choosing. Moreover, their understanding of spiritual growth as growth toward likeness made models necessary—the apostles, the early church, Moses and Aaron, the saints, and Christ in his earthly life. Therefore, for twelfth-century writers, change of self had to take place in the context provided by other Christians.

Recent scholarship has emphasized the variety of twelfth-century cultural life. This emphasis and the increasing dissatisfaction of some scholars with any precise definition of the period exactly because of its variety finds some support in my picture of writers elaborating new statements about groups and roles as well as about individuals and self.[60] But, in the final analysis, my argument about the twelfth century is not merely a reiteration of its diversity nor a plea that historians broaden the number of items to which they give attention. It is also an effort to give a more specific definition of the concerns for self and community by locating each in the context of the other. Just as the discovery of self is not a twentieth-century awareness of personality, so the emphasis on models, types, and ways of affiliating with groups cannot be the modern sense of personal lifestyle. Not only is it possible to spec-

60. See Southern, "Humanism."

ify something of the particular nature of twelfth-century culture by the phrase "discovery of self"; it is possible to delineate the period even more precisely when "discovery of self" is coupled with and understood in the context of "discovery of model for behavior" and "discovery of consciously chosen community."

The formulation I have suggested helps to locate twelfth-century religious developments in the broader sweep of medieval history. The interpretation advanced by Southern, Morris, Brown, Radding, Hanning, and others locates in the religious life and writing of the period 1050 to 1200 an awareness of self similar to that which Burckhardt claimed for the Italian Renaissance. Much recent scholarship supports this point, by stressing continuities between twelfth and fifteenth-century piety.[61] But, if my analysis above is correct, we need both a broader picture of twelfth-century religion and a description of its relationship to the later Middle Ages that stresses discontinuity as well as influence and parallels. I have argued that twelfth-century religious thinkers stress individual decision, lifestyle, and experience as part of a search for institutions and practices that embody these, and that the goal of development to a twelfth-century person is the application to the self of a model that is simultaneously, exactly because it *is* a model, a mechanism for affiliation with a group. This argument suggests that the optimism and self-confidence of the period lie in the fact that a personal religious vision tends to be an imitation of Christ, an identification with the ultimate example, and therefore that, *in what one is* as imitator of Christ, one is not an isolated or lone individual but an evangelizer, teacher, and frequently even a founder of a new group or revitalizer of an old. Thus the twelfth century is *not* (as it is sometimes pictured) the beginning of a march toward a more and more private and individualistic piety which increasingly bypasses ecclesiastical struc-

61. See Charles Trinkaus, *In Our Image and Likeness: Humanity and Divinity in Italian Humanist Thought*, 2 vols. (Chicago, 1970); and Giles Constable, "Twelfth-Century Spirituality and the Late Middle Ages," *Medieval and Renaissance Studies* 5: *Proceedings of the Southern Institute of Medieval and Renaissance Studies, Summer, 1969* (1971): 27–60, reprinted in idem, *Religious Life and Thought (11th–12th Centuries)*, Variorum Reprints (London, 1979).

tures.[62] No period was ever busier creating structures for its piety than the twelfth century. It is the Fourth Lateran Council's prohibition of new orders in 1215 that signals the end of the twelfth-century equilibrium between self and group and the beginning of a new period in which individual experience breaks away from or undercuts, rather than issues in or coincides with, community.[63] The individualism historians usually find in the later Middle Ages, Renaissance, and Reformation is not only in continuity with the twelfth-century discovery of self; it is also, I would suggest, in certain ways in contrast with the twelfth-century equilibrium between interior and exterior, self and community.

62. Much recent discussion seems to be moving toward this interpretation; see, for example, Brown, "Society and the Supernatural," pp. 146–47.
63. Throughout the thirteenth century there were, of course, groups that found ways around the prohibition.

IV

Jesus as Mother
and Abbot as Mother:
Some Themes
in Twelfth-Century
Cistercian Writing

———

IN 1949, André Cabassut published an article on a little known medieval devotion: the devotion to Jesus our Mother.[1] In the years immediately following the appearance of Cabassut's study, the devotion remained "little known"; where it did attract attention, it aroused distaste. The article on the humanity of Christ, published in the *Dictionnaire de spiritualité* in 1969, calls it "a devotion that makes theologians wince."[2] In recent years, several scholars have

This chapter is a greatly expanded version of "Jesus as Mother and Abbot as Mother: Some Themes in Twelfth-Century Cistercian Writing," *Harvard Theological Review* 70 (1977): 257–84, copyright 1979 by the President and Fellows of Harvard University, reprinted by permission. Some of the material I have added was used in "Feminine Names for God in Cistercian Writing: A Case Study in the Relationship of Literary Language and Community Life," paper presented at the York University Conference on Consciousness and Group Identification in High Medieval Religion, 7–9 April, 1978 [hereafter: Conference on Consciousness]. I would like to thank Karl F. Morrison of the University of Chicago and my students in Church History 224 at the Harvard Divinity School, especially Sharon A. Farmer, John Martin, Catherine Mooney, and Carol G. Rucker, for their criticisms and suggestions.

1. André Cabassut, "Une dévotion médiévale peu connue: la dévotion à 'Jésus Notre Mère,'" *Mélanges Marcel Viller*, RAM 25 (1949): 234–45.
2. André Rayez, "Humanité du Christ," DS 7.1: col. 1070. For a discussion of the embarrassment modern scholars have felt about this devotion, see Eleanor C. McLaughlin, "'Christ My Mother': Feminine Naming and Metaphor in Medieval Spirituality," *Nashota Review* 15

become deeply interested in this aspect of medieval piety, impelled in part by a feminist theology that either calls for androgynous God-language or condemns the image of "God our Father."[3] This new enthusiasm for the "mother Jesus" of medieval religious writers has usually concentrated on thirteenth- and fourteenth-century uses of the image, especially on the sophisticated theology developed around it by the anchoress Julian of Norwich († after 1416), and has often implied that such a devotional tradition is particularly congenial to women and therefore must have been developed by or for or about them.[4] The first flowering of the image after

(1975): 246–47. This embarrassment seems to continue in the most recent and by far the fullest and most penetrating examination of the theme: the introduction and critical apparatus to Edmund Colledge and James Walsh, eds., *A Book of Showings to the Anchoress Julian of Norwich*, 2 vols. (Toronto, 1978).

3. Recent works in which the theme of mother Jesus is treated include, in addition to the studies cited in nn. 1 and 2 above, Giles Constable, "Twelfth-Century Spirituality and the Late Middle Ages," *Medieval and Renaissance Studies* 5 (1971): 45–47; J. Bugge, *Virginitas* (The Hague, 1975) especially pp. 100–5; Ritamary Bradley, "The Motherhood Theme in Julian of Norwich," *Fourteenth-Century English Mystics Newsletter* 2.4 (1976): 25–30; idem, "Patristic Background of the Motherhood Similitude in Julian of Norwich," *Christian Scholar's Review* 8 (1978): 101–13; Elaine H. Pagels, "What Became of God the Mother? Conflicting Images of God in Early Christianity," *Signs: Journal of Women in Culture and Society* 2 (1976): 293–303; idem, *The Gnostic Gospels* (New York, 1979), pp. 48–69; Jean Leclercq, Preface to Julian of Norwich, *Showings*, ed. Edmund Colledge and James Walsh, The Classics of Western Spirituality (New York, 1978), pp. 8–11; Kari Elizabeth Børresen, "Christ notre mère, la théologie de Julienne de Norwich," *Mitteilungen und Forschungsbeiträge der Cusanus-Gesellschaft* 13 (Mainz, 1978): 320–29; Eleanor C. McLaughlin, "Women, Power and the Pursuit of Holiness in Medieval Christianity," *Women of Spirit: Female Leadership in the Jewish and Christian Traditions*, ed. Rosemary Ruether and Eleanor C. McLaughlin (New York, 1979), pp. 100–30. The study of iconographic traditions of a female Christ by Rudolph Berliner ("God is Love," *Essays in Honor of Hans Tietze 1880–1954*, ed. E. Gombrich, J. S. Held, O. Kurz [New York, 1958], pp. 143–60) is disappointing.

4. See Mary M. McLaughlin, "Survivors and Surrogates: Children and Parents from the Ninth to the Thirteenth Centuries," *The History of Childhood*, ed. L. DeMause (New York, 1974), pp. 101–81 passim; Pagels, "God the Mother," pp. 293–303; Bugge, *Virginitas*, pp. 100–5; Der-

the patristic period, however, appears to have come in the twelfth century in the works of men: the Cistercian monks Bernard of Clairvaux (†1153), Aelred of Rievaulx (†1167), Guerric of Igny († ca. 1157), Isaac of Stella († ca. 1169), Adam of Perseigne (†1221), and Helinand of Froidmont († ca. 1235); William of St. Thierry († ca. 1148), a black Benedictine who became a Cistercian only late in life; and the Benedictine, Anselm of Canterbury (†1109), from whom the Cistercians perhaps borrowed the idea of mother Jesus.[5]

The question I would like to ask is why the use of explicit and elaborate maternal imagery to describe God and Christ, who are usually described as male, is so popular with twelfth-century Cistercian monks. It will be necessary to give two different kinds of answers to this question. First—because the imagery is in no sense uniquely Cistercian (as the examples of Anselm and even William of St. Thierry prove)—I shall argue that such language must be understood in the context of very broad changes in religious imagery, devotion, and theology in the high Middle Ages. Second—because in the twelfth century the imagery is particularly prominent in Cistercian writing and has there characteristics noticeably different from those it takes on in other hands—I shall argue that it is related to the specific concerns and themes of Cistercian life. As Cabassut himself pointed out, maternal imagery was applied in the Middle Ages to male religious authority figures, particularly abbots, bishops and the apostles, as well as to God and Christ. Moreover, the use of maternal imagery to talk about male figures was developed in the twelfth century by cloistered authors with

yck Hanshell, "A Crux in the Interpretation of Dame Julian," *Downside Review* 92 (1974): 91; Børresen, "Christ notre mère;" E. McLaughlin, "Women, Power . . . ," pp. 122–27.

5. This was Cabassut's conclusion, "Une dévotion peu connue," p. 239. The general influence of Anselm, particularly Anselm's prayers, on the Cistercians is well known: see J. Lewicki, "Anselme et les doctrines des Cisterciens du XIIe siècle," *Analecta Anselmiana* 2 (1970): 209–16; S. Vanni Rovighi, "Notes sur l'influence de saint Anselme au XIIe siècle," *Cahiers de civilisation médiévale* 8 (1965): 43–58. Of the texts studied here, Guerric of Igny's treatment of Peter and Paul (see below n. 37) is so close to Anselm's (see n. 8) as to suggest that the similarity cannot be coincidental.

particular reference to a cloistered setting. Thus we must locate the Cistercian devotion to mother Jesus not merely against the background of the growing affective spirituality of the high Middle Ages but also in the context of a Cistercian ambivalence about authority and a Cistercian conception of community.

Examples of Maternal Imagery

Let me begin by giving six examples of twelfth-century authors who use the idea of motherhood (physiological or psychological) to talk about figures usually described in "male" language. Anselm of Canterbury, who in his *Monologion* objects to calling God "mother" both because male is superior to female and because the father contributes more to the child than the mother in the process of reproduction,[6] nonetheless speaks in a particularly lyrical prayer of both Paul and Jesus as mothers to the individual soul. In this passage Anselm associates "mother" as well as "father" with engendering and stresses the mother as one who gives birth, even dying to give the child life, but the contrast that he draws between Jesus as father and Jesus as mother stresses the father as one who rules and produces, the mother as one who loves. In an association of images that continues throughout the twelfth century,[7] Anselm describes the consoling, nurturing Jesus as a hen gathering her chicks under her wing (Matt. 23:37) and suggests that mother Jesus revives the soul at her breast.

> . . . You [Paul] are among Christians like a nurse who not only cares for her children but also gives birth to them a second time by the solicitude of her marvelous love.

6. Anselm, *Monologion*, chap. 42, *Opera omnia*, ed. F. S. Schmitt, 6 vols. (Edinburgh, 1940–1961) 1:58. This view of the respective male and female contributions to reproduction was the common one in the Middle Ages; see Vern L. Bullough, "Medieval Medical and Scientific Views of Women," *Viator* 4 (1973): 487–93.

7. See below nn. 29 and 49. Even in Helinand of Froidmont, who uses less feminine imagery, the hen-and-chicks reference occurs to describe both Christ's advent in the human heart and the parallel roles of Christ and abbot: see Helinand, sermons 6 and 14, PL 212: cols. 531D and 591–94.

. . . Gentle nurse, gentle mother, who are these sons to whom you give birth and nurture if not those whom you bear and educate in the faith of Christ by your teaching? . . . For, as that blessed faith is born and nurtured in us by the other apostles also, how much more by you, because you have labored and accomplished more in this than all the others. . . . O mother of well known tenderness, may your son feel your heart [*viscera*] of maternal piety. . . .

But you, Jesus, good lord, are you not also a mother? Are you not that mother who, like a hen, collects her chickens under her wings? Truly, master, you are a mother. For what others have conceived and given birth to, they have received from you. . . . You are the author, others are the ministers. It is then you, above all, Lord God, who are mother.

Both of you [Paul and Jesus] are therefore mothers. . . . For you accomplished, one through the other, and one through himself, that we, born to die, may be reborn to life. Fathers you are then by result, mothers by affection; fathers by authority, mothers by kindness; fathers by protection, mothers by compassion. You [Lord] are a mother and you [Paul] are also. Unequal by extent of love, you do not differ in quality of love. . . . You have given birth to me when you made me a Christian, . . . you [Lord] by the teaching coming from you and you [Paul] by the teaching he inspires in you. . . .

Paul, mother, . . . lay then your dead son [i.e., the sinful soul] at the feet of Christ, your mother, for he is her son. Or rather throw him into the bosom [*sinus*] of Christ's love, for Christ is even more his mother. Pray that he may revive this dead son, not so much yours as his. Do, mother of my soul, what the mother of my flesh would do. . . .

And you also, soul, dead by yourself, run under the wings of your mother Jesus and bewail your sorrows under his wings.

Christ, mother, who gathers under your wings your little ones, your dead chick seeks refuge under your wings. For by your gentleness, those who are hurt are comforted; by your perfume, the despairing are reformed. Your warmth resuscitates the dead; your touch justifies sinners. . . . Console your chicken, resuscitate your dead one, justify your sinner. May your injured one be consoled by you; may he who of himself despairs be comforted by you and reformed through you in your complete and unceasing grace. For the consolation of the wretched flows from you, blessed, world without end, Amen.[8]

Bernard of Clairvaux, whose use of maternal imagery for male figures is more extensive and complex than that of any other twelfth-century figure, uses "mother" to describe Jesus, Moses, Peter, Paul, prelates in general, abbots in general, and, more frequently, himself as abbot.[9] To Bernard, the maternal image is almost without exception elaborated not as giving birth or even as conceiving or sheltering in a womb but as nurturing, particularly suckling.[10] Breasts, to Bernard, are a symbol of the pouring out towards others of affectivity or of instruction and almost invariably suggest to him a discussion of the duties of prelates or abbots. Bernard not only develops an elaborate picture of the abbot (he usually has himself in mind) as mother, contrasting *mater* to *magis-*

8. Anselm, prayer 10 to St. Paul, *Opera omnia* 3: 33 and 39–41; see also *Méditations and prières de saint Anselme*, trans. A. Castel, Introd. by A. Wilmart, Collection Pax 11 (Paris, 1923), pp. i–lxii and 48–61. Colledge and Walsh suggest that the source of Anselm's devotion is Augustine's exegesis of Ps. 101:7; see *A Book of Showings* 1:153–54.

9. JESUS: Bernard of Clairvaux, letter 322, *Epistolae*, ed. J. Mabillon, PL 182: col. 527C; Bernard, sermon 9 on the Song of Songs, pars. 5–10, and sermon 10, pars. 1–4, OB 1:45–50. MOSES: sermon 12, par. 4, ibid., pp. 62–63. PETER: letter 238, PL 182: col. 429C-D. PAUL: sermon 12, par. 2, OB 1:61; sermon 85, par. 12, ibid., p. 315. PRELATES OR ABBOTS: sermon 9, par. 9, ibid., p. 47; sermon 10, pars. 2–3, ibid., pp. 49–50; sermon 23, pars. 2 and 7–8, ibid., pp. 139–40 and 142–44; sermon 41, pars. 5–6, OB 2:31–32. SELF: letter 1, PL 182: col. 76A-B; letter 71, cols. 183B–84A; letter 110, col. 253; letter 146, col. 303B–C; letter 152, col. 312A; letter 201, col. 369B–C; letter 258, cols. 466B–67A; and sermon 29, par. 6, OB 1:207. See also Suibert Gammersbach, "Das Abtsbild in Cluny und bei Bernhard von Clairvaux," *Cîteaux in de Nederlanden* 7 (1956): 85–101; Gervais Dumeige, "Bernard de Clairvaux, 'Père et Mère' de ses moines," *Études* 277 (June, 1953): 304–20; and Fracheboud, "Je suis la chimère," COCR 16 (1954):45–52, 128–36, 183–91. Extensive discussions of CHARITY AS MOTHER are found in: letter 2, PL 182: cols. 79D–81A, and letter 7, cols. 93D–94C.

10. Passages in which Bernard sees mothering as "giving birth with pain": letter 146, PL 182: col. 303B–C; sermon 29 on the Song of Songs, par. 6, OB 1:207. In letter 144, col. 301A–B, Bernard refers to the pain of having children torn away before the proper time for weaning, but this is clearly a nursing image.

ter or *dominus* and stating repeatedly that a mother is one who cannot fail to love her child;[11] he also frequently attributes maternal characteristics, especially suckling with milk, to the abbot when he refers to him as father. He does not, however, reject the conception of the father as disciplinarian.[12]

Many of Bernard's references to himself as mother occur casually in letters. He admonishes the parents of Geoffrey of Péronne: "Do not be sad about your Geoffrey or shed any tears on his account, for he is going quickly to joy and not to sorrow. I will be for him both a mother and a father, both a brother and a sister. I will make the crooked path straight for him and the rough places smooth."[13] He explains to his own monks his absence and his love for them: "Sad is my soul until I shall return, and it does not wish to be comforted until I come to you. . . . Behold this is the third time, unless I am mistaken, that my sons have been torn from my heart [*avulsa . . . a me viscera mea*], little ones, weaned before their time [*parvuli ablactati . . . ante tempus*]."[14] To abbot Baldwin of Rieti he writes: "As a mother loves her only son, so I loved you, when you clung to my side pleasing my heart [*haerentem lateri meo, placentem cordi meo*]."[15] To Robert, whom he fears he has driven away by harshness, he explains (weaving together images of "father" and "mother"):

> Who else would not scold your disobedience and be angry at your desertion . . . ? But I know your heart. I know that you can be led more easily by love than driven by fear. . . .
>
> And I have said this, my son, not to put you to shame, but to help you as a loving father, because if you have many masters in Christ, yet you have few fathers. For if you will allow me to say so, I begot you in religion by word and example. I nourished

11. Sermon 12 on the Song of Songs, par. 4, OB 1:62–63; sermon 23, par. 2, ibid., pp. 139–40; sermon 26, par. 6, ibid., p. 173; letter 258, PL 182: cols. 466A–67A; letter 300, col. 502A–C.

12. Letter 1, PL 182: cols. 67–79; letter 238, cols. 427D–31A; sermon 16, pars. 4–8, OB 1:91–94.

13. Letter 110, PL 182: col. 253; trans. Bruno Scott James, *The Letters of St. Bernard of Clairvaux* (London, 1953), letter 112, p. 169.

14. Letter 144, PL 182: cols. 300B and 301A.

15. Letter 201, PL 182: col. 369B–C.

you with milk when, while yet a child, it was all you could take. . . . But alas! how soon and how early you were weaned. . . . Sadly I weep, not for my lost labor but for the unhappy state of my lost child. . . . My case is the same as that of the harlot Solomon judged, whose child was stealthily taken by another who had overlain and killed her own. You too were torn from my breast, cut from my womb. My heart cannot forget you, half of it went with you. . . .[16]

His letters also contain passing references to the motherhood of God: "Do not let the roughness of our life frighten your tender years. If you feel the stings of temptation. . . . suck not so much the wounds as the breasts of the Crucified [. . . *suge non tam vulnera quam ubera Crucifixi*]. He will be your mother, and you will be his son."[17]

But Bernard's most complex use of maternal imagery occurs in his sermons on the Song of Songs. Here he repeatedly chooses to explain references to breasts that are erotic in the Biblical text with lengthy discussions of the obligation of prelates, especially abbots, to "mother" the souls in their charge. Commenting on the verse "For your breasts are better than wine, smelling sweet of the best ointments" (Song 1:1–2), he first associates nursing with Christ the bridegroom: "She [the bride, i.e., the soul] would seem to say to the bridegroom [Christ]: 'What wonder if I presume to ask you for this favor, since your breasts have given me such overwhelming joy?' . . . When she said, then, 'Your breasts are better than wine,' she meant: 'The richness of the grace that flows from your breasts contributes far more to my spiritual progress than the biting reprimands of superiors.'"[18] From this he moves to a discussion of "those who have undertaken the direction of souls":

. . . how many [of them] there are today who reveal their lack of the requisite qualities: . . . They display an insatiable passion for gains. . . . Neither the peril of souls nor their salvation gives

16. Letter 1, PL 182: cols. 72 and 76A–C; trans. James, letter 1, pp. 3 and 7, with my changes.
17. Letter 322, PL 182: col. 527.
18. Sermon 9, pars. 5–6, OB 1:45–46; trans. Kiliam Walsh, *On the Song of Songs* 1, The Works of Bernard of Clairvaux 2, Cistercian Fathers Series 4 (Spencer, Mass., 1971):57–58.

them any concern. They are certainly devoid of the maternal instinct. . . . There is no pretense about a true mother, the breasts that she displays are full for the taking. She knows how to *rejoice with those who rejoice*, and to be sad with those who sorrow [Rom. 12:15], pressing the milk of encouragement without intermission from the breast of joyful sympathy, the milk of consolation from the breast of compassion.[19]

A number of sermons later Bernard returns to a discussion of breasts, which suggest to him the subject of mothers; and once again mothers suggest to him the responsibility of prelates:

Here is a point for the ear of those superiors who wish always to inspire fear in their communities and rarely promote their welfare. *Learn, you who rule the earth* [Ps. 2:10]. Learn that you must be mothers to those in your care, not masters [*domini*]; make an effort to arouse the response of love, not that of fear; and should there be occasional need for severity, let it be paternal rather than tyrannical. Show affection as a mother would, correct like a father [*matres fovendo, patres . . . corripiendo . . .*]. Be gentle, avoid harshness, do not resort to blows, expose your breasts: let your bosoms expand with milk not swell with passion. . . . Why will the young man, bitten by the serpent, shy away from the judgement of the priest, to whom he ought rather to run as to the bosom of a mother? If you are spiritual, instruct him in a spirit of gentleness. . . .[20]

And, still later, Bernard returns to breasts and nursing as symbols of preaching:

Take note however that she [the bride] yearns for one thing and receives another. In spite of her longing for the repose of contemplation she is burdened with the task of preaching; and despite her desire to bask in the bridegroom's presence she is entrusted with cares of begetting and rearing children. [Just as once before, she is reminded that] she [is] a mother, that her duty [is] to suckle her babes, to provide food for her children. . . . We learn from this that only too often we must interrupt the sweet kisses to feed the needy with the milk of doctrine.[21]

19. Sermon 10, par. 3, OB 1:49–50; trans. Walsh, *Song* 1:62–63.
20. Sermon 23, par. 2, OB 1:139–40; trans. Walsh, *Song* 2:27.
21. Sermon 41, pars. 5–6, OB 2:31–32; trans. Walsh, *Song* 2:208.

118

In contrast to Bernard, William of St. Thierry avoids explicit references to God as mother, using "father and child" or "bride-groom and bride" to describe the soul's relationship to God.[22] But, like Bernard, William expounds the references to breasts in the Song of Songs as descriptions of Christ feeding and instructing the individual soul.[23]

> . . . it is your breasts, O eternal Wisdom, that nourish the holy infancy of your little ones. . . . Since that everlasting blessed union and the kiss of eternity are denied the Bride on account of her human condition and weakness, she turns to your bosom; and not attaining to that mouth of yours, she puts her mouth to your breasts instead. . . .[24]

Like Bernard, William uses such references to breasts as opportunities to discuss the burdens of the abbacy.[25] And elsewhere in his works, despite the fact that "Eve" or "woman" is frequently for him a symbol of weakness or of the flesh,[26] he includes references to Christ nursing his children, to the fostering wings of Jesus, and references (perhaps with womb overtones) to the soul entering the side of Christ.

> It was not the least of the chief reasons for your incarnation that your babes in the church, who still needed your milk rather than

22. Colledge and Walsh, *A Book of Showings* 1:155, and 2:582, n. 12, are misleading when they say that "there appears to be no attribution to the Son of motherhood before that of William of St. Thierry," although they are correct in seeing William's stress on the cooperation of operations in the Trinity as a precursor of Julian's theology of motherhood.
23. William of St. Thierry, *Exposé sur le Cantique des Cantiques*, ed. J.M. Déchanet, SC 82, Sér. mon. 8 (Paris, 1962), chaps. 37–38, pp. 120–24; chaps. 44–46, pp. 132–36; and chap. 52, p. 144 (cf. chap. 83 on the breasts of the bride, pp. 200–2).
24. William, *Sur le Cantique*, chap. 38, pp. 122–24; trans. Mother Columba Hart, *The Works of William of St. Thierry* 2: *Exposition on the Song of Songs*, Cistercian Fathers Series 6 (Spencer, Mass., 1970):30.
25. William, *Sur le Cantique*, chap. 52, p. 144, and see n. 153 below.
26. William, *Meditativae Orationes*, chaps. 4 and 5, PL 180: cols. 216A and C and 221C; see also William, *La contemplation de Dieu: l'oraison de Dom Guillaume*, ed. J.Hourlier, SC 61, Sér. mon. 2 (Paris, 1959), chap. 3, p. 64; and William, *Epistola ad fratres de Monte Dei*, ed. J. Déchanet, SC 223, Sér. mon. 45 (Paris, 1975), pt. 1, chap. 2, pars. 52–53, p. 186.

solid food, who are not strong enough spiritually to think of you in your own way, might find in you a form not unfamiliar to themselves.[27]

Those unsearchable riches of your glory, Lord, were hidden in your secret place in heaven until the soldier's spear opened the side of your Son our Lord and Savior on the cross, and from it flowed the mysteries of our redemption. Now we may not only thrust our fingers or our hand into his side, like Thomas, but through that open door may enter whole, O Jesus, even into your heart, the sure seat of your mercy. . . .

. . . Open to us your body's side, that those who long to see the secrets of your Son may enter in, and may receive the sacraments that flow therefrom, even the price of their redemption.[28]

Lord, whither do you draw those whom you thus embrace and enfold, save to your heart? The manna of your Godhead, which you, O Jesus, keep within the golden vessel of your all-wise human soul, is your secret heart. . . . Blessed are the souls whom you have hidden in your heart, that inmost hidingplace, so that your arms overshadow them from the disquieting of men and they hope only in your covering and fostering wings.[29]

Guerric abbot of Igny († ca. 1157) is, after Bernard, the Cistercian who makes most frequent and complex use of maternal imagery to speak of God and male authority figures. Guerric uses "motherhood" to describe the relationship of Christ, Peter and Paul, and prelates in general to the soul of the individual believer; he also reverses the image, using "maternity" to describe the birth or incorporation of Christ in the individual soul.[30]

27. *Meditativae Orationes*, chap. 10, PL 180: col. 236A; trans. Sister Penelope, *The Works of William of St. Thierry* 1: *On Contemplating God . . .*, Cistercian Fathers Series 3 (Spencer, Mass., 1971):152–53.

28. *Meditativae Orationes*, chap. 6, PL 180: cols. 225D–26A; trans. Sister Penelope, *Works* 1:131. See n. 34 below.

29. *Meditativae Orationes*, chap. 8, PL 180: col. 230C; trans. Sister Penelope, *Works* 1:141.

30. Guerric, third Christmas sermon, chaps. 4–5, *Sermons*, 2 vols., ed. J. Morson and H. Costello, SC 166 and 202, Sér. mon. 31 and 43 (Paris, 1970 and 1973) 1:196–200; first Epiphany sermon, chap. 6, *Sermons* 1:250; second sermon for Lent, chap. 2, *Sermons* 2:30; fourth sermon

Give to the church, he [Solomon] says, the living infant, for she is its mother. Whoever does his will [Christ's], he is his mother and brother and sister.

Lord Solomon, you call me mother. . . . And indeed I will show myself a mother by love and anxious care to the best of my ability. . . .

Brethren, this name of mother is not restricted to prelates, although they are charged in a special way with maternal solicitude and devotion; it is shared by you too who do the Lord's will. Yes, you too are mothers of the child who has been born for you and in you, that is, since you conceived from the fear of the Lord and gave birth to the spirit of salvation.[31]

Unlike Bernard, Guerric is fascinated by images of pregnancy and of the womb. He not only speaks at length of the soul hiding in the wounds and heart of Christ; he also explicitly associates heart and womb and produces a bizarre description of the soul as child incorporated into the bowels of God the father.[32]

He [God the father] draws them [the wretched] into his very bowels and makes them his members. He could not bind us to himself more closely, could not make us more intimate to himself than by incorporating us into himself.[33]

He [Christ] is the cleft rock . . . do not fly only to him but into him. . . . For in his loving kindness and his compassion he opened his side in order that the blood of the wound might give you life, the warmth of his body revive you, the breath of his heart flow into you. . . . There you will lie hidden in safety. . . .

---

for Palm Sunday, chap. 5, *Sermons* 2:210–14; second sermon for SS. Peter and Paul, chaps. 1–6, *Sermons* 2:380–94; second sermon for the Nativity of Mary, chaps. 3–5, *Sermons* 2:490–96.

31. Guerric, third Christmas sermon, chaps. 4–5, *Sermons* 1:198; trans. the monks of Mount St. Bernard abbey, in Guerric of Igny, *Liturgical Sermons*, 2 vols., Cistercian Fathers Series 8 and 32 (Spencer, Mass., 1970–71), 1:52.

32. Second sermon for the Annunciation, chap. 4, *Sermons* 2:140: "Haec est ad uterum cordis via spiritus concipiendi"; see also second and third sermons for the Annunciation, pp. 126–62 passim.

33. Second sermon for Lent, chap. 2, *Sermons* 2:30; trans. the monks of Mount St. Bernard abbey, *Liturgical Sermons* 1:142.

There you will certainly not freeze, since in the bowels of Christ charity does not grow cold.[34]

Thus, to Guerric, the maternity that is associated with the womb is a symbol of fertility, security, and union more than a symbol of separation, suffering, or sacrifice. And Guerric, like Bernard, uses maternal attributes to expand and change what he means by "father."[35] But Guerric also, when he contrasts "fathering" and "mothering," associates engendering and authority with the father, nursing and loving with the mother;[36] and his most extensive images are images of breasts and milk.

> The Bridegroom [Christ] . . . has breasts, lest he should be lacking any one of all duties and titles of loving kindness. He is a father in virtue of natural creation . . . and also in virtue of the authority with which he instructs. He is a mother, too, in the mildness of his affection, and a nurse. . . .
>
> But behold all at once the Holy Spirit was sent from heaven like milk poured out from Christ's own breasts, and Peter was filled with an abundance of milk. Not long afterwards Saul became Paul, the persecutor became the preacher, the torturer became the mother, the executioner became the nurse, so that you might truly understand that the whole of his blood was changed into the sweetness of milk, his cruelty into loving kindness.[37]

The image of God as mother is less important to Aelred of Rievaulx (†1167) than to Guerric; meditation on the infancy and

34. Fourth sermon for Palm Sunday, *Sermons* 2:212–14; trans. the monks of St. Bernard abbey, *Liturgical Sermons* 2:77–78. In psychoanalytic theory, "bowels" is a standard womb symbol; see Sigmund Freud, "On the Sexual Theories of Children" (1908), *The Standard Edition of the Complete Psychological Works of Sigmund Freud*, ed. James Strachey and Anna Freud, 24 vols. (London, 1953–74) 9:207–26, especially 219. *Viscera* in the Vulgate usually means the source of feelings of compassion, which we moderns might translate "heart" (e.g., Gen. 43:30; Isa. 63:15), although the same Hebrew word that is translated *viscera* is also translated *venter* and *uterus* (Gen. 25:23; Isa. 48:19).
35. Second sermon for Lent, *Sermons* 2:26–36.
36. Second sermon for SS. Peter and Paul, *Sermons* 2:380–94, and first sermon for the Assumption, ibid. 2:414–26.
37. Second sermon for SS. Peter and Paul, chap. 2, *Sermons* 2:384–86; trans. the monks of Mount St. Bernard abbey, *Liturgical Sermons* 2:155.

childhood of Jesus is more important. But Aelred elaborates the idea of Jesus as nursing mother as well as the image of Jesus our brother suckled at the Virgin's breasts.[38]

> On your altar let it be enough for you to have a representation of our Savior hanging on the cross; that will bring before your mind his Passion for you to imitate, his outspread arms will invite you to embrace him, his naked breasts will feed you with the milk of sweetness to console you.[39]

In a complex discussion of John reclining on Jesus's breast, Aelred says that John drinks the wine of knowledge of God, whereas the soul of the ordinary believer feeds on the milk that flows from Christ's humanity.[40] The blood that flows from the wound in Christ's side becomes wine, the water becomes milk; and the soul not only draws nurture from Christ but also flees for refuge into the wound in the wall of his body.

> Then one of the soldiers opened his side with a lance and there came forth blood and water. Hasten, linger not, eat the honeycomb with your honey, drink your wine with your milk. The blood is changed into wine to gladden you, the water into milk to nourish you. From the rock streams have flowed for you, wounds have been made in his limbs, holes in the wall of his body, in which, like a dove, you may hide while you kiss them one by one. Your lips, stained with blood, will become like a scarlet ribbon and your word sweet.[41]

And Aelred, like other Cistercian authors, moves naturally from a discussion of parents and nursing to a discussion of the heavy burdens borne by religious leaders.

---

38. *De Jesu puero duodenni*, sect. 3, par. 31, in Aelred, *Opera omnia*, 1, ed. A. Hoste and C. H. Talbot, CCCM 1 (Turnhout, 1971): 277–78 (cf. ibid., par. 30, 1:276); *De institutione inclusarum*, chap. 26, *Opera omnia* 1:658, and chap. 31, 1:668–71; *Speculum caritatis*, bk. 2, chap. 12, *Opera omnia* 1:79–80.

39. *De institutione*, chap. 26, *Opera omnia* 1:658; trans. M. P. Mcpherson in *The Works of Aelred of Rievaulx* 1: *Treatises and Pastoral Prayer*, Cistercian Fathers Series 2 (Spencer, Mass., 1971):73.

40. *De institutione*, chap. 31, *Opera omnia* 1:668.

41. Ibid., p. 671; trans. Mcpherson, *Works* 1:90–91.

But while the holy soul lingers in these delights [i.e., the child Jesus remains behind in Jerusalem] its mother and foster-father grieve, complain and search; when at length they find it they upbraid it with gentle reproaches and take it back to Nazareth. This can be applied in particular to those spiritual men who have been entrusted with preaching God's Word and caring for souls. Further, our foster-father I would interpret most readily as the Holy Spirit, and nothing is better fitted to serve as our mother than charity. These cherish and make us advance, feed and nourish us, and refresh us with the milk of twofold affection: love, that is, for God and for neighbor.[42]

His biographer reports that his dying words to his own monks were: "I love you all . . . as earnestly as a mother does her sons."[43]

Adam, abbot of Perseigne (†1221), is the only twelfth-century Cistercian writer to emphasize the pains of labor when he uses maternal imagery or to draw extensively on the Biblical reference to the woman in travail (John 16:21). In this he is closer to Anselm than are the earlier Cistercian writers. But in contrast to Anselm's stress on Christ's suffering for the soul, Adam's use of giving birth as an image is almost completely restricted to discussion of the soul's fertility in good works or of the solicitude of abbots or bishops for their charges.[44] Adam insists that a good father must also be a good mother (i.e., prelates must give birth as well as impregnate).[45] When he turns to the soul's relationship to God, however, it is nursing, not giving birth, that becomes the dominant image and, to Adam, the nurse is usually the Virgin. We, the children, drink Christ, the milk, at the Virgin's breasts and so become the brothers of Christ in a special sense, those who nurse at the breast alongside him.[46] "Do you think," writes Adam, "that this most loving of all children would refuse to his nursing broth-

42. *De Jesu puero duodenni*, sect. 3, par. 30, *Opera omnia* 1:276; trans. Berkeley, *Works* 1:37.

43. Walter Daniel, *The Life of Ailred of Rievaulx*, ed. and trans. F. M. Powicke, Medieval Classics (New York, 1950), p. 58.

44. Adam of Perseigne, letter 2, *Correspondance*, ed. J. Bouvet, *Archives historiques du Maine* 13 (1952):20–22; letter 11, pp. 77–78; letter 41, p. 410; letter 50, p. 519 and PL 211: col. 623.

45. *Correspondance*, letter 2, pp. 20–22.

46. *Correspondance*, letter 35, pp. 305–7, and PL 211: cols. 602–3; letter 45, p. 443, and PL 211: col. 624; letter 48, pp. 471–74 and 477, and PL

ers the womb or the breasts of his mother, when he has chosen her precisely for mother so that she may be the nurse of the humble?"[47] Adam also speaks of the prelate as nurturing, using the hen-and-chicks metaphor (which he supplements with references to the strength of eagles).[48] He reprimands the bishop of Le Mans: "Besides, in what way are you yourself named father or mother of little ones, you who do not jealously watch over your chicks with tender affection as a hen does, or like an eagle provoking her chicks to fly flutter over them and bear upwards in your wings both by word and example those little ones commended to you?"[49]

Biblical and Patristic Background

Any explanation of the medieval theme of God as mother must begin by noting that it is not an invention of twelfth-century devotional writers. In the Old Testament, God frequently speaks of himself as mother, bearing the Israelites in his bosom, conceiving them in his womb (e.g., Isa. 49:1, 49:15, and 66:11–13).[50] The wisdom of God is a feminine principle; in Ecclesiasticus she says: "I am the mother of fair love, and of fear, and of knowledge, and of holy hope. . . . Come over to me, all ye that desire me: and be filled with my fruits" (Ecclus. 24:24–26).[51] In the New Testament such imagery is nonexistent. The gospel of John does apply to Christ some of the titles of the Old Testament wisdom literature (e.g., John 14:6),[52] but it uses no feminine language. Christ is, however, described as a hen gathering her chicks under her wings

---

211: cols. 635–36 and 638; letter 53, pp. 541–43 and 545–46, and PL 211: cols. 604–5 and 607; letter 54, pp. 553–55. See also letter 64, pp. 629–30, and PL 211: col. 651, which refers to Christ at the Virgin's breast but says that we receive our milk from the Word itself.

47. *Correspondance*, letter 53, p. 542.

48. *Correspondance*, letter 2, p. 22; letter 4, p. 30.

49. *Correspondance*, letter 4, p. 30. In addition to the authors discussed above, Gilbert of Hoyland, *Sermones in Canticum Salomonis*, sermon 5, PL 184: col. 32C, sees Jesus as the nurse preparing pap for the child.

50. See Phyllis Trible, "God, Nature of, in the Old Testament," *Interpreter's 'Dictionary of the Bible*, supplementary vol. (Nashville, 1976), pp. 368–69, and Cabassut, "Une dévotion peu connue," pp. 236–37.

51. Colledge and Walsh, *A Book of Showings* 1:154.

52. Ibid.

in Matt. 23:37.[53] And the contrast drawn in the Epistles between milk and meat as symbols of types of instruction (1 Cor. 3:1–2; Heb. 5:12; 1 Pet. 2:2) seems to have suggested to later writers that the apostles responsible for the Epistles, Peter and Paul, themselves provided the milk for beginners and should therefore be seen as mothers. The possibly gnostic *Odes* of Solomon, the apocryphal third-century Acts of Peter, and the writings of Clement, Origen, Irenaeus, John Chrysostom, Ambrose, and Augustine all describe Christ as mother.[54] In general the Greek fathers, particularly those influenced by gnosticism, seem to have been more at home with maternal metaphors.[55] The Latin translator of the Acts of Peter suppressed "mother" in his list of titles for Christ,[56] and the passing references to Christ's maternal love in Augustine and Ambrose in no way compare to the elaborate and lengthy passages that Clement of Alexandria devotes to the nursing Christ.[57] With the exception of Bede's references to God's wisdom as feminine,[58] the theme is unimportant in the early Middle Ages. Early medieval texts do, however, occasionally refer to religious leaders as

53. Mark 3:35, where Christ refers to any faithful follower as his mother or brother, is a very different use of mother as symbol, although one on which twelfth-century Cistercians probably draw; cf. the passages cited in nn. 28, 30, 31, 49, and 97.

54. See Cabassut, "Une dévotion peu connue"; E. McLaughlin, "'Christ My Mother'"; Bradley, "Motherhood Theme"; Pagels, "God the Mother," and *Gnostic Gospels*; Eleanor McLaughlin, "God's Body and Ours: Possibilities for Reformation in Medieval Spirituality," unpublished lecture, Vanderbilt Theological School, October 1976; Colledge and Walsh, *A Book of Showings*. To their references, I add: Irenaeus, *Adversus haereses*, bk. 3, chap. 24, par. 1, *Patrologia graeca*, ed. J.-P. Migne, 7: cols. 966–67; and Augustine, *In Iohannis Evangelium Tractatus CXXIV*, chap. 15, par. 7, chap. 16, par. 2, chap. 18, par. 1, and chap. 21, par. 1, Corpus christianorum 36 (Turnhout, 1954), pp. 153, 165, 179, and 212.

55. Pagels, "God the Mother," and *Gnostic Gospels*.

56. Cabassut, "Une dévotion peu connue," p. 237.

57. Compare, for example, Ambrose, *De virginibus*, bk. 1, chap. 5, PL 16: col. 205, with Clement of Alexandria, *Paedagogus*, bk. 1, chap. 6, *Clemens Alexandrinus*, 2 vols., ed. Otto Stählin, Die griechischen christlichen Schriftsteller der ersten drei Jahrhunderte 12 and 15 (Leipzig, 1936–39) 1:104–21.

58. Colledge and Walsh, A *Book of Showings* 1:154.

mothers. The *Regula magistri* and later monastic texts use maternal metaphors to describe the abbot;[59] Hincmar of Rheims refers in passing to both bishop and Christ as mother.[60] Moreover, the popular theme of the church as virgin mother, common in the early patristic period probably because it expressed so perfectly the nature of an entity withdrawn from the world (virgin) yet expanding and converting (mother), continued to be influential throughout the early Middle Ages.[61] Although it is not a female image applied to a male figure, it suggested to twelfth-century authors an association of instruction and pastoral responsibility with maternity and nurturing.

Furthermore, inversion of language and therefore of values is a New Testament literary technique ("Hath not God made foolish the wisdom of this world?" 1 Cor. 1:20; "But many that are first shall be last" Mark 10:31; etc.), which twelfth-century authors such as Adam and Bernard used quite consciously.

> I rightly apply to myself those words of the Prophet: . . . *Play the mountebank I will* . . . [2 Kings 6:22]. A good sort of playing this . . . by which we become an object of reproach to the rich and of ridicule to the proud. In fact what else do seculars think we are doing by playing when what they desire most on earth, we fly from; and what they fly from, we desire? [We are] like acrobats and jugglers, who with heads down and feet up, stand or walk on their hands. . . . And we too play this game that we

59. Cabassut, "Une dévotion peu connue," p. 235. For a Carolingian example of the abbot as mother, see Paschasius Radbertus, *Vita sancti Adalhardi*, chap. 71, PL 120: col. 1543D.
60. Hincmar, *Opusculum LV Capitulorum adversus Hincmarum Laudunensem*, chap. 51, PL 126: col. 488, and *De praedestinatione Dei et libero arbitrio, posterior dissertatio*, chap. 35, PL 125: col. 375; see Karl F. Morrison, "'Unum ex multis': Hincmar of Rheims' Medical and Aesthetic Rationales for Unification," *Nascita dell'Europa ed Europa carolingia: un'equazione da verificare*, Settimana di Studio del Centro Italiano di Studi sull'Alto Medioevo 27 (Spoleto, 1980), to appear.
61. See J. A. Jungmann, "The Defeat of Teutonic Arianism and the Revolution of Religious Culture in the Early Middle Ages," *Pastoral Liturgy* (New York, 1962), pp. 48–63; see also Mary Douglas, *Purity and Danger: An Analysis of Concepts of Pollution and Taboo* (New York, 1966), p. 157.

may be ridiculed, discomfited, humbled, until he comes who puts down the mighty from their seats and exalts the humble.[62]

When he distinguishes monks and clergy by calling monks women and clergy men, Bernard means to suggest that monks have a weakness and unworldliness that is valued in God's eyes as humility.[63] Thus sexually inverted images (e.g., calling men women) were part of a tradition of using inverted language to express personal dependence and the dependence of one's values on God.

But the mere existence of earlier literary techniques or "maternal" texts does not explain why twelfth-century authors chose to borrow them. And closer exploration reveals some basic differences between patristic and twelfth-century uses of maternal imagery. By far the fullest patristic elaboration of the theme of God as mother (fuller in fact than any of the twelfth-century references) occurs in Clement of Alexandria's *Paedagogus*, but Clement nowhere moves from a discussion of Christ as a pedagogue and mother to a discussion of the responsibilities of prelates or clergy.[64] And Origen's commentary on the Song of Songs, which opens with a discussion of levels of knowledge as "milk" and "meat," does not elaborate these references into a discussion of either prelates or Christ as mother; nor does Origen choose to explain the breasts of the bridegroom (Song 1:2) as a nursing image, let alone use it, as do Bernard and William, to introduce a discussion of the burdens of pastoral responsibility.[65]

62. Bernard, Letter 87, PL 182: col. 217C–D; trans. James, letter 90, p. 135.
63. Sermon 12, par. 9, OB 1:66 (he compares monks to women who remain at home spinning while their husbands, i.e., bishops, go out to war). See also ibid., par. 8, pp. 65–66, where Bernard calls himself a woman as an indication of his weakness and of his need for contemplation. For a discussion of inverted imagery used by women, see Jo Ann McNamara, "Sexual Equality and the Cult of Virginity in Early Christian Thought," *Feminist Studies* 3.3/4 (1976): 145–58.
64. Clement of Alexandria, *Paedagogus*, bk. 1, chap. 6, *Clemens Alexandrinus* 1:104–21; see also *Paedagogus*, bk. 1, chap. 5, 1:96–104.
65. Origen, *Commentarium in Canticum Canticorum*, prologue and bk. 1, and *Homilia in Canticum Canticorum*, first homily, chap. 5, *Origenes Werke* 8, ed. W. Baehrens, Die griechischen christlichen Schriftsteller der ersten drei Jahrhunderte 33 (Leipzig, 1925): 61–70, 90–95, and 34–35.

Thus the theme of mother Jesus, as it is used by Bernard, Guerric, Anselm, and others, is not merely a repetition of patristic ideas. Indeed, the presence of maternal metaphors in twelfth-century devotional texts seems less an aspect of that looking back to the early church that is such a prominent motive in twelfth-century spirituality than an aspect of certain broad trends that are, so far as we can tell, new.[66] These two trends are the rise of affective spirituality and the feminization of religious language.

The Theme of "Mother Jesus" as a Reflection of Affective Spirituality

Several of the scholars who have noticed the use of maternal imagery in medieval authors from Anselm of Canterbury to Julian of Norwich have associated this particular image with the rise, from the eleventh century on, of a lyrical, emotional piety that focuses increasingly on the humanity of Christ.[67] Descriptions of God as a woman nursing the soul at her breasts, drying its tears, punishing its petty mischief-making, giving birth to it in agony and travail, are part of a growing tendency to speak of the divine in homey images and to emphasize its approachability. If Christ presents himself to us as a child playing in a carpenter's shop or a young man stopping, dusty and tired, for a meal with friends, what can possibly be wrong with earthy metaphors that associate his love with that of female as well as male parents, his sustenance with milk as well as meat? Seeing Christ or God or the Holy Spirit as female is thus part of a later medieval devotional tradition that is characterized by increasing preference for analogies taken from human relationships,[68] a growing sense of God as loving and accessible, a general tendency toward fulsome language, and a more

66. On "reform" and "return to the early church" as themes in twelfth-century spirituality, see above chapter 3, n. 47.
67. Cabassut, "Une dévotion peu connue"; Constable, "Twelfth-Century Spirituality"; E. McLaughlin, "'Christ My Mother'"; idem, "Women, Power . . .," pp. 122–27.
68. This has been pointed out by R. Javelet, *Image et ressemblance au douzième siècle de saint Anselme à Alain de Lille*, 2 vols. (Paris, 1967).

accepting reaction to all natural things, including the physical human body.[69] But the idea of mother Jesus is not merely an aspect of increasing attention to the human Christ. It also expresses quite specifically certain of the emphases that underlay the affective spirituality of the twelfth to the fourteenth centuries.[70]

The affective piety of the high Middle Ages is based on an increasing sense of, first, humankind's creation "in the image and likeness" of God and, second, the humanity of Christ as guarantee that what we are is inextricably joined with divinity. Creation and incarnation are stressed more than atonement and judgment. Christ is seen as the mediator who joins our substance to divinity and as the object of a profound experiential union; God is emphasized as creating and creative; the cooperation of the Trinity in the work of creation is stressed. The dominant note of piety is optimism and a sense of momentum toward a loving God. Concentration on the eucharist and on Christ's suffering in the Passion, which increases in thirteenth- and fourteenth-century devotions, is not primarily a stress on the sacrifice needed to bridge the enormous gap between us in our sin and God in his glory; it is rather an identification with the fact that Christ is what we are. Moreover, both the imaginative identification with Christ's humanity, which is so stressed by late medieval preachers and devotional writers, and the increased theological emphasis on creation and incarnation are answers to the major heresies of the twelfth to fourteenth centuries. Affirmation of God's creation of all things and of the joining of physicality to divinity countered Cathar dualism; affirma-

69. This latter point is stressed by E. McLaughlin, "'Christ My Mother'," and "Women, Power. . . ." It should not, however, be misunderstood. From the twelfth century on, negative attitudes toward sexuality, at least among the religious, probably increased; see John Boswell, *Christianity, Social Tolerance, and Homosexuality: Gay People in Western Europe from the Beginning of the Christian Era to the Fourteenth Century* (Chicago, 1980).

70. Of those scholars who have written on maternal imagery, Bradley ("Motherhood Theme" and "Patristic Background of Motherhood Similitude"), Børresen ("Christ notre mère"), and Colledge and Walsh (*A Book of Showings*) have been concerned with the theological tradition more than the devotional; all three treat this through a search for the sources of Julian of Norwich's trinitarian theology, which is expressed through the motherhood metaphor.

tion of the centrality of the eucharist countered the neglect or abandonment of the church's rituals that was implicit in various antisacerdotal movements and in Free Spirit antinomianism. In addition to expressing and evoking the emotional response so highly valued in the twelfth and thirteenth centuries, the devotion to mother Jesus conveyed the specific emphases of this piety on mystical union and the eucharist.

In spiritual writers from Anselm to Julian, we find three basic stereotypes of the female or the mother: the female is generative (the foetus is made of her very matter) and sacrificial in her generation (birth pangs);[71] the female is loving and tender (a mother cannot help loving her own child);[72] the female is nurturing (she feeds the child with her own bodily fluid).[73] This threefold concept of

71. Anselm, prayer 10, *Opera omnia* 3: 33 and 39–41; Marguerite of Oingt, *Pagina meditationum*, chaps. 30, 32–33, 36–37 and 39, *Les oeuvres de Marguerite d'Oingt*, ed. and trans. Antonin Duraffour, P. Gardette and P. Durdilly, Publications de l'Institut de Linguistique Romane de Lyon 21 (Paris, 1965), pp. 77–79; and Julian of Norwich, *A Book of Showings*, the long text, passim and especially chaps. 58–60, 2:582–600. On the complex problems of the text of Julian's revelations, see also E. Colledge and J. Walsh, "Editing Julian of Norwich's Revelations: A Progress Report," *Mediaeval Studies* 38 (1976): 404–27. The theme of God as mother is developed in the later, longer version.

72. *Ancrene Riwle: The English Text of the Cotton Nero A. XIV*, ed. Mabel Day, Early English Text Society 225 (London 1952), p. 103 (and see also p. 180); Hugh Lacerta, *Liber de doctrina vel liber sententiarum seu rationum beati viri Stephani primi patris religionis Grandmontis*, chap. 10, CCCM 8 (Turnhout, 1968), p. 14; Bernard of Clairvaux, sermon 12, par. 4, OB 1:62–63; sermon 23, par. 2, 1:139–40; sermon 26, par. 6, 1:173; letter 258, PL 182: cols. 466A–67A; and *De diligendo Deo*, chap. 7, par. 17, OB 3:134; Julian, *A Book of Showings*, the long text, especially chaps. 61 and 63, 2:601–9 and 614–18; Gertrude the Great, *Revelationes Gertrudianae ac Mechtildianae* 1: *Sanctae Gertrudis magnae virginis ordinis sancti Benedicti Legatus divinae pietatis . . .*, ed. the monks of Solesmes [Dom Paquelin] (Paris, 1875), bk. 4, chap. 5, p. 314; and bk. 5, chap. 28, p. 546; Mechtild of Hackeborn, *Revelationes Gertrudianae ac Mechtildianae* 2: *Sanctae Mechtildis virginis ordinis sancti Benedicti Liber specialis gratiae*, ed. the monks of Solesmes (Paris, 1877), bk. 2, chap. 16, pp. 149–50; bk 3, chap. 9, p. 208; bk. 4, chap. 7, p. 264; and bk. 4, chap. 59, p. 311.

73. See the passages cited in nn. 16, 19, 20, 37, 41, 142, and 143; Gertrude the Great, *Oeuvres spirituelles*, vols. 2 and 3: *Le Héraut*, SC 139 and 143,

the female parent seems to have been particularly appropriate to convey the new theological concerns, more appropriate in fact than the image of the male parent if we understand certain details of medieval theories of physiology.

People in the high Middle Ages argued that the ideal child-rearing pattern was for the mother to nurse her own child; in medieval medical theory breast milk is processed blood.[74] According to medieval understanding of physiology, the loving mother, like the pelican who is also a symbol for Christ, feeds her child with her own blood. Thus, the connection of blood and milk in many medieval texts is based on more than merely the parallelism of two bodily fluids. Clement of Alexandria as early as the second century makes explicit the connection between breast milk and the blood supplied to the foetus in order to use the nursing Christ as an image of the eucharist.[75] In medieval legends like the lactation of St. Bernard[76] and in medieval devotions like the sacred

---

Sér. mon. 25 and 27 (Paris, 1968), bk. 3, chap. 4, 3:24; Richard Rolle, "Richard Rolle's Comment on the Canticles, Edited From MS Trinity College, Dublin, 153," ed. Elizabeth M. Murray (Ph.D. Dissertation, Fordham, 1958), pp. 29–30 and 33; and Julian, *A Book of Showings*, the long text, chap. 60, 2:596–97.

74. M. McLaughlin, "Survivors and Surrogates," pp. 115–18; Michael Goodich, "Bartholomaeus Anglicus on Child-rearing," *History of Childhood Quarterly: The Journal of Psychohistory* 3 (1975): 80.

75. Clement, *Paedagogus*, bk. 1, chap. 6, *Clemens Alexandrinus* 1: 104–21.

76. See Léon Dewez and Albert van Iterson, "La lactation de saint Bernard: Legende et iconographie," *Cîteaux in de Nederlanden* 7 (1956): 165–89. We should also note in this connection the legend, found in a work attributed to John Chrysostom and repeated by Guerric, that the apostle Paul bled milk rather than blood when he was beheaded (see Guerric of Igny, *Liturgical Sermons* 2:154, n.7). St. Catherine of Alexandria is also supposed to have bled milk when decapitated: see G. Bardy, "Catherine d'Alexandrie," DHGE 11 (Paris, 1949): cols. 1503–5. Moreover lactation as an act of filial piety (an adult female offering the breast to a parent or an adult in a desperate situation) was a solemn theme in the literature and religion of pagan antiquity; Adolphe de Ceuleneer, "La Charité romaine dans la littérature et dans l'art," *Annales de l'Académie Royale d'archéologie de Belgique* 67 (Antwerp, 1919): 175–206. On medieval devotion to the Virgin's milk, see P. V. Bétérous, "A propos d'une des légendes mariales les plus répandues: le 'lait de la Vierge,'" *Bullétin de l'association Guillaume Budé* 4 (1975): 403–11.

heart,[77] milk and blood are often interchangeable, as are Christ's breasts and the wound in his side.[78] What writers in the high Middle Ages wished to say about Christ the savior who feeds the individual soul with his own blood was precisely and concisely said in the image of the nursing mother whose milk *is* her blood, offered to the child.

Medieval images of the maternal also stressed mother-love as instinctive and fundamental: the mother is tender and loving, sometimes dying to give the child life; she tempts or disciplines only with the welfare of the child in mind. Such imagery could, of course, be highly sentimental and was apt to bring affective response. It was peculiarly appropriate to a theological emphasis on an accessible and tender God, a God who bleeds and suffers less as a sacrifice or restoration of cosmic order than as a stimulus to human love.

Moreover, in medieval physiological theories—however confused they may be on the subject—the female in some sense provides the matter of the foetus, the male the life or spirit.[79] Medieval theologians sometimes stressed that, as Eve came from the matter of Adam, so Christ came from the matter of Mary.[80] Thus, the mother was, to medieval people, especially associated with the

77. See Jean Leclercq, "Le sacré-coeur dans la tradition bénédictine au moyen âge," *Cor Jesu: Commentationes in litteras encyclicas Pii PP. XII 'Haurietis aquas'*, 2 vols. (Rome, 1959), 2:3–28; see also Cyprien Vagaggini, "La dévotion au sacré-coeur chez sainte Mechtilde et sainte Gertrude," ibid., pp. 31–48.

78. For examples of this interchangeability, see Guerric of Igny, second sermon for SS. Peter and Paul, chap. 2, *Sermons* 2:384–86; Aelred, *De institutione*, chap. 31, *Opera omnia* 1:671; the monk of Farne, *Meditations*, chap. 40, "The Meditations of the Monk of Farne," ed. Hugh Farmer, *Studia Anselmiana* 41–42, *Analecta monastica* 4 (1957): 182–83.

79. Bullough, "Medieval Medical and Scientific Views." See also John F. Benton, "Clio and Venus: An Historical View of Medieval Love," *The Meaning of Courtly Love*, ed. F. X. Newman (Albany, 1969), p. 32, and Charles T. Wood, "Menstruation in the Middle Ages," *Speculum*, to appear.

80. M.-T. d'Alverny, "Comment les théologiens . . . voient la femme?" *Cahiers de civilisation médiévale* 20 (1977): 115–24. See also Basile Studer, "Consubstantialis Patri, consubstantialis Matri: Une antithèse christologique chez Léon le Grand," *Revue des études Augustiniennes* 18 (1972): 87–115; and Morrison, "Hincmar."

procreation of the physicality, the flesh, of the child. Here again, the emphases of physiological theory were particularly useful, given the devotional concerns of the later Middle Ages. For a theology that stressed the humanity of Christ as a taking up into divinity of humankind's fleshliness, female generativity could be an important symbol. For a theology that maintained—over against Cathar dualism—the goodness of creation in all its physicality, a God who is mother and womb as well as father and animator could be a more sweeping and convincing image of creation than a father God alone. (It could also, of course, be dangerous, with implications of pantheism or antinomianism.) Thus, the growth of maternal names for God in the later Middle Ages reflects the general tendency to see God as "accessible" and "like man," to apply to him homey metaphors and anthropomorphic analogies; it also reflects the fact that what medieval authors assume the female to be coincided with what they increasingly wished to emphasize about God the creator and about the Incarnation.

We must be careful not to overemphasize the affective aspects of later medieval piety. Even in writers, like Marguerite of Oingt, who give the images very concrete development, the notion of Christ as mother, like that of Christ as bridegroom, remains allegorical. Moreover, the humanity of Christ is not as absent in early medieval devotion as many twelfth-century scholars have suggested, following Southern.[81] Piety from the later Middle Ages is not as literal in its use of images or as filled with weeping and ecstasy as scholars since Huizinga have thought.[82] Nor did affective response to Christ's humanity or a stress on creation and

81. See R. W. Southern, *The Making of the Middle Ages* (New Haven, 1959), pp. 219–57. Southern's emphases have been continued by C. Morris, *The Discovery of the Individual: 1050–1200* (New York, 1972), who pushes devotion to Christ's humanity back in time somewhat. Southern was in many ways following A. Wilmart, *Auteurs spirituels et textes dévots du moyen âge latin* (Paris, 1932). For a different view, see Jungmann, *Pastoral Liturgy*, pp. 1–101, and Christopher L. Chase, "'Christ III,' 'The Dream of the Rood,' and Early Christian Piety," *Viator* 11 (1980): pp. 11–33.

82. Johan Huizinga, *The Waning of the Middle Ages: A Study of the Forms of Life, Thought and Art in France and the Netherlands in the XIVth and XVth Centuries* (1921; English trans., London, 1924); see also Lucien Febvre, "Sensibility and History . . ." (1941) and "The Origins of the

incarnation always employ maternal imagery. In a mystic like Ruysbroeck (†1381), for example, whose writings are filled with metaphors from the natural world but studiously avoid physiological (including erotic or nuptial) imagery, we find the same theological and devotional emphases expressed so differently that we suspect throughout an implicit critique of the tradition I have just been describing.[83] Nonetheless, in a number of medieval writers from the twelfth to the fourteenth centuries and even beyond, maternal imagery is a part of a new sense of God, which stresses his creative power, his love, and his presence in the physical body of Christ and in the flesh and blood of the eucharist.

The Feminization
of Religious Language
and Its Social Context

There is a second, very broad trend against which we must locate the maternal imagery not only of twelfth-century male Cistercians but also of later medieval authors—male and female. We can perhaps call this trend the feminization of religious language.

It is well known, of course, that medieval theological, medical, and scientific views of woman as compared to man were negative. Woman was physiologically and spiritually weaker, defective in body and moral fortitude, although she was equal in capacity for salvation.[84] For example, John Gerson (†1429), writing perhaps with Catherine of Siena in mind, remarks that:

the female sex is forbidden on apostolic authority [1 Tim. 2:12] to teach in public, that is either by word or by writing. . . . All

French Reformation . . ." (1929), reprinted in L. Febvre, *A New Kind of History*, ed. P. Burke (New York, 1973), pp. 12–26 and 44–107.

83. The critical edition of Ruysbroeck is J. B. Poukens, L. Reypens, D. A. Stracke, M. Schurmans, J. Van Mierlo, eds., *Jan van Ruusbroec: Werken*, 4 vols. (Amsterdam, 1932). On Ruysbroeck, see Eric Colledge, Introd., Jan Van Ruysbroeck, *The Spiritual Espousals*, Classics of the Contemplative Life (New York, n.d.), pp. 9–42; and Louis Cognet, *Introduction aux mystiques rhéno-flamands* (Paris, 1968), pp. 233–81.

84. Bullough, "Medieval Medical and Scientific Views"; Kari Elisabeth Børresen, *Subordination et equivalence: nature et rôle de la femme d'après*

women's teaching, particularly formal teaching by word and by writing, is to be held suspect unless it has been diligently examined, and much more fully than men's. The reason is clear: common law—and not any kind of common law, but that which comes from on high—forbids them. And why? Because they are easily seduced, and determined seducers; and because it is not proved that they are witnesses to divine grace.[85]

Female as well as male authors in the high Middle Ages accepted such generalizations, although religious women were usually little deterred by them.[86] For example, Julian of Norwich, whose vision of God as mother is one of the greatest reformulations in the history of theology, feels that her theological creativity is *in spite of* her sex.[87] But, alongside the theory of women as inferior, we find an increasing presence in later medieval religious literature of images taken from uniquely female experiences (childbearing, nursing, female sexual surrender or ecstasy), of female characteristics or experiences used to describe males, and of actual female figures.

From the twelfth century on, as is well known, increased importance was given to the Virgin Mary.[88] Even in the early Middle Ages she was seen as mediating between souls and Christ. But

Augustin et Thomas d'Aquin (Oslo, 1968); Eleanor McLaughlin, "Equality of Souls, Inequality of Sexes: Women in Medieval Theology," *Religion and Sexism: Images of Women in the Jewish and Christian Traditions*, ed. Rosemary Ruether, (New York, 1974), pp. 213–66; d'Alverny, "Les théologiens . . . voient la femme," pp. 103–29.

85. John Gerson, *De examinatione doctrinam*, pt. 1, considerations 2a and 3a, *Joannis Gersonii . . . omnia opera*, ed. Louis Ellies-Dupin, 5 vols. (Antwerp, 1706), 1:14–26; quoted in Colledge and Walsh ed., *A Book of Showings* 1:151.

86. See below pp. 226–7 and 251–2.

87. Julian, *A Book of Showings*, short version, chap. 6, 1:222. But Julian seldom refers to female incapacity, and this description is deleted in the longer version. See also Margery Kempe, *The Book of Margery Kempe*, ed. S. B. Meech and Hope Emily Allen, Early English Text Society 212 (London 1940), chap. 52, pp. 125–26.

88. See Hilda Graef, *Mary: A History of Doctrine and Devotion*, 2 vols. (London, 1963) 1:esp. 210–64; Penny S. Gold, "*Mater Christi* to *Sponsa Christi*: The Iconography of the Virgin Mary in Twelfth- and Thirteenth-Century Architectual Sculpture in France," *Paideia*, to appear; and T. Koehler, "Marie (sainte Vierge): Du moyen âge aux temps modernes," DS 10 (Paris, 1977): cols. 440–59.

then she was pictured as the majestic queen of heaven; closer to the people were the saints. In the twelfth century she begins to be described as a human mother with a baby, and gradually, in popular religion, she becomes so central that her mediation is "automatic" and "ethically irrational." In keeping with the medieval view that women were above and below reason, she saves her loyal favorites, even if they fail to meet the standards of contrition and penitence. The twelfth-century Cistercians studied here felt a particular devotion to Mary as the gateway by which salvation entered the world. Guerric of Igny described his fellow monks as "curled up against her breast."[89] Aelred of Rievaulx wrote: "It is she . . . who has given us life, who nourishes and raises us; . . . she is our mother much more than our mother according to the flesh."[90]

But the Virgin Mary was not the only female figure who increased in popularity; devotion to female saints increased also. For example, many twelfth- and thirteenth-century churches were dedicated to Mary Magdalene, patron of hermits and repentant sinners, and the office that was written for her at this time described her as *apostle* to the apostles.[91] In the second half of the eleventh century the percentage of saints who were women was 9.8; the proportion rose to 14.6% in the twelfth century, 15% by 1250, 24% by 1300, and 29% by the period 1400–1449.[92] In contrast to the early Middle Ages, there were more female than male *lay* saints in the period between 1215 and 1500.[93] Married women

89. Guerric, first sermon for the Assumption, chap. 4, *Sermons* 2:422; quoted in M. A. Lassus, "Le mystère de la virginité dans la pensée cistercienne," COCR 20 (1958): 4.

90. Aelred, sermon 20: second sermon for the Nativity of the Virgin, PL 195: col. 323A and C; quoted in Lassus, "Le mystère," p. 6. See also Albert van Iterson, "L'Ordre de Cîteaux et le Coeur de Marie," COCR 20 (1958): 219–312 and 21 (1959): 97–120.

91. Victor Saxer, *Le culte de Marie Madeleine en-Occident des origines à la fin du moyen âge*, Cahiers d'archéologie et d'histoire 3, 2 vols. (Auxerre, 1959).

92. Jane Tibbetts Schulenburg, "Sexism and the Celestial Gynaeceum from 500 to 1200," *Journal of Medieval History* 4 (1978): 122, 127, and 131, n.11.

93. Pierre Boglioni reporting on his research, Discussion, Conference on Consciousness.

saints, almost nonexistent in the early Middle Ages, also grew in numbers and influence.[94]

If we look beyond female saints to female images, we find, as Joan Ferrante has recently argued, that allegorical literature in the twelfth century shows an increase in the personification of key concepts as women.[95] We also find that the soul is usually pictured as female by both female and male writers. This is in part because the gender of *anima* is feminine in Latin. But the gender of *anima* does not explain why twelfth-century writers *elaborate* the idea of the soul as female. For example, when they comment on the Song of Songs, they turn away from the older tradition of identifying the bride with the church to an identification of her with the individual soul.[96] Moreover, we find monks and friars as well as nuns and beguines speaking of themselves as "weak women," where the context makes it clear that weakness is a positive description of humility. (This is not, of course, to deny that the weakness of women continues to be a negative description as well, but, as a negative description too, it is applied to males in the twelfth and thirteenth centuries.)[97] And finally, increasing steadily from the twelfth century on, we find female erotic and sexual experience used to describe the soul's union with Christ.

These feminine metaphors and symbols of the high Middle Ages seem the inverse, the mirror image, of earlier medieval language. Whereas twelfth-century monks sometimes call themselves women, early medieval women sometimes call themselves men. In the patristic period we find cases of women having visions of themselves standing before the throne of God as *males*—a sign

94. Marc D. Glasser, "Marriage in Medieval Hagiography," unpublished paper.

95. Joan M. Ferrante, *Woman as Image in Medieval Literature from the Twelfth Century to Dante* (New York, 1975).

96. Rosemary Herde, "Das Hohelied in der lateinischen Literatur des Mittelalters bis zum 12. Jahrhundert," *Studi Medievali* 3.8.2 (1967): 957–1073.

97. See below pp. 148–9, and n. 63 above. Guerric speaks of monks as mothers to Christ: Guerric, third Christmas sermon, chaps. 4–5, *Sermons* 1:198. Francis of Assisi says we are Christ's mother when we bear him in our hearts: Francis, *Epistola* 1, *Opuscula* (Quaracchi, 1904), p. 93.

that they are saved.[98] And early literature has several stories of women masquerading as men in order to enter monasteries.[99] Whereas twelfth- to fourteenth-century texts call Jesus mother, in the Carolingian period we find an iconographic tradition of the bearded Mary, the mother of God with a male attribute.[100] Whereas tenderness and comfort are stressed in later medieval spirituality, images of warfare—which were to medieval people clearly male images—were dominant in the monastic spirituality of the tenth and eleventh centuries.[101]

Thus the presence of maternal imagery in medieval texts is only partially explained by the increased importance of certain theological emphases for which the stereotype of the mother was an appropriate expression. It is also a result of a general feminization of language. Scholars who have noticed this feminization have sometimes suggested that it reflects an increasingly positive attitude toward women in medieval society;[102] or that it is an imagery developed especially for women;[103] or that it is particularly promi-

98. McNamara, "Sexual Equality and the Cult of Virginity," pp. 145–58. Even within the Gnostic tradition, which Pagels has seen as so sympathetic to women and the feminine (Gnostic Gospels, pp. 48–69), there is a tradition of seeing conquest of the passions as "the female becoming male": see Michael A. Williams, "'Gnosis' and 'Askesis,'" Aufstieg und Niedergang der römischen Welt 2.22: Religion (Gnostizismus und Verwandtes), ed. Wolfgang Haase, to appear; and Elisabeth Schüssler Fiorenza, "Word, Spirit and Power: Women in Early Christian Communities," Women of Spirit, ed. R. Ruether and E. C. McLaughlin (New York, 1979), pp. 44–51.

99. John Anson, "The Female Transvestite in Early Monasticism: The Origin and Development of a Motif," Viator 5 (1974): 1–32. Anson argues, correctly I think, that these stories are a projection of male fantasies and fears. See also Vern L. Bullough, "Transvestites in the Middle Ages," American Journal of Sociology 79 (1974): 1381–94.

100. Jonathan Smith, unpublished paper. And see McNamara, "Sexual Equality and the Cult of Virginity," pp. 150–54.

101. Barbara H. Rosenwein and Lester K. Little, "Social Meaning in the Monastic and Mendicant Spiritualities," Past and Present 63 (May 1974): 20–32.

102. For example, M. McLaughlin, "Survivors and Surrogates," pp. 101–81 passim; Pagels, "God the Mother," pp. 293–303, and Gnostic Gospels, pp. 48–69.

103. Bugge, Virginitas, pp. 100–5.

nent in works by female authors and is therefore related to the increasing numbers of women in religious life.[104] There are, however, problems with each of these interpretations.

As the discussion above makes clear, it was not women who originated female images of God. And a list of the medieval authors in whom modern scholars have found the image of God as mother makes it clear that such language is in no way the special preserve of female writers: Anselm, Peter Lombard, the biographer of Stephen of Muret, Bernard, William of St. Thierry, Aelred, Guerric of Igny, Isaac of Stella, Adam of Perseigne, Helinand of Froidmont, Gilbert of Hoyland, Guigo II the Carthusian, Albert the Great, Bonaventure, Aquinas, Gertrude the Great, Mechtild of Hackeborn, Mechtild of Magdeburg, Marguerite of Oingt, the monk of Farne, Richard Rolle, William Flete, Dante, Ludolph of Saxony, Catherine of Siena, Bridget of Sweden, Margery Kempe, Julian of Norwich, the *Ancrene Riwle*, the *Stimulus Amoris*, the *Chastising of God's Children*, and a number of anonymous English poems and sermons.[105] Although the most sophisticated use of the theme is Julian of Norwich's trinitarian theology, there is no reason to assert, as some have done, that the theme of the motherhood of God is a "feminine insight."[106] Moreover it is not at all clear, although many scholars assume it, that women are particularly drawn to feminine imagery. Bridal imagery is more common in women's writing than in men's in the thirteenth and fourteenth centuries,[107] but there is no evidence that women were

104. Hanshell, "Crux," p. 91; Børreson, "Christ notre mère"; E. McLaughlin, "Women, Power . . ."
105. This list is compiled from the studies cited in nn. 1–3 above plus my own research, which has supplied the references to Stephen of Muret (see n. 72 above), the Cistercian monks, Guigo (see n. 136 below), and the Helfta nuns. Rupert of Deutz, *De glorificatione Trinitatis*, PL 169: col. 186D, sees the Holy Spirit as maternal. Abelard, *Expositio in Hexaemeron*, PL 178: cols. 735D–36B, gives an extended metaphor of the Holy Spirit as a bird hatching an egg, which has maternal overtones. Hildegard of Bingen also sees the Holy Spirit as feminine (see below n. 113). Elisabeth of Schönau saw Christ's humanity as a virgin (*Die Visionen der hl. Elisabeth . . . von Schönau*, ed. F. W. E. Roth [Brünn, 1884], pp. 60ff.).
106. Hanshell, "Crux," p. 91.
107. See above Introduction, n. 25.

especially attracted to devotion to the Virgin or to married women saints. (Indeed there is some evidence that they were less attracted than men.)[108] And there is no evidence that the idea of God as mother was developed especially in writings that men addressed to women (although the image of the soul as female and Christ as its bridegroom was particularly popular in works for nuns).[109]

Brautmystik (the use of nuptial and erotic imagery to describe the soul's union with God), the use of maternal names for God, and devotion to the Virgin did not occur together in medieval texts; the presence of some kinds of feminine imagery seems to have inhibited the presence of other kinds. Julian's recent editors point out that Marian commentaries on the Song of Songs perhaps competed with a theology of motherhood,[110] and a perceptive recent interpreter of Julian notes the virtual absence in her thought of bridal imagery and the minor importance attributed to the Virgin.[111] Among the nuns of Helfta, those who pay most attention to Christ as bridegroom and the soul as bride are least likely to stress Christ as mother.[112] The major female theologian of the twelfth century, Hildegard of Bingen, is not attracted to the idea of Christ as mother, although she develops the idea of God's charity and wisdom as feminine and emphasizes the sacred heart.[113] Hildegard is convinced both that women are less concupiscent than men and that women's religious role is contemplative (to serve as Christ's

108. Simone Roisin, *L'Hagiographie cistercienne dans le diocèse de Liège au XIIIᵉ siècle* (Louvain, 1947). See below, p. 162.

109. See Bugge, *Virginitas*, pp. 100–5. It is true that Aelred's *De Institutione*, which uses maternal imagery, was written for anchoresses and that Adam of Perseigne uses such imagery in writing to women (see Adam, *Correspondance*, letter 45 and 55, pp. 441–44 and 571–80; and PL 211: cols. 623–24 and 659–64). But I find in the twelfth century no general pattern of using female imagery especially when addressing women.

110. Colledge and Walsh, *A Book of Showings* 1:155.

111. Børresen, "Christ notre mère."

112. See below, pp. 225–6 and 242–6.

113. See above, pp. 91–94, and Leclercq, "Le sacré-coeur." In the *Scivias*, Hildegard sees the blood from Christ's side as washing the church and making possible her marriage to Christ the spouse: *Scivias*, pt. 2, vision 6, chaps. 1 and 29–30, ed. A Führkötter and A. Carlevaris, CCCM 43, 2 vols. (Turnhout, 1978), 1:232–33 and 258–60. I am

bride); women are unsuited, she argues, for priesthood. Thus it is not surprising that Hildegard does not emphasize Christ as mother. Her positive sense of the religious capacities and role of women is based in a sense of female otherness from male authority. Her "feminine" images for divine aspects refer either to the Spirit, which inspires us, or to the creative work of the entire Trinity, not to Christ, who is ruler, judge and pedagogue.

There is some reason to hold that the increased use of marriage and motherhood as metaphors in the twelfth century reflects a more positive evaluation of these institutions in society. Twelfth-century theology and canon law move toward a new emphasis on marriage as a sacrament at the moment when marriage becomes a powerful spiritual metaphor.[114] Saints' lives begin to emphasize the influence of mothers on children at the moment when motherhood becomes an important image of God's activity.[115] Moreover, the use of female metaphors by both men and women undoubtedly has roots in the social changes of the period. Both erotic and maternal metaphors become prominent at a time when many spiritual writers have grown up in families, known their own mothers, and gone through puberty in the world; some may even have been parents themselves. In the twelfth century the new monastic orders, in contrast to the old, preferred to recruit adults, and the percentage of monks and nuns who had been married before their conversion appears to have become much higher.[116] But we have only to remember the deterioration of the political and legal status

---

grateful to Barbara Newman of Northwestern University for sharing with me part of her forthcoming dissertation on Hildegard; her discussion gives to the issue of Hildegard's view of the "feminine divine" a precision and a subtlety I cannot introduce here.

114. Constable, "Twelfth-Century Spirituality," pp. 42 and 51; Glasser, "Marriage."

115. M. McLaughlin, "Survivors and Surrogates," pp. 115–18. But we should note that the author who reports one of Gertrude's visions of Christ describing himself as mother reports also that Gertrude could not answer when Christ asked her: "Have you not seen a mother caress her children?" Gertrude, who had entered the convent at five, did not remember ever having seen it: *Héraut*, bk. 3, chap. 30, *Oeuvres*, 3:160–62. See below, chapter 5, n. 124.

116. Leclercq, *Monks and Love in Twelfth-Century France* (Oxford, 1979), pp. 8–12.

of women in the later Middle Ages and the continuation of misogynist reactions to have hesitations about relating increasingly positive and even sentimentalized feminine images directly to a positive role for, or influence of, women in society. We should also remember that the great increase in groups of religious women and in female followers of wandering preachers, heterodox and orthodox, was accompanied by male resistance as well as male support and by increased articulations and enforcement of the prohibition of clerical status to women.[117]

There is little evidence that the popularity of feminine and maternal imagery in the high Middle Ages reflects an increased respect for actual women by men. Saints' lives might romanticize mothers, but there was in the general society no mystique of motherhood; both medical texts and exhortations to asceticism dwell on the horrors of pregnancy and the inconveniences of marriage.[118]

117. Brenda M. Bolton, "*Vitae Matrum*: A Further Aspect of the *Frauenfrage*," *Medieval Women: dedicated and presented to Professor Rosalind M. T. Hill . . .* , ed. D. Baker (Oxford, 1978), pp. 253–73, and see below, chapter 5, nn. 33, 291, and 292. Pagels, *Gnostic Gospels*, relates the presence of feminine images for God in gnostic texts to greater respect for women and greater opportunities for them to participate in cult. The later Middle Ages shows a more complex situation: feminization of language, growth of certain religious opportunities for women (not without male opposition), yet, alongside this, aggrandizement of the clerical role and clearer exclusion of women from it.

On the general decline of women's political and social power in the later Middle Ages, see Eileen Power, "The Position of Women," *The Legacy of the Middle Ages*, eds. G. C. Crump and E. F. Jacobs (Oxford, 1926), pp. 401–34; Jo Ann McNamara and Suzanne Wemple, "The Power of Women Through the Family in Medieval Europe, 500–1100," *Feminist Studies* 1 (1973): 126–41; and idem, "Sanctity and Power: The Dual Pursuit of Medieval Women," *Becoming Visible: Women in European History*, eds. R. Bridenthal and C. Koonz (Boston, 1977), pp. 90–118.

118. M. McLaughlin, "Survivors and Surrogates," pp. 124–39; Alice A. Hentsch, *De la littérature didactique du moyen âge s'adressant spécialement aux femmes* (Cahors, 1903); Philippe Delhaye, "Le dossier antimatrimonial de l'*Adversus Jovinianum* et son influence sur quelques écrits latins du XIIᵉ siècle," *Mediaeval Studies* 13 (1951): 65–86; Bullough, "Medieval Medical and Scientific Views," pp. 485–501; Goodich, "Bartholomaeus Anglicus," p. 80. See also Hildegard of Bingen, *Hildegardis Causae et Curae*, bk. 2, ed. P. Kaiser, Bibliotheca scriptorum graecorum et romanorum Teubneriana (Leipzig, 1903), pp. 104–5 and 108–9.

Even authors who speak of the parent-child relationship as a kind of love see it as a lower form—lower, that is, than friendship or the love of husband and wife.[119] Those same authors who equate motherhood or the Virgin Mary with compassion and nurture also use woman as a symbol of physical or spiritual weakness, of the flesh, of sin, of inability to bear burdens or resist temptation.

The males who popularized maternal and feminine imagery were those who had renounced the family and the company of women; the "society" out of which their language comes is a substitute for (and implicitly a critique of) the world. This is what Bernard means when he describes his monks as mountebanks, walking on their hands: their life and their images invert the values of the world. To call monks women, as Bernard does, is to use the feminine as something positive (humility) but also to imply that such is *not* the opinion of society. The wisdom of the world is not the wisdom of God.[120] Moreover, we should note that some of the same saints who are described by their biographers as influenced by their mothers grow up to write in strident tones about renouncing mother and father for God.[121] And it is from the safety of the cloister that Abelard, Bernard, Aelred of Rievaulx, and Rupert of Deutz argue anew for the spiritual equality of women.[122] Religious writing by cloistered males in the twelfth and thirteenth

119. See William of St. Thierry, *De natura et dignitate amoris*, PL 184: cols. 379–408 passim, especially chap. 7, cols. 391A–C. The same view is expressed later by Bonaventure, *Commentarius in Evangelium S. Ioannis*, chap. 15, par. 20, *Opera omnia* 6 (Quaracchi, 1893): 450.

120. See above nn. 62 and 63.

121. See below nn. 125 and 126. Psychoanalysts note that a close relationship between mother and son is often connected with hostility toward women: Karen Horney, "The Dread of Women . . . ," *International Journal of Psychoanalysis* 13 (1932): 348–60; see also Douglas, *Purity and Danger*, pp. 166–87. Such a theory suggests that a literary tradition of misogyny and a literary tradition of idealizing motherhood are not in any way inconsistent.

122. D'Alverny, "Les théologiens . . . voient la femme." On Abelard, see also M. McLaughlin, "Peter Abelard and the Dignity of Women: Twelfth-Century 'Feminism' in Theory and Practice," *Pierre Abélard, Pierre le Venerable: Les courants . . .* , Colloques internationaux du centre national de la recherche scientifique 546 (Paris, 1975), pp. 287–333, and John Benton, "Fraud, Fiction and Borrowing in the Correspondence of Abelard and Heloise," ibid., pp. 469–506. Aelred makes the argument

centuries shows at least as much hostility toward actual mothers and actual women as it does romanticizing of them.[123] Although Bernard wrote with graciousness and tact to individual women about their religious yearnings, he also feared contamination from women. In his commentary on the Song of Songs, he warned monks: "To be always with a woman and not to have sexual relations with her is more difficult than to raise the dead. You cannot do the less difficult; do you think I will believe that you can do what is more difficult?"[124] Bernard links receptivity to the "mothering" of Jesus with renunciation of earthly mothers. The passage from letter 322 quoted above (". . . suck not so much the wounds as the breasts of the Crucified . . .") continues:

He [Christ] will be your mother. . . . But a man's household are his own enemies [Matt. 10:36]. These are they who love not you but the satisfaction they derive from you. . . . And now hear what blessed Jerome says: "If your mother should lie prostrate at the door, if she should bare her breasts, the breasts that gave you suck, . . . yet with dry eyes fixed upon the cross go ahead and tread over your prostrate mother and father. It is the height of

---

for spiritual equality in *De spirituali amicitia*, bk. 1, *Opera omnia* 1: 298–99. See also Jean Leclercq, "S. Pierre Damien et les femmes," *Studia monastica* 15 (1973): 43–55.

123. The emphasis on *replacing* one's earthly mother with mother-Jesus or mother-Mary (see n. 90 above and nn. 125 and 126 below) can of course be seen as an expression of hostility against earthly mothers who fail. David Herlihy has suggested that medieval religious movements are part of a general rebellion against the family: "Alienation in Medieval Culture and Society," *Alienation: Concept, Terms and Meanings*, ed. Frank Johnson (New York, 1973), pp. 125–40, reprinted in *The Social History of Italy and Western Europe 700–1500*, Variorum reprints (London, 1978); a similar approach is taken by Michael Goodich, "Childhood and Adolescence among the Thirteenth-Century Saints," *History of Childhood Quarterly* 1 (1974): 285–309. The argument seems to somewhat oversimplify a complex phenomenon.

124. Sermon 65, par. 4, OB 1:174–75. Bernard continues: "Quotidie latus tuum ad latus iuvenculae est in mensa, lectus tuus ad lectum eius in camera, oculi tui ad illius oculos in colloquio, manus tuae ad manus ipsius in opere; et continens vis putari? . . . Scandalo mihi es . . . Tu Ecclesiam scandalizas . . ." For a different evaluation, see Jean Leclercq, "S. Bernard et le féminin," *Nouveau visage de Bernard de Clairvaux: Approches psycho-historiques* (Paris, 1976), pp. 127–54.

piety to be cruel for Christ's sake." Do not be moved by the tears of demented parents who weep because from being a child of wrath you have become a child of God.[125]

Isaac of Stella links the parenthood of God with even harsher rejection of earthly family:

> For myself I declare that I am a stranger and pilgrim here below. . . . I am not a son of man but a son of God hidden under the appearance and resemblance of man; henceforth I am not the son of my father and mother, nor the brother of my brother, even if they say, affirm and swear falsely that I am theirs. If they produce witnesses and if they signal with recognizable marks on my skin and in my flesh, I have awareness myself of my origin and I persist in denying; I protest that I am not what they say. . . . Indeed we are all orphans; we have no father on earth for our father is in heaven and our mother is a virgin. It is from there that we have our origins. . . .[126]

It therefore seems that the somewhat sentimentalized maternal imagery of twelfth- to fourteenth-century religious writing does not tell us—at least not *primarily*—about the lives of (or even the attitudes toward) actual women.

The Basic Characteristics of Cistercian Usage

Up to this point I have argued that the maternal names and metaphors found in twelfth-century Cistercian writing are reflections of two far-reaching trends in medieval religion: the rise of affective piety and the feminization of religious imagery. And such generalizations are probably as far as we can go toward explaining the idea of mother Jesus if we simply jump from author to author and century to century. But if—a far more difficult and time-consuming task—we study the way in which the precise use of

125. Letter 322, PL 182: col. 527C–D; trans. James, letter 378, p. 449, with my changes; see n. 17 above. See also letter 104, PL 182: col. 240A–C.
126. Isaac of Stella, sermon 29, *Sermons*, ed. A. Hoste and G. Salet, 2 vols. to date, SC 130 and 207, Sér. mon. 20 and 44 (Paris, 1967 and 1974) 2:172 (col. 1785C–D).

imagery differs from author to author, group of authors to group of authors, and period to period, we may then be able to relate the image to the social and psychological as well as the literary and theological context within which it occurs.

When we look more closely at the idea of God as mother in the writings of twelfth-century male Cistercians, we discover that it has three specific characteristics that are different, at least in emphasis, from the idea as it occurs in the Greek and Latin Fathers, in twelfth-century scholastic authors, and in later writers, both Cistercian and non-Cistercian, male and female. The first characteristic of twelfth-century Cistercian use of the mother-Jesus theme has to do with the other images among which it occurs. Mothering imagery was, of course, popular with Cistercians to describe both the Virgin and the church. But more relevant to the idea of God as mother is the fact that many *male* figures are referred to as mother, or described as nursing, conceiving, and giving birth. Male figures so described are invariably figures whom both medieval and modern readers would recognize to be authority figures. Thus Cistercians refer to prelates—that is, abbots and bishops—as mothers. They also use maternal imagery when they wish to describe male figures from the Old or New Testament in their capacity as leaders or teachers; one of the most powerful and elaborate uses of maternal imagery in the twelfth century is Guerric of Igny's meditation on Peter and Paul (probably influenced by Anselm's similar meditation).[127] And Cistercian authors not only refer to a variety of male figures in maternal adjectives; they also tend to link discussions of God as mother with discussions of authority figures, chiefly abbots or the apostles Peter and Paul. Moreover certain biblical passages, especially the hen gathering her chicks under her wings (Matt. 23:37) and the reference to the delights of the Bridegroom's breasts in the Song of Songs (Song 1:1-2), are as likely to trigger in the minds of these authors reference to the burdens of pastoral responsibility as to the motherhood of God. It is significant that, in Bernard's commentary on the Song of Songs, which I discussed above, the breasts of the bridegroom repeatedly call forth not erotic but maternal metaphors.[128] It is also significant that

127. See above nn. 8 and 37.
128. This point is emphasized by Leclercq, *Monks and Love*, pp. 27–61.

these passages call forth discussions of prelates: "Learn, you who rule the earth . . . let your bosom expand with milk, not swell with passion."[129] In Cistercian texts, therefore, references to mothering often occur as a way of describing a figure or institution (God, Christ, the abbot, Moses, the church, etc.) that teaches or exercises authority, and in such passages *mater* is usually quite explicitly a complement to *pater* or *magister* or *dominus*. Furthermore, the tendency of these Cistercian authors to associate in the same discussion God's motherhood and the pastoral burdens of clergy or abbots is in marked contrast to patristic authors, who do not connect Jesus' mothering with the mothering of earthly men. Nor do the many authors from the thirteenth and fourteenth centuries who use maternal imagery for Jesus tend to apply this imagery to priests or bishops or even, in any elaborate and metaphorical way, to abbesses.[130]

The second general characteristic of maternal imagery in twelfth-century Cistercian writing is the consistency of the sexual stereotypes that lie behind it. In other words, certain personality characteristics are seen by these authors as female and certain others as male. Throughout contemporary sermons and treatises, gentleness, compassion, tenderness, emotionality and love, nurturing and security are labeled "female" or "maternal"; authority, judgment, command, strictness, and discipline are labeled "male" or "paternal"; instruction, fertility, and engendering are associated with both sexes (either as begetting or as conceiving). Moreover, these stereotypes remain the same whether they are evaluated as positive or negative. Thus to Adam of Perseigne, the maternal and female is strong;[131] to William of St. Thierry, the female is a symbol of both weakness and penitence.[132] And Helinand of Froid-

129. See above, p. 118.
130. See below, pp. 158–9. Julian of Norwich implies that a spiritual counselor should share the fatherhood and motherhood of God (Colledge and Walsh, *A Book of Showings* 1:185), but this is not, to her, a central concern.
131. Adam, *Correspondance*, letter 2, pp. 20–22; Adam here associates women with strength and fecundity. But in letter 30, pp. 221–22, he gives the standard exegesis of Eve as the lower part of the soul, Adam the higher.
132. For the use of woman or Eve or the feminine as a symbol of spiritual weakness combined with penitence see n. 24 above. In William,

mont gives a complex and repeated explanation of *mulier* as related to *molis* ("soft" in the sense of weak) and *malleus* ("hammer" in the sense of scourge)—an explanation that is intended to interpret the tenderness of women in a very pejorative light.[133] Because these sexual stereotypes are constant throughout twelfth-century Cistercian literature, it seems clear that these authors spoke of fathers as nursing or joined "mother" to "father" in their descriptions (whether of God, the apostles, prelates, or themselves) in order to add a specific dimension (i.e., nurture) to their general conception of leadership, authority, and pastoral concern. In contrast to this twelfth-century usage, we find that later medieval writing by women is much less likely to identify nurture with the female and discipline with the male, or to have any consistent sense of certain actions or traits as associated with one gender or the other. Gertrude of Helfta, for example, sees God the mother as disciplinarian.[134]

There is a third characteristic of maternal imagery in twelfth-

---

Sur le Cantique, chap. 63, p. 152, *mulier* is related to *molis*, which seems to mean "weak" as well as "delicate." See also n. 63 above.

133. Helinand of Froidmont, sermon 20, PL 212: cols. 646–52; and *Epistola ad Galterum*, ibid., col. 753B. (The etymology is borrowed from Varro.) See also sermon 27, ibid., col. 622B: "Ecce Deus homines mulieribus comparat; nec solum homines molles et fluxos, sed et fortes et robustos; nec mulieribus tantum, sed mulieribus menstruatis. Vae nobis omnibus a fragilitate corruptionis et corruptione fragilitatis, qui mulieres appellamur!"

134. See below, pp. 189–90. What I argue there about Gertrude and Mechtild of Hackeborn is also true of Marguerite of Oingt, who appears to have had little sense of male and female differences. When she writes of herself as a mother cradling the infant Jesus in her arms (Marguerite, letter 129, *Oeuvres*, p. 139), the language expresses a yearning I have not found in male writers; and there is one passage that can be interpreted as an expression of gratitude for her freedom from subjection to any man (*Pagina*, chap. 102, *Oeuvres*, p. 87). But in general she seems unconcerned with her own gender. Her mother Jesus is primarily an image of sacrifice (see n. 144 below).

Anthropologists argue that, in patrilineal societies, "woman" represents the "affectional," soft side whereas "man" represents the "hard" line of authority and property transfer; see Victor and Edith Turner, *Image and Pilgrimage in Christian Culture: Anthropological Perspectives* (New York, 1978), pp. 161 and 199.

century Cistercian writing that is closely related to the second. To these authors, breasts and nurturing are more frequent images than conceiving or giving birth. And where birth and the womb are dominant metaphors, the mother is described as one who conceives and carries the child in her womb, not as one who ejects the child into the world, suffering pain and possibly death in order to give life. Conceiving and giving birth, like suckling, are thus images primarily of return to, union with, or dependence upon God, not images of Christ's sacrifice or of human alienation. References to God as mother usually occur not in the context of castigation of sinners or elaboration of the gulf between human and divine but rather as part of a general picture of the believer as child or beginner, totally dependent on a loving and tender God. Indeed, descriptions of the soul as nursing child are even more common in Cistercian writing than explicit references to the breasts of God: when the soul is described as Christ's brother, for example, it is usually seen as a brother of the nursing, not the adult Christ.[135] In the twelfth-century *Ladder of Monks* by Guigo II the Carthusian, which echoes many Cistercian themes, the single reference to Christ as mother is a nursing image, which occurs in the context of a host of eating metaphors.[136] Moreover, other physiological images, such as Guerric's references to the bowels of God or Aelred's to hiding inside Christ, express not merely the compassion or love that God offers man but also the closest possible binding of self to God.[137] As an extreme case of this stress on union, Isaac of Stella goes beyond images of souls drawn into the womb or bowels or side of Christ to develop a theory of the mystical body that claims that Christ himself is not complete until we are all incorporated into him.[138] In contrast, when these authors apply

---

135. See, for example, Adam of Perseigne, *Correspondance*, letter 35, pp. 305–7 (cf. PL 211: cols. 602–3); letter 45, p. 443 (cf. PL 211: col. 624); letter 48, pp. 471–74 and 477 (cf. PL 211: cols. 635–38); letter 53, p. 544 (cf. PL 211: col. 606); letter 54, pp. 553–55; letter 64, pp. 629–30 (cf. PL 211: col. 651).

136. Guigo II, *Scala*, chap. 8, in *Lettre sur la vie contemplative . . . Douze méditations*, ed. E. Colledge and J. Walsh, SC 163, Sér. mon. 29 (Paris, 1970) p. 98, lines 190–93.

137. See above nn. 34 and 41.

138. Isaac, sermon 14, *Sermons* 1:270–80; sermon 34, 2:232–54, es-

maternal imagery to prelates, that imagery is more apt to stress the pain of giving birth. But even in these references, the image most often expresses that tender and affective bond between mother-abbot and child that prepares for the similar bond between soul and God.

Thus the most frequent meaning of mother-Jesus to twelfth-century Cistercians is compassion, nurturing, and union. This appears to contrast with other medieval uses of the theme. Anselm of Canterbury's strong emphasis on Christ's sacrifice (the mother who dies in giving birth to the soul), which is frequently found in later writers, is not very prominent in twelfth-century Cistercians.[139] Nor is the charming image of mother-God playing games with the baby-soul, teasing it and protecting it from harm, which is found, for example, in Stephen of Muret, the *Ancrene Riwle*, Richard Rolle, Catherine of Siena, and Bridget of Sweden.[140] Moreover, the use of maternal language that we find in twelfth- and thirteenth-century scholastic writers (e.g., Peter Lombard, Abelard, Albert, Thomas, and Bonaventure) also seems to convey a different meaning and be part of a somewhat different tradition. In these texts much of the maternal imagery refers to Christ as the Wisdom of God or to the Holy Spirit; it speaks primarily of God as creator of life or illuminator of knowledge. It is on this tradition, more theological than devotional, that Julian of Norwich draws in the late fourteenth century when she uses motherhood to speak of the action of the trinity.[141]

Even when we find motherhood and especially nursing used by later authors to talk of compassion and union there are differences of emphasis. In thirteenth- and fourteenth-century literature, nursing tends to become nursing with blood, not milk; giv-

---

pecially 234; and sermon 42, PL 194: col. 1829D; sermon 51, PL 194: cols. 1862–63A.

139. See nn. 8, 141 and 142.

140. See Colledge and Walsh, *A Book of Showings* 1:159; and n. 72 above. It is important to note that later authors who were influenced by the *Ancrene Riwle* were especially attracted by its maternal imagery; see Peter Hackett, "The Anchoresses' Guide," in *Pre-Reformation English Spirituality*, ed. James Walsh (New York, n.d.), p. 70.

141. Bradley, "Motherhood Theme." Hildegard of Bingen probably belongs in this tradition also; see above nn. 105 and 113.

ing birth in great agony is emphasized along with cuddling and suckling. By the fourteenth century, discussions of purgatory or hell and of predestination occur more frequently alongside insistence on the possibility of union with mother Jesus. For example, Lutgard of Aywières (†1246), at crucial turning points in her own life, has visions of Christ baring his chest or dying on the cross; and she nurses, drinking in sweetness and strength with the blood.[142] The monk of Farne (probably later fourteenth century) writes:

> . . . little ones . . . run and throw themselves into their mothers' arms . . . Christ our Lord does the same with us. He stretches out his hands to embrace us, bows down his head to kiss us, and opens his side to give us suck; and though it is blood he offers us to suck we believe that it is health-giving and *sweeter than honey and the honey-comb* [Ps. 18:11]. Do not wean me, good Jesus, from *the breasts of thy consolation* [Isa. 66:11] as long as I live in this world, for all who suffer this abide in death, as thou thyself didst testify in the gospel saying: *Unless you eat the flesh of the son of man and drink his blood, you shall not have life in you* [John 6:54].
>
> . . . I will say to my Lord: "There is safety for me in hastening to thine embrace. . . . it is the greatest delight to me to suck the breast of the king, who has been *my hope from the bosom of my mother*, and *upon whom I was cast from the womb* [Isa. 49:1; Isa. 49:23; Ps. 21:10–11]. But I also need to enter again into the womb of my Lord and be reborn unto life eternal, if I am to be amongst the members of the church whose names are in the book of life." . . . So precisely because I am a sinner . . . thou dost stretch out thine arms to receive me and bend down thy head to kiss me; thou dost bleed that I may have to drink, and open thy side in thy desire to draw me within.[143]

The Carthusian prioress, Marguerite of Oingt (†1310), speaks thus of mother Jesus:

142. Thomas of Cantimpré, *Vita S. Lutgardis*, AASS: June, vol. 4 (Paris, 1867): 189–210, especially bk. 1, chap. 1, sec. 2, pp. 191F–92A, and bk. 1, chap. 1, sec. 13, pp. 193C–E. See also Ursmer Berlière, *La dévotion au sacré-coeur dans l'Ordre de St. Benoît*, Collection Pax 10 (Paris, 1923), pp. 20–23.

143. The monk of Farne, "Meditations," chaps. 40 and 50–51, ed. Farmer, pp. 182–83 and 189–90; trans. a Benedictine nun of Stanbrook, *The Monk of Farne: The Meditations of a Fourteenth-Century Monk*, ed.

My sweet Lord, I gave up for you my father and my mother and
my brothers and all the wealth of the world. . . . You know, my
sweet Lord, that if I had a thousand worlds and could bend them
all to my will, I would give them all up for you . . . for you are
the life of my soul. Nor do I have father or mother besides you
nor do I wish to have. For are you not my mother and more than
my mother? The mother who bore me labored in delivering me
for one day or one night but you, my sweet and lovely Lord,
labored for me for more than thirty years. Ah, my sweet and
lovely Lord, with what love you labored for me and bore me
through your whole life. But when the time approached for you
to be delivered, your labor pains were so great that your holy
sweat was like great drops of blood that came out from your
body and fell on the earth. . . . Ah! Sweet Lord Jesus Christ,
who ever saw a mother suffer such a birth! For when the hour of
your delivery came you were placed on the hard bed of the cross
. . . and your nerves and all your veins were broken. And truly
it is no surprise that your veins burst when in one day you gave
birth to the whole world.[144]

By the late fourteenth century, devotional use of the theme of
mother Jesus is different in certain ways from twelfth-century
male Cistercian usage. Later medieval writing stresses suckling
with blood and is more frankly eucharistic.[145] More emphasis is
placed on Christ's suffering; much attention is devoted to sin, seen
more as separation from than as rebellion against God,[146] and the

---

Hugh Farmer, The Benedictine Studies (Baltimore, 1961), pp. 64 and
73–74.

144. Marguerite, *Pagina*, chaps. 30–39, *Oeuvres*, pp. 77–79.

145. On the growing eucharistic devotion of the later twelfth and thirteenth centuries, see below, pp. 192–3 and 256–7.

146. Julian and Mechtild of Magdeburg have trouble understanding
how sin can really be; for sin is, to them, pain and loss—which neither
God nor man would desire. See Hanshell, "Crux," pp. 77–91; Conrad
Pepler, *The English Religious Heritage* (St. Louis, 1958), pp. 321–27; and
Eric Colledge, *The Medieval Mystics of England* (New York, 1961), p. 87.
What the love of mother-God expresses most frequently to these writers is less the ecstasy of union than the impossibility of ever being really
lost or alone. But in contrast to the calm tone of the twelfth-century
sermons and treatises examined above, the threat of sin (which is itself
suffering) seems graver in these later authors, and Christ suffers more
cruelly in order to overcome it.

comfort offered by mother Jesus is not merely love but also a place among the elect. Male and female characteristics are less clearly and specifically delineated in the maternal and paternal images. The whole theme of mother Jesus occurs less frequently in the context of examination of the nature of authority, human or divine.[147] By drawing these contrasts between twelfth-century usage and later writers, I do not mean to suggest that there was a single late medieval use of the theme of mother Jesus. But a glance at some of the thirteenth- to fifteenth-century usages helps us to underline quite precisely what characterized twelfth-century images.

In the Cistercian writings analyzed here, maternal imagery is used, to put it simply, to talk about authority (good and bad) and dependence (good and bad). In the discussion that follows, I shall argue that the roots of these specific characteristics of Cistercian usage lie in two things: the ambivalence of these authors (all of them abbots) about the exercise of pastoral responsibility, and hence about authority in general, and their deep sense of the life of the cloister as cut off from the world.

Maternal Imagery and the Cistercian Concept of Authority

All twelfth-century Cistercian writers use maternal imagery to add something to authority figures qua rulers or fathers, and the something added is always nurturing, affectivity, and accessibility. Thus the specific context in which maternal imagery appears suggests not only that these authors saw God and prelates as rulers but also that they felt that rule needed to be softened or complemented by something else. These authors appear to have supplemented their image of God with maternal metaphors because they needed to supplement their image of authority with that for which the maternal stood: emotion and nurture. To make this argument is not, of course, to propose that their concept of God is merely a projection of their own psyches. But it is to say that the language

147. See below, pp. 158–9, 189–90, 209, and 225–7 and above, nn. 130 and 134.

in which they chose to speak of their relationship to God expressed the particular ideals and problems of the religious life they lived.

That the need to supplement authority with love is the motive behind much Cistercian use of maternal imagery is perhaps clearest in the case of Bernard.[148] As I pointed out earlier, Bernard's mind frequently leaps to the topic of pastoral responsibility when it finds maternal metaphors in the Bible; it leaps to maternal or feminine imagery when it must discuss rule or discipline (either human or divine). Moreover, explicit claims to be mother as well as father and brother to his monks form one of his favorite self-descriptions.[149] Bernard reveals himself in his letters as a person who worried more about whether he loved adequately than about whether he was loved;[150] some of his tendency to supplement images of rule or command with images of nurture and affectivity may express his own particular psychological needs. But the concern to add affectivity to rule in descriptions of God, prelates, and self occurs also in William of St. Thierry, Guerric of Igny, Aelred of Rievaulx, Adam of Perseigne, and Isaac of Stella.[151] On his deathbed, Aelred chose to describe his own role as maternal.[152]

148. Gammersbach has suggested that the reason for Bernard's parallel descriptions of Christ and abbot lies in an explicit conception, found in the Benedictine Rule itself, of the abbot as image of Christ to his monks; Gammersbach, "Das Abtsbild," pp. 85–101. This is certainly correct. But this concept by itself does not explain why the description of both Christ and abbot has the content it does.

149. Bernard, letters 1, 71, 110, 146, 152, 201, and 258, PL 182: cols. 76A–B, 183B–84A, 253, 303B–C, 312A, 369B–C, 466B–67A; and sermon 29 on the Song of Songs, par. 6, OB 1:207. See also Gammersbach, "Das Abtsbild."

150. We see this especially in letter 85, PL 182: cols. 206C–10A; letter 87, cols. 211–17; letter 258, cols. 466–67; and in letter 73, cols. 187–88, where Bernard says that loving ought to be difficult. Bernard's own ambivalence comes out clearly in letter 72, col. 186D, where he admits that he is the father but refuses fatherly authority because, he says, he and all the monks are brothers.

151. In addition to the passages cited above, nn. 126 and 138, see Isaac of Stella, sermon 27, *Sermons* 2:150–52 (col. 1780D): "[Abbas] pater sit filii Dei in nobis et nutritor et paedagogus et tutor, quanto tempore parvulus est . . ." But in the same passage Isaac also describes the abbot as executioner and flagellator.

152. Walter Daniel, *Life of Ailred*, p. 58.

When we look at actual Cistercian life in the twelfth century we find much evidence of intense concern with and anxiety over authority. Every Cistercian author in whose writings maternal imagery plays a prominent role was himself an abbot (and in some cases a novice master as well). Moreover, in several of these authors, the effort to expand or supplement the conception of rule occurs in conjunction with intense and articulated ambivalence about their own exercise of leadership. William of St. Thierry several times expressed feelings of exhaustion and a desire to leave his abbacy, a desire upon which he finally acted.[153] Bernard wished to renounce the cares of pastoral responsibility and return to contemplation, yet he issued violent rebukes to other abbots who acted upon such yearnings. His ambivalence is at times acute enough to seem a self-hatred, an antagonism toward the gift for administration and preaching that he knows himself to possess.[154] And even Aelred, who had a sunnier disposition than Bernard or William, expresses differing views of the value of administration and pastoral responsibility depending upon his audience. At least when writing for hermits and recluses, he speaks of such activities in most pejorative terms.[155] Furthermore, there are institutional indications that the abbatial role was seen as a heavy burden in the twelfth century. We know that a number of abbots resigned, Cistercians prominent among them. And by the thirteenth century many of the new orders began to move toward election of abbots for a limited term rather than for life—clearly a response to twelfth-century feelings that lifelong rule was too great a burden for both the abbot and his sons.[156]

153. William of St. Thierry, *De natura et dignitate amoris*, chap. 8, PL 184: cols. 393–95: *Meditativae Orationes*, chap. 11, PL 180: cols. 237–42; and *Sur le Cantique*, chap. 52, p. 144.

154. Letter 87, PL 182: cols. 211–17, and letter 233, cols. 420–21; see also the citations from the sermons on the Song of Songs in nn. 11 and 18–21 above; and sermons 52 and 53, OB 2:90–102.

155. Compare Aelred's tolerant view of the demands of administration in *De Jesu puero duodenni*, sect. 3, par. 31, *Opera omnia* 1:277–78, with his harsh description of it as a "dung heap" in his *De institutione*, chap. 28, *Opera omnia* 1:660–61.

156. Pierre Salmon, *The Abbot in Monastic Tradition: A Contribution to the History of the Office of Religious Superiors in the West*, trans. Claire Lavoie, Cistercian Studies Series 14 (Washington D.C., 1972), pp. 46–

The reasons for this Cistercian anxiety about rule are complex. Ambivalence about taking on pastoral care inside the monastery or outside (often expressed as a debate between the active and contemplative lives) was part of the monastic tradition. Monks were supposed to feel such ambivalence. And twelfth-century monks, attracted by a new ideal of evangelism, suffered more acutely than monks of an earlier day from conflict between this desire to preach and the traditional monastic commitment to flight from the world. Awareness of such conflict may lie behind some of the most creative of Cistercian ideas: Aelred's new sense of the active life and the new emphasis, in many writers, on love of neighbor.[157] Moreover, as is well known, Cistercians rejected the institution of child oblates and put a greater emphasis on adult choice and conversion. It is probable that this resulted in more pressure on abbots to offer spiritual guidance to sensitive souls who worried about the quality of their inner life, about whether their conversion was genuine. Aelred of Rievaulx writes, drawing on his own experience as novice master, of a novice who worries because his gift of tears has dried up upon entering the monastery. Both Bernard and Adam of Perseigne speak of similarly delicate problems of spiritual direction.[158] Such discussions indicate that, whatever the reason, Cister-

---

104, especially 95–99. Monastic ambivalence about the exercise of pastoral authority may be a contributing cause in another trend. By the end of the twelfth century the number of bishops who came from the regular clergy had declined in both France and England. See Marcel Pacaut, *Louis VII et les élections episcopales dans la royaume de France* (Paris, 1957), pp. 111–12; and Thomas Callahan, Jr., "The Renaissance of Monastic Bishops in England, 1135–1154," *Studia monastica* 16 (1974): 55–67.

157. See C. Dumont, "L'equilibre humain de la vie cistercienne d'après le bienheureux Aelred de Rievaulx," COCR 18 (1965): 177–89; A. Squire, "Aelred of Rievaulx and the Monastic Tradition Concerning Action and Contemplation," *Downside Review* 72 (1954): 289–303; Constable, "Twelfth-Century Spirituality," pp. 40–45; and above, chapter 2.

158. Aelred, *Speculum caritatis*, bk. 2, chap. 17, *Opera omnia* 1:86–91, and see Louis Bouyer, *The Cistercian Heritage*, trans. E. A. Livingstone (Westminster, Md., 1958), p. 13, and A. Squire, "The Composition of the *Speculum caritatis*," *Cîteaux: commentarii cistercienses* 14 (1963): 229–30. Adam of Perseigne, *Correspondance*, letter 24, pp. 169–73. Bernard, sermon 9, par. 2, OB 1:43. See also Leclercq, *Monks and Love*, pp. 8–16.

cian abbots were in fact increasingly called upon to respond with qualities that medieval men considered feminine. Anxious, even guilty about ruling, these religious leaders tried to create a new image of authority (both their own and God's) that would temper that authority with compassion and "mothering." Ironically, of course, the new image may have actually made the role of ruler even harder to fill.[159]

This thesis—that the Cistercian description of God as *pater* and *mater* has its roots at least partially in the need of Cistercian abbots for a new image of authority—finds further support when we contrast these Cistercians with thirteenth- and fourteenth-century women. Female writers do not use the idea of God as mother to complement judgment with nurture, nor does the image occur in their writings in conjunction with a picture of prelates as mothers. There are undoubtedly many reasons for this—among them, a growing sense in thirteenth- and fourteenth-century piety of God's accessibility. But the absence of this particular use of the theme is perhaps also a reflection of the fact that women did not feel the conflict about the exercise of leadership that twelfth-century Cistercian males experienced. Women in general did not struggle, caught in a tension between the desire to preach and serve and the desire to be humble and subservient and grow toward God. At the simplest level, this is because women were not priests or preach-

---

159. The supplementing of authority with nurture, harshness with affection, which we find in male Cistercian images of God and of the monastic official, has parallels in twelfth-century descriptions of bishops. See, for example, Gerhoh of Reischersberg, *De aedificio Dei*, ed. Sackur, *Monumenta Germaniae Historica, Libelli de lite* 3:201. Landulf Senior, *Historia Mediolanensis usque ad a. 1085* (written around 1110) speaks of archbishop Aribert and the church of Milan in maternal, particularly nursing, images: bk. 2, chaps. 26 and 34, *Monumenta Germaniae Historica, Scriptores* 7 (Hanover, 1848): 64 and 69–70.

To speak much more broadly, there are also parallels in secular literature to this pairing of personality characteristics. The male role as delineated in the twelfth-century romance was certainly no less military than the male role in the somewhat earlier epic; but the knight of the romance was required to supplement leadership and prowess with good manners, affection, and social graces. All this suggests a general ambivalence about authority and about male roles in twelfth-century society.

ers, nor were they subject to being tempted out of the cloister by offers of bishoprics. The women in whose writings or visions we find maternal imagery were not, for the most part, even abbesses, although many of them did in fact advise other nuns or practice the "apostolate of the pen." [160] But it seems that even women who took on leadership roles as abbesses or novice mistresses or informal spiritual advisers had a built-in guarantee that they would remain, psychologically speaking, pupils as well as teachers, followers as well as leaders. That guarantee was the male priest and confessor, on whom they were dependent for spiritual guidance, before whom they were docile and humble. By definition women were considered unfit to be priests and theologians; perhaps this obviated the guilt any "beginner in the school for the service of God," male or female, would feel if he or she really became teacher and master.

This is not to argue that abbesses felt no anxiety about exercising authority. Many nuns felt a great reluctance and sense of unworthiness when confronted with the opportunity to govern. [161] Nor is this to argue that women were unable to be leaders simply because they could not be clerics. In the twelfth to fourteenth centuries, many were visionaries or prophets through whom God spoke directly. And they had very positive images of these roles. Strangely enough, the contrast is not the simple one: males have authority and feel ambivalent about it; women neither have authority nor feel ambivalent. The contrast is rather: men have authority, based on office, and desire to temper it; women have something analogous, based directly on divine inspiration, and seem to feel less anxiety about it. [162]

160. Gertrude the Great, Mechtild of Hackeborn, Mechtild of Magdeburg, and Julian of Norwich, as far as we know, had no official teaching or governing position. Marguerite of Oingt, whose writings reveal no anxiety about care for others, began her meditations in 1286; in 1288 a document gives her the title "prioress" but it is impossible to know whether she was a prioress two years earlier when she wrote her lengthy descriptions of Christ as mother; see Duraffour *et al.*, Pref., Marguerite, *Oeuvres*, p. 12.

161. Thomas of Cantimpré, *Vita S. Lutgardis*; see n. 142 above. Hildegard of Bingen in the twelfth century felt great consternation at the idea of becoming abbess.

162. See below, pp. 226–7 and 247–62.

Maternal Imagery and
True and False Dependence

The tendency of twelfth-century Cistercian monks to pair the authority of prelates and the authority of God is not the only salient characteristic of their use of maternal imagery. In addition to being an image that complements authority with compassion, their image of God as mother is also an image of dependence and union—of hanging on God's breast as a suckling child, even of crawling inside God's body. An explanation of this aspect of Cistercian usage lies partly in certain fundamental characteristics of twelfth-century theology and spirituality, partly in the psychological needs of monks, and partly in the nature of the Cistercian concern for community.

As Robert Javelet has recently pointed out, monastic writing in the twelfth century is optimistic and dynamic.[163] Whatever the particular theological issue under discussion, a twelfth-century spiritual writer (at least when addressing monks) is apt to use it to describe the route to God. Thus, for example, both predestination and free will are used to convince readers that God is a goal toward which they are in fact moving. Such an attitude tends to use references to sin to stimulate not despair or guilt but a sense of progress toward and dependence on God. Whatever basic assumptions lie behind this optimism (and some of them are clearly neo-Platonic), it is well captured in the idea of God's motherhood as Bernard understood it: a mother cannot fail to love her child; sin is a tarnishing of what the child should be, a naughtiness, but the fundamental bond of mother-child remains.[164] Moreover, the traditional emphasis on monks as beginners certainly influenced Cistercian authors to elaborate for their fellow monks a picture of the soul at the very first stage of growth (for which the unweaned infant is an

163. Javelet, *Image et ressemblance*, especially 1:451–61; see also Southern, *Medieval Humanism and Other Studies* (New York, 1970) pp. 29–60; and Morris, *Discovery*.

164. See Bernard, *De diligendo Deo*, chap. 7, par. 17, OB 3:134, lines 10–11, where Bernard gives as examples of love that does what it freely desires: a hungry man eating, a thirsty man drinking, and a mother nursing her child. See also the references cited in n. 11 above; letter 300 is addressed to a woman and discusses maternal affection literally.

obvious metaphor).[165] Adam of Perseigne, for example, suggests that when the soul is itself a "child," it contemplates the humanity of Christ as a nursing baby; awareness of suffering and crucifixion (the adult Christ) can come only when the soul is an adult, ready for "meat," not "milk."[166] The calm tone of this twelfth-century usage contrasts vividly with the increasing emphasis in thirteenth- and fourteenth-century writers on the suffering that mother Christ must undergo to give life to—and to feed—the sinful soul.

We may also suspect another reason for the Cistercian choice of the mother-child image to speak of dependence and union. Given the twelfth-century partiality for metaphors drawn from human relationships, religious males had a problem. For if the God with whom they wished to unite was spoken of in male language, it was hard to use the metaphor of sexual union unless they saw themselves as female. We do have occasional examples of monks describing what appears to us to be a sexual union with a male God. (Rupert of Deutz's vision of embracing the crucifix is a case in point.)[167] We also have many examples of monks describing themselves or their souls as brides of Christ—that is, as female. But another solution (which kept images drawn from human relationships central and did not require the male to describe himself in a female image) was of course to see God as female parent, with whom union could be quite physical (in the womb or at the breast). We should not ignore the possibility that in such

---

165. The fact that the authors considered in this article were writing for those already in the cloister undoubtedly contributes to the tone of optimism.

166. See n. 135 above.

167. Rupert, *Commentaria in Matthaeum*, bk. 12, PL 168: cols. 1590–91. The crucified Christ supposedly appeared to Bernard, lifted him up and embraced him: see Herbert of Torres, *De miraculis*, bk. 2, chap. 19, PL 185.2: col. 1328. Bugge, *Virginitas*, p. 108, points out that one poem in the middle English Katherine group depicts the virgin monk as bridegroom of the Virgin Mary.

John Boswell has recently made us aware of the gay subculture of the twelfth century, many of whose members were clerics or monks. Gay males may, of course, have found erotic attachment to a male God an attractive metaphor. See Boswell, *Christianity, Social Tolerance, and Homosexuality*.

writings males could express as males certain sexual desires: play at the breast and entry into the female body.

Once again, a comparison with thirteenth- and fourteenth-century women helps to strengthen the point. For women do not use the image of mother-Jesus as one of their primary ways of speaking of union (although it does sometimes mean this).[168] To them, Christ is the bridegroom, and all kinds of passionate sexual language serves as metaphor for union with a male God. Simone Roisin's study of thirteenth-century Cistercian hagiography demonstrates that women are particularly likely to emphasize the handsome, young, human Christ, whereas male religious more frequently have visions of the Virgin Mary.[169] Thus, to some extent, males seem to have been attracted to female images and women to male images. But we must be careful not to push such arguments too far. Medieval authors do not seem to have drawn as sharp a line as we do between sexual responses and affective responses or between male and female. Throughout the Middle Ages, authors found it far easier than we seem to find it to apply characteristics stereotyped as male or female to the opposite sex. Moreover, they were clearly not embarrassed to speak of all kinds of ecstasy in language *we* find physical and sexual and therefore inappropriate for God. We cannot assume that twelfth-century monks associated the feminine with the female to the extent that we do or that they associated certain physical or affective responses with sexuality in the way that we do.[170]

Nevertheless, it seems clear that the psychological needs of religious males provide a partial explanation for the Cistercian theme of mother-Jesus and the concern for union that it expresses. But we should also locate this concern for dependence and union against the background of Cistercian life. For in the particular Cistercian authors I have studied, dependence on God is expressed in a number of relational and bodily images, some of which are not feminine, and the more concerned an author is with images of dependence and incorporation, the more likely he is to stress detachment from, independence from, withdrawal from the world.

168. See n. 146 above.
169. Simone Roisin, *Hagiographie*, pp. 108 and 111–13.
170. Bugge, *Virginitas*, does not seem to have borne this point sufficiently in mind.

Thus maternal imagery is part of a broad concern with dependence/independence, incorporation/withdrawal (or, to put it another way, with true and false dependence). And this concern lies behind not only the language these authors employ but also their way of life.

If we look at the structure of Cistercian monasticism as it emerges in the early twelfth century, we find a concern for independence from the world coupled with a concern for intense and humble dependence within church and cloister. In their economic and administrative arrangements, Cistercians tried to withdraw from power relationships with laity (as embodied in property relationships); yet they submitted themselves to episcopal authority, refusing at least initially to seek exemptions. They stressed solitude and withdrawal to the desert: of the authors studied here, Guerric was attracted to the solitary life; Isaac of Stella withdrew to a tiny, austere island community; and Adam of Perseigne and William of St. Thierry both changed orders in adulthood to seek a life of deeper withdrawal from the world.[171] Again and again their writings stress the renunciation of all family ties. Yet Cistercians in general opposed the eremitical movement, emphasizing the importance of dependence and interdependence within a community—an interdependence in which all are servants and learners.[172] Thus, Cistercians seem to have viewed themselves as renouncing dependence on the world in order to embrace dependence within religious community as a way of learning dependence on God. Aelred of Rievaulx draws explicitly the connection between perfect detachment from the world and perfect union with both neighbor and God.[173]

It is exactly this sense of renunciation of false dependence (on the world) in order to create true dependence (on God and com-

171. See Bouyer, *Cistercian Heritage*. On Adam of Perseigne, see J. Bouvet, "Biographie d'Adam de Perseigne," COCR 20 (1958): 16–26 and 145–52.

172. See above, chapter 2.

173. Aelred, *De institutione*, chap. 28, *Opera omnia* 1:661: "Itaque totum mundum uno dilectionis sinu complectere, ibi simul omnes qui boni sunt considera et gratulare, ibi malos intuere et luge." This example is all the more remarkable because it occurs in a work addressed to recluses, not to the cloistered.

munity) that the imagery of Cistercian writings conveys. Bernard, William, Guerric, Aelred, Isaac, and Adam of Perseigne each emphasizes physical withdrawal from and renunciation of the world. Each uses maternal imagery to express an intense emotional dependence of the child-soul on God, a dependence for which the affective bond of abbot and monk is preparation. Frequently these authors choose images that express the relationship of the soul to God in a way that also joins the soul with other souls (as, for example, nursing brothers of Christ). Indeed it seems no accident that the twelfth-century Cistercian author who writes with the greatest passion of the necessity for solitude and for the austere isolation of a tiny community—Isaac of Stella—has the most radical imagery of incorporation.[174] Isaac, who also uses images of bride (the soul) and bridegroom (Christ), mother (the Virgin Mary) and child (the soul),[175] claims that our incorporation into the mystical body is the "completion" of Christ.[176] Similarly, when Aelred of Rievaulx writes of Christ on the crucifix feeding the soul with milk, he immediately associates this feeding with the virginity of the watching soul, symbolized by John and Mary, and suggests that Christ from the cross gives the two virgins to each other for mutual love and comfort. This complex passage thus couples virginity (renunciation of the world), the motherhood of Christ, and the union of virgin souls in love not only with Christ but also with

174. See sermon 2, *Sermons* 1:98–102 (cols. 1693D–94D); sermon 14, 1:276–80 (cols. 1737–38A); sermon 15, 1:286–93 (cols. 1739B–40D); sermon 18, 2:18–20 (cols. 1752A–B); sermon 37, 2:296–304 (cols. 1816A–17D); and sermon 50, PL 194: cols. 1858–62A, for Isaac's intense sense of renunciation of the world. See also F. Bliemetzrieder, "Isaak von Stella, Beiträge zur Lebensbeschreibung," *Jahrbuch für Philosophie und spekulative Theologie* 18 (1904): 1–35.

175. See sermon 11, *Sermons* 1:242–44 (cols. 1728B–D); sermon 42, PL 194: col. 1832B; sermon 45, PL 194: col. 1841C–D; sermon 51, PL 194: col. 1863A.

176. Sermon 29, *Sermons* 2:166–80 (cols. 1784–87C); sermon 34, 2:232–54, especially 234 (col. 1801A–B); sermon 42, PL 194: col. 1829D; sermon 51, PL 194: cols. 1862–63A. We should note that sermon 14, 1:270–80 (cols. 1735B–38A) joins in the same discussion the "corps mystique" theme and almost frantic exhortation to renounce the world. It is no accident that Isaac sees sin, the loss that is the opposite of union (incorporation) with God, as fragmentation.

each other.[177] On the other hand, the only Cistercian author I have found who lacks the intense interiority and sense of incorporation with God that characterizes his fellow Cistercians lacks also any interest in the cloister (either as solitude or as community) and uses little feminine imagery. This writer, the former troubador Helinand of Froidmont,[178] was far more interested in the organization of the church and the life of the clergy and discussed these issues in the kind of building imagery that was popular with some regular canons.[179] Thus, it seems that those Cistercian authors who use maternal imagery for God develop it as part of an interest in affectivity and dependence that is tied to their sense of the cloister as independent of the world.

Twelfth-century Victorines, Premonstratensians, and some Benedictine authors as well (e.g., Hildegard of Bingen) are fond of images of houses and cities, underlining with such language not only the variety of mansions and roles in the edifice of God but also the stages of personal growth and of Christian history. Such imagery frequently expresses a concern to sort out the significance of various obligations within the church or society. Cistercians and Carthusians are also fond of images of stages—steps of ladders, levels of the Ark, and so forth. But Cistercians and Carthusians, with the important exception of the former Cistercian Joachim of Flora, are less concerned with stages of history than with personal growth, less concerned with what is appropriate to different roles than with how community functions as a setting for growth. They

177. Aelred, *De institutione*, chap. 26, *Opera omnia* 1:658–59.

178. See Helinand of Froidmont, Sermons, PL 212: cols. 481–720. The description of Helinand in François Vandenbroucke, *La morale monastique du XIᵉ au XVIᵉ siècle*, Analecta Mediaevalia Namurcensia 20 (Louvain, 1966), p. 165, which has become standard in reference works, seems to be based entirely on the first Christmas sermon: "Helinand . . . attest un attachement en quelque sorte chevaleresque à Marie." If all the sermons are considered together a very different picture emerges.

179. Helinand, sermon 23, PL 212: cols. 670–71; sermon 25, cols. 685–87; sermon 26, cols. 693–97 (and cf. sermon 11, col. 580B–C); sermon 27, cols. 700–2; sermon 28, cols. 711–16. See Gerhard Bauer, *Claustrum Animae: Untersuchungen zur Geschichte der Metapher vom Herzen als Kloster*, 1 (Munich, 1973). Helinand is also fond of military imagery. Building and military images occur in his sermons for clergy, references to the Virgin in his sermons for monks.

are far more inclined to pour out their love of God in images of bodily closeness—eating God's honeycomb, drinking from his breast, nestling in his side or under his wings, sleeping with him as his bride. The experience from which they learn is not so much temptation as the touching and tasting of God; sin to them is fragmentation, rupture, assertion of one's differentness from the image of God that one is in the process of becoming. The idea of Christ as nursing or pregnant mother is for Cistercians one among a host of images that articulate a process of return through love of others to true dependence, a return made possible by the breaking of false dependence on the difference and otherness of the world. Aelred of Rievaulx, in a rush of metaphors that expresses many Cistercian themes, writes of the love of Jesus (*dilectio, affectus, mirae suavitatis gutta*):

> . . . at [that] sweet taste all bitterness flees, the heart is enlarged, the mind penetrated, and the ability to rise prepared in a marvelous way. . . . The whole mind begins to wish to be dissolved and be with Christ. . . . Thus the legislator gives his blessing, administering to beginners the wine of compunction with his fear, to the proficient milk from the breasts of his consolation, and when they have been torn from the milk, they will be dinner guests at the banquet of the coming of his glory.[180]

Conclusion

In this analysis, I have discussed the ways in which one image (which turns out to be a cluster of images) expresses some of the basic values that are implicit in the life of a religious community. Twelfth-century Cistercians drew their maternal imagery from earlier literature, particularly Anselm and the Bible. But I have tried to argue that they used it to express immediate concerns: a need for affectivity in the exercise of authority and in the creation of community, and a complex rhythm of renouncing ties with the world while deepening ties with community and between the soul and God. My analysis does not, I realize, answer all questions about maternal imagery in twelfth-century spiritual writing. It

180. Aelred, *Speculum caritatis*, bk. 2, chap. 12, *Opera omnia* 1:79–80.

does not try to say what in society or in the depths of the human psyche led to the consistent association of women with tenderness or of mothers with closeness; nor does it say why values such as emotionality and dependence on God, among others, became central in a religious community intended to renounce the values and ties of worldly society. To answer those questions would be to write another essay—one which would have to consider a far greater range of phenomena than I have explored here. But this analysis should make clear why we cannot isolate an image from its intellectual or its institutional context and why we cannot take it as literal comment on the objects or situations from which the metaphor is constructed. The maternal imagery of medieval monastic treatises tells us that cloistered males in the twelfth century idealized the mothering role, that they held consistent stereotypes of femaleness as compassionate and soft (either weak or tender), and that they saw the bond of child and mother as a symbol of closeness, union, or even the incorporation of one self into another. But it would be unwarranted to argue that this imagery tells us what monks thought of actual women or of their own mothers. If religious symbols express the values of communities that use them and if those communities transmute or invert the values of the world, then the monastic idea of mother-Jesus tells us, at least directly, only what monks thought about Jesus and about themselves.

Modern interest in women and their history led scholars first to study an aspect of male history—that is, male conceptions of and definitions of women and of the female. This was natural, at least for the Middle Ages, for most of the primary source material had been produced by men. But the commendable desire to study women led scholars to try to squeeze from male attitudes information about women's experience. Some even went further, attempting to correlate conceptions of the feminine or female images with real opportunities for women either in society at large or within the Christian community. A simple distinction was often lost sight of: the female (or woman) and the feminine are not the same. The former is a person of one gender; the latter may be an aspect of a person of either gender. Thus the attitudes of a man toward the feminine (as distinct from women) may reflect not so much his attitudes toward his mother, his sister, females in his community, what attracts him sexually, and so forth, as his sense of the feminine aspects of himself. In working on twelfth-century Cistercians, I have been conscious of studying the attitudes of males toward themselves—that is, studying the Cistercian conception of the feminine (in particular the maternal), not Cistercian policy toward women in religious life. It should not surprise us that Aelred of Rievaulx, who writes of the spiritual equality of women, can tell without comment the brutal story of the nun of Watton, who was beaten and forced to castrate her lover.[181] Nor should the slow, complex history of the efforts of Cistercian nuns to gain support and supervision surprise us either.[182] The Cistercian conception of Jesus as mother and abbot as mother reveals not an attitude toward women but a sense (not without ambivalence) of a need and obligation to nurture other men, a need and obligation to achieve intimate dependence on God.

The theme of God's motherhood is a minor one in all writers of the high Middle Ages except Julian of Norwich. Too long neglected or even repressed by editors and translators, it is perhaps now in danger of receiving more emphasis than it deserves. And yet, through exploring it, we have penetrated to some very deep anxieties, delights, and commitments felt by the Cistercian monks who used it. If we are ever to know how late medieval religious people felt about themselves—to understand their self-definitions, their assumptions, their tensions and anxieties, their deepest values and pleasures—we have no better source than their vivid imagery, produced for members of their own communities and shaped by

181. Giles Constable, "Aelred of Rievaulx and the Nun of Watton: An Episode in the Early History of the Gilbertine Order," *Medieval Women*, ed. D. Baker, (Oxford, 1978), pp. 205–26.

182. Micheline Pontenay de Fontette, *Les religieuses à l'âge classique du droit canon: Recherches sur les structures juridiques des branches féminines des ordres* (Paris, 1967), pp. 27–64; Noreen Hunt, "Notes on the History of Benedictine and Cistercian Nuns in Britain," *Cistercian Studies* 8 (1973): 157–77; Sally Thompson, "The Problem of the Cistercian Nuns in the Twelfth and Early Thirteenth Centuries," *Medieval Women*, ed. D. Baker, (Oxford, 1978), pp. 227–52; Brenda Bolton, "*Vitae Matrum*," ibid., pp. 253–73; John B. Freed, "Urban Development and the 'Cura Monialium' in Thirteenth-Century Germany," *Viator* 3 (1972): 311–27.

imagination and the unconscious as well as by established theological tradition. What I have attempted here—the close examination of one, relatively minor image in the context of other images and of the life of the religious community that produced
them—may provide an example of what we can learn from looking at the way in which religious groups use metaphors and names
for the God they worship.

V

Women Mystics
in the
Thirteenth Century:
The Case of
the Nuns of Helfta

———

The State of the Question

𝔉ᴇᴡ ᴍᴇᴅɪᴇᴠᴀʟ women before the thirteenth century speak to us directly about their inner religious experiences.[1] After 1200 the situation slowly changes, owing in part to the emergence of the vernaculars as literary languages.[2] There appear in increasing numbers saints' lives about and sometimes by women, prayers and meditations by women, and accounts of the mystical experi-

---

This essay has grown out of a paper prepared for the 1978 faculty seminar on religion at the University of Washington, which was funded by the National Endowment for the Humanities. I am grateful to members of the seminar for their advice, especially to its director, Charles Keyes. Time to complete the essay was provided by the American Council of Learned Societies, which awarded me a fellowship for fall and winter, 1978–79. I am also grateful to Susan Dickman of the Massachusetts Institute of Technology, Thomas Head, Robert E. Lerner of Northwestern University, Lester K. Little of Smith College, Mary Martin McLaughlin, Royal Rhodes of Kenyon College, and Karen Scott for their help and suggestions.

1. For the twelfth century, there are only three major female religious writers (if we exclude Heloise): Hildegard of Bingen (†1179), Elisabeth of Schönau (†1164), and Herrad of Hohenbourg (or Landsberg) (†1191).
2. The classic treatment is Herbert Grundmann, "Die Frauen und die Literatur im Mittelalter: Ein Beitrag zur Frage nach der Entstehung des Schrifttums in der Volkssprache," *Archiv für Kulturgeschichte* 26 (1936): 129–61.

ences of women ecstatics and visionaries, sometimes told in their own words or in the words of their fellow beguines or nuns.[3] Scholars have not failed to notice this phenomenon, and most textbook accounts of medieval mysticism include a short section on "female mysticism," as if it were one among many types of late medieval piety and synonymous with "nuptial mysticism" (i.e., mysticism that makes use of bridal or erotic imagery drawn from the Song of Songs).[4] Nor have scholars failed to judge it. Protestant historians have stressed its individualism;[5] Catholic historians its affective and liturgical aspects.[6] William James saw it as the nadir of Christian devotion—"theopathic, absurd and puerile."[7] A recent Italian theologian, Cyprien Vagaggini, has seen in it a model for reforming present-day Catholic piety.[8] What has been missing is an effort to put this flowering of female piety into historical perspective. And because its historical context has been neglected, its specifically historical significance has been missed. For the female mysticism of the thirteenth century was not merely one type among many, nor was it characterized primarily or universally by the use of bridal images. Where careful comparative study

3. Major thirteenth-century women whose own words survive include the Cistercian Beatrice of Nazareth (†1268), Hadewijch, Marguerite of Oingt (†1310), and Marguerite Porete (burned at Paris in 1310). For other thirteenth-century women about whose spiritual teaching we know something see below n. 28.

4. See, for example, J. Leclercq, F. Vandenbroucke and L. Bouyer, *La spiritualité du moyen âge* (Paris, 1960), pp. 430–38 and 448–54; A. Rayez, "Humanité du Christ," DS 7.1: cols. 1088–90; David Knowles and Dimitri Obolensky, *The Middle Ages*, The Christian Centuries: A New History of the Catholic Church 2 (New York, 1968), p. 258.

5. Wilhelm Preger, *Geschichte der deutschen Mystik im Mittelalter . . .* 3 vols. (Leipzig, 1874–93), 1:70–132.

6. See the works cited in nn. 4 above and 8 below.

7. William James, *The Varieties of Religious Experience: A Study in Human Nature* (1902, reprint ed., New York, 1961), p. 275. For a similarly negative assessment, see William R. Inge, *Studies of English Mystics: St. Margaret's Lectures 1905* (London, 1906), p. 52, where he calls Gertrude's *Legatus* "a paltry record of sickly compliments and semi-erotic endearments."

8. Cyprien Vagaggini, *Initiation théologique à la liturgie*, 2 vols., trans. R. Gantoy (Bruges, 1959–63), 2:190–93 and 206–39.

of saints' lives and spiritual treatises has been done, it indicates that in the thirteenth century women were more likely than men to be mystics, to gain reputations based on their mystical abilities, and to have paramystical experiences (such as trances, levitations, stigmata, etc.). Moreover, these women mystics were primarily responsible for encouraging and propagating some of the most distinctive aspects of late medieval piety: devotion to the human, especially the infant, Christ and devotion to the eucharist (frequently focused in devotion to the wounds, blood, body, and heart of Jesus).[9]

These are striking facts. For the first time in Christian history we can document that a particular kind of religious experience is more common among women than men. For the first time in Christian history certain major devotional and theological emphases emanate from women and influence the basic development of spirituality. The questions suggested by these facts are obvious: why were women so prominent in thirteenth-century mysticism? and why did their piety have the particular characteristics that it did? Insofar as historians have asked these questions at all, they seem to have assumed that the answer lies in some kind of inherent female "emotionalism" or in some kind of affinity between women and female imagery.[10] But these answers will not do. If

9. Louis Gougaud, *Devotional and Ascetic Practices in the Middle Ages*, trans. G. C. Bateman (London, 1927), pp. 75–130; Grundmann, "Die Frauen und die Literatur"; E. Amann, "Stigmatisation," DTC 14.2: col. 2617; S. Roisin, *L'Hagiographie cistercienne dans le diocèse de Liège au XIII*ᵉ *siècle* (Louvain, 1947); idem, "L'efflorescence cistercienne et le courant féminin de piété au XIIIᵉ siècle," RHE 39 (1943): 342–78; E. W. McDonnell, *The Beguines and Beghards in Medieval Culture with Special Emphasis on the Belgian Scene* (1954: reprint ed., New York, 1969); Jean-Baptiste M. Porion, "Hadewijch," DS 7.1: col. 20; Ernst Benz, *Die Vision: Erfahrungsformen und Bilderwelt* (Stuttgart, 1969); R. De Ganck, "The Cistercian Nuns of Belgium in the Thirteenth Century," *Cistercian Studies* 5 (1970): 169–87; Frederick M. Stein, "The Mysticism of Engelthal," unpublished; Brenda Bolton, "*Vitae Matrum*," *Medieval Women: dedicated and presented to Professor Rosalind M. T. Hill . . .* , ed. D. Baker, (Oxford, 1978), pp. 253–73; Wolfgang Riehle, *The Middle English Mystics*, trans. B. Standring (London, 1981), pp. 1–33.

10. The assumption that women are more emotional than men seems to underlie many standard accounts: for example, Rayez, "Humanité du Christ," cols. 1088–90. Cf. I. M. Lewis, *Ecstatic Religion* (Harmonds-

women become mystics because they are intrinsically more emotional, imaginative, religious, or hysterical than men, why did it take centuries for this to emerge? If women are particularly attracted by images of women, why is it that monks refer more frequently to the virgin Mary, while women concentrate especially on the infant or adolescent Christ?[11] Clearly other answers are needed. On the basis of my investigation of the Benedictine/Cistercian nuns of the Saxon monastery of Helfta I think I can begin to suggest what those answers may be.[12] The nuns of Helfta are an

worth, Middlesex, England, 1971), p. 32. The assumption that women need female images is also common: see, for example, E. Pagels, "What Became of God the Mother?" *Signs* 2 (1976): 293–303; E. C. McLaughlin, "Women, Power and the Pursuit of Holiness in Medieval Christianity," *Women of Spirit*, ed. R. Ruether and E. C. McLaughlin (New York, 1979), pp. 99–130; David Herlihy, "Women in Medieval Society," pp. 12–14, reprinted in *The Social History of Italy and Western Europe 700–1500*, Variorum Reprints (London, 1978); and the generally unreliable article by Carol P. Christ, "Heretics and Outsiders: The Struggle Over Female Power in Western Religion," *Soundings* 61.3: *Dilemmas of Pluralism* (1978): 260–80.

11. See above p. 162; Roisin, *Hagiographie*, pp. 108 and 111–13; and Rayez, "Humanité du Christ." None of the three twelfth-century women listed in n. 1 above shows as much affinity with affective spirituality in general and feminine imagery in particular as Cistercian and Carthusian monks from the same period.

12. Many of the standard English works on mysticism pay little attention to the Helfta nuns because they did not produce "mystical theology," defined in a technical sense. The nuns are discussed in Lina Eckenstein, *Woman Under Monasticism: Chapters on Saint-Lore and Convent Life Between A.D. 500 and A.D. 1500* (Cambridge, 1896), pp. 328–53; Lucie Félix-Faure Goyau, *Christianisme et culture féminine* (Paris, 1914), pp. 165–210, reprinted with additions from idem, "Une école de littérature mystique au XIIIᵉ siècle: Le monastère d'Helfta," *Revue française* (25 May 1913), pp. 207–13; Jean Martial Besse, *Les mystiques bénédictins des origines au XIIIᵉ siècle*, Collection Pax 6 (Paris, 1922), pp. 216–75; Pierre Pourrat, *La spiritualité chrétienne*, 4 vols. (Paris, 1927–31), 2:126–36; Leclercq, Vandenbroucke and Bouyer, *La spiritualité*, pp. 448–54 and 537–43; P. Schmitz, *Histoire de l'ordre de saint Benoît*, 7 vols. (Maredsous, 1942–56) 7: *Les moniales*: 293–301; Benz, *Die Vision*; and mentioned in Ailbe J. Luddy, *The Cistercian Nuns: A Brief Sketch of the Order from Its Foundation to the Present Day* (Dublin, 1931), p. 17, and Hilda Graef, *The Light and the Rainbow: A Study in Christian Spirituality from Its Roots . . . to Recent Times* (London, 1959), p. 242. In his classic work,

obvious place to start in exploring female mysticism in the thirteenth century, for their reports of visions and inner experiences or meditations form the largest single body of women's mystical writing in the period.

Our knowledge of Helfta as an institution is limited. The monastery was founded at Mansfeld in 1229 by Count Burchard of Mansfeld and his wife Elisabeth for a small group of nuns from Halberstadt who intended to practice the Cistercian rule.[13] The

---

Geschichte der deutschen Mystik 1:70–132, Wilhelm Preger treats them as forerunners of Protestantism; Friedrich-Wilhelm Wentzlaff-Eggebert, *Deutsche Mystik zwischen Mittelalter und Neuzeit: Einheit und Wandlung ihrer Erscheinungsformen* (Berlin, 1944), pp. 47–59, sees Mechtild of Magdeburg as part of one basic strain of German mysticism, the mysticism of "union," which leads into modern pietism (as opposed to the other strain, speculative mysticism); Vagaggini, *Initiation à la liturgie* 2:190–93 and 206–39, finds in Gertrude an example of a liturgical piety he recommends to modern Catholics. The best single study of any of these women remains Jeanne Ancelet-Hustache, *Mechtilde de Magdeburg (1207–1282): Étude de psychologie religieuse* (Paris, 1926). The most extensive discussion of the Helfta mystics has been in the context of the cult of the sacred heart. See Ursmer Berlière, *La dévotion au Sacré-Coeur dans l'Ordre de Saint Benoît*, Collection Pax 10 (Paris, 1923), pp. 24–53; Gougaud, *Devotional and Ascetic Practices*, pp. 75–130; Cyprien Vagaggini, *La dévotion au Sacré-Coeur," Cor Jesu*, 2 vols. (Rome, 1959), 2:31–48; and Auguste Hamon, "Coeur (sacré)," DS 2: cols. 1023–46.
13. The account of Helfta that follows is based on H. Grössler, *Die Blütezeit des Klosters Helfta bei Eisleben*, Jahres-Bericht über das Königliche Gymnasium zu Eisleben von Ostern 1886 bis Ostern 1887 . . . (Eisleben, 1887); Félix-Faure Goyau, *Christianisme et culture féminine*, pp. 165–210; Ancelet-Hustache, *Mechtilde de Magdeburg*; Pierre Doyère, "Gertrude d'Helfta (sainte)," DS 6: cols. 331–39; idem, Introd. to Gertrude of Helfta, *Oeuvres spirituelles* 2: *Le Héraut*, SC 139, Sér. mon. 25 (Paris, 1968): 9–98; and the charters in Max Krühne, ed., *Urkundenbuch der Klöster der Grafschaft Mansfeld*, Geschichtsquellen der Provinz Sachsen und angrenzender Gebiete 20 (Halle, 1888), pp. 129–92. Historians are now in agreement that the earlier controversy over whether Helfta was Benedictine or Cistercian is a meaningless question given the nature of thirteenth-century monasticism for women (see J. B. Freed, "Urban Development and the 'Cura monialium' in Thirteenth-Century Germany," *Viator* 3 [1972]: 311–27; and M. Pontenay de Fontette, *Les religieuses à l'âge classique du droit canon* [Paris, 1967], pp. 27–63). Helfta was not incorporated into the Cistercian order nor did it follow Cister-

house was never incorporated into the Cistercian order, although it followed Cistercian practice (with variations) and adopted the grey habit; many of the nuns appear to have felt a special reverence for the greatest twelfth-century Cistercian, Bernard. By the late thirteenth century its confessors were Dominicans, probably from Halle or Magdeburg. The nuns moved to Rodarsdorf (or Rossdorf) in 1234 and in 1258 to Helfta near Eisleben in Saxony, which was given to them by two powerful nobles, brothers of the then abbess Gertrude of Hackeborn.[14] Historians agree that the house was a large and prosperous one, although subject (as we can see from the nuns' own writings) to pillage by the turbulent nobility and pressure (including an interdict in 1295) from powerful local ecclesiastical bodies. The nuns were probably recruited primarily from wealthy, noble families in Thuringia and Saxony; a number were learned. There may have been more than a hundred sisters by the last decades of the thirteenth century, and the house was already large enough in 1262 to send out a group of twelve sisters to the monastery of Hedersleben in the Hartz.[15] It was linked in spiritual confraternity with a number of German houses.[16] Probably under the religious supervision of the bishop of Halberstadt, who celebrated mass for the nuns on the occasion of the convent's move

---

cian practice in every detail but it was very much under the influence of Cistercian spirituality. The earliest charters speak of "Cistercian nuns" and "grey sisters": see Krühne, *Urkundenbuch*, pp. 129–31. Mechtild of Hackeborn and Gertrude speak of their house as part of the order of Benedict: see Gertrude, *Legatus*, bk. 4, chap. 26, *Revelationes Gertrudianae ac Mechtildianae* 1: *Sanctae Gertrudis magnae virginis ordinis sancti Benedicti Legatus divinae pietatis . . .*, ed. the monks of Solesmes [Dom Paquelin] (Paris, 1875) [hereafter *Legatus*]: 353, and below nn. 42 and 162. Gertrude indicates both her enormous respect for Bernard of Clairvaux and the fact that not all the nuns revered him as much as she did: see *Legatus*, bk. 4, chap. 49, pp. 445–48; and below n. 108.

14. Not to be confused with Gertrude the Great (also called Gertrude of Helfta), the subject of my study; see Jacques Hourlier and Albert Schmitt, Introd. to Gertrude of Helfta, *Oeuvres spirituelles* 1: *Les Exercices*, SC 127, Sér. mon. 19 (Paris, 1967): 8, n. 4 [hereafter *Oeuvres* 1: *Exercices*].

15. Krühne, *Urkundenbuch*, p. 133, and Félix-Faure Goyau, *Christianisme et culture féminine*, p. 171.

16. Krühne, *Urkundenbuch*, pp. 129–59 passim.

to Helfta,[17] the house was endowed with land by the archbishop of Magdeburg and protected throughout the century by the counts of Mansfeld and the relatives of Gertrude of Hackeborn. Under the forty-year rule of abbess Gertrude (†1291), the house prospered materially (as we can see from charter evidence) and developed the intense intellectual and spiritual life we find reflected in the Helfta revelations.[18] Books were collected, manuscripts copied and illustrated; the names of several scribes and miniaturists (for example, Sophie and Elisabeth of Mansfeld) have come down to us. Although a *praepositus* (for the late thirteenth century a certain Otto by name) acted for the abbess in material acquisitions, neither the charters nor the revelations suggest that confessors, chaplains, or neighboring abbots or friars were the primary sources of the nuns' intellectual life. Indeed clergy and laity, powerful and humble, seem to have had recourse to the nuns and to have crowded into the part of the church open to them to attend the mass, which was celebrated frequently, in line with abbess Gertrude's intense eucharistic piety.[19] Insofar as we can tell from influences traceable in the surviving literature, the nuns appear to have read the great spiritual writers of the past, especially Augustine, Gregory the Great, Bernard, and Hugh of St. Victor.[20]

There are four works that come from Helfta in the late thirteenth century; three are of complex and in some sense collective

17. Ibid., pp. xvi and 132; see also Pontenay de Fontette, *Les religieuses*, pp. 31–4. Since Helfta was not incorporated into the Cistercian order, it would have remained under the diocesan.

18. The convent was destroyed in 1343 by the bands of Otto of Brunswick in a struggle over the episcopal see of Halberstadt. The nuns then built new Helfta near the walls of Eisleben. It was invaded and partially burned by peasants in 1525; twenty years later, the community ceased to exist.

19. M. Camille Hontoir, "La dévotion au saint Sacrement chez les premiers cisterciens (XIIe–XIIIe siècles)," *Studia eucharistica DCC anni a condito festo Sanctissimi Corporis Christi, 1246–1946* (Antwerp, 1946), pp. 146–47.

20. Theresa A. Halligan, ed., *The Book of Gostlye Grace of Mechtild of Hackeborn*, Pontifical Institute of Medieval Studies, Studies and Texts 46 (Toronto, 1979), p. 35; Félix-Faure Goyau, *Christianisme et culture féminine*, pp. 167–76.

authorship. The earliest, *The Flowing Light of the Godhead*,[21] seems
to have been written in low German by Mechtild of Magdeburg
(† about 1282 or 1297), primarily during her years as a beguine
in Magdeburg, and collected—and rearranged—by a Dominican,
Henry of Halle, about whom nothing else is known. A seventh
book (i.e., section) was composed after she retreated to Helfta in
about 1270 at the advice of her Dominican directors. We have the
work in a Latin translation (which does not contain the seventh
book), perhaps made while Mechtild was at Helfta, and in a high
German version made in the fourteenth century by the secular
priest Henry of Nördlingen, who was the center of an important
mystical group in Basel and helped to spread Mechtild's fame
among his followers.[22] Mechtild of Magdeburg's visions differ
from the other Helfta works: they are written in the vernacular,
compiled by a man (although apparently from segments produced
by Mechtild herself), and composed primarily in a nonmonastic
milieu. Her spirituality—which has affinities with the great German visionaries of the twelfth century, Hildegard of Bingen and
Elisabeth of Schönau—is quite different from that of her younger
contemporaries, Gertrude and Mechtild of Hackeborn, who entered the monastery as children (five and seven years old). Far

21. I have used the (admittedly inadequate) German edition of Gall
Morel, *Offenbarungen der Schwester Mechtild von Magdeburg oder Das
fliessende Licht der Gottheit* (1869; reprint ed., Darmstadt, 1963) [here-
after *Licht*]; the partial English translation by Lucy Menzies, *The Revelations of Mechtild of Magdeburg (1210–1297) or The Flowing Light of
the Godhead* (London, 1953) [hereafter *Light*]; and the Latin version in
Revelationes Gertrudianae ac Mechtildianae, ed. the monks of Solesmes,
2 (Paris, 1877): 435–707. The Latin translation does not give the same
order of chapters as the German and appears to be less close to the
original; see Hans Neumann, "Problemata Mechtildiana," *Zeitschrift für
deutsches Altertum und deutsche Literatur* 82 (1948/50): 143–72, and idem,
"Beiträge zur Textgeschichte des 'Fliessenden Lichts der Gottheit' und
zur Lebensgeschichte Mechtilds von Magdeburg," *Altdeutsche und Altnie-
derländische Mystik*, ed. Kurt Ruh (Darmstadt, 1964), pp. 175–239.
22. Ancelet-Hustache, *Mechtilde de Magdeburg*, pp. 1–56, and H. Neumann, "Problemata," pp. 153–72. On Mechtild, see also Heinz Till-
mann, *Studien zum Dialog bei Mechtild von Magdeburg* (Marburg, 1933),
and James C. Franklin, *Mystical Transformations: The Imagery of Liquids
in the Works of Mechtild von Magdeburg* (Madison, New Jersey, 1978).

more lyrical, erotic and nuptial in her imagery, less pastoral in her concern, Mechtild is more apocalyptic and prophetic, more inclined (in part owing to her experience of persecution during her more than forty years in Magdeburg) to emphasize suffering. But Mechtild was deeply admired at Helfta, and her mysticism clearly influenced the way in which the religious life of the convent developed in the 1280s and 1290s when the compilers of the other volumes of visions were at work.

The second work from Helfta is the revelations of another Mechtild, Mechtild of Hackeborn (†1298 or 1299), sister of the abbess Gertrude of Hackeborn. Known as *The Book of Special Grace*, it was confided in 1291, when Mechtild was more than fifty years old, to two nuns, who wrote it down in Latin.[23] Many scholars have thought that one of these confidantes was Gertrude "the Great" (†1301 or 1302), not to be confused with abbess Gertrude of Hackeborn. Gertrude the Great, also known as Gertrude of Helfta, had received her first vision in 1281 at the age of twenty-five and had discussed her experiences with Mechtild of Hackeborn. Gertrude herself wrote (probably in Latin) a set of rich and complex prayers or meditations, called *exercitia* by her sixteenth-century editor.[24] She also composed in 1289 an account of her own

23. *Revelationes Gertrudianae ac Mechtildianae* 2: *Sanctae Mechtildis virginis ordinis sancti Benedicti Liber specialis gratiae*, ed. the monks of Solesmes (Paris, 1877): 1–422 [hereafter *Lib. spec. grat.*]. There is a French translation with a good introduction by the monks of Solesmes, *La Livre de la grâce spéciale: Revelations de sainte Mechtilde Vierge de l'ordre de saint Benoît* . . . (1878, reprint ed., Tours, 1920). On Mechtild's work and its diffusion, see Phillip Strauch, "Mechtild von Hackeborn," *Allgemeine deutsche Biographie* 21 (Berlin, 1970): 156–58; C. A. J. Armstrong, "The Piety of Cicely, Duchess of York: A Study in Late Medieval Culture," *For Hilaire Belloc: Essays in Honor of His 71st Birthday*, ed. Douglas Woodruff (1942; reprint ed., New York, 1969), pp. 75 and 82; and Halligan, ed., *The Book of Gostlye Grace*.

24. The most recent edition is Gertrude, *Oeuvres* 1: *Exercices*. There is an English translation by a Benedictine nun of Regina Laudis, *The Exercises of Saint Gertrude, Introduction, Commentary, and Translation* (Westminster, Md., 1956). We have no manuscript of the *Exercises* nor any mention of a manuscript in the earliest edition by the Carthusian Johannes Lanspergius in 1536. The title and original language of the work are uncertain. The recent editors argue convincingly for Gertrude as

spiritual life, which appears as the second book of a massive Latin work known as *The Herald of Divine Love* or the *Revelations*.[25] The remainder of the *Herald* is a biography of Gertrude (book 1) written almost certainly by a nun of Helfta and a series of prayers and revelations (books 3–5), some of which appeared to people other than Gertrude and many of which concern members of the convent or its friends. The compiler (or compilers) of books 3–5, perhaps the same as the author of book 1, worked from Gertrude's own writings and oral confidences and from the confidences of others in the circle that surrounded Gertrude.[26]

Both Gertrude and Mechtild of Hackeborn were pressured by their sisters into permitting the books of revelations to be written. The nuns themselves were quick to get a testimonial approving Gertrude's work from Dominican and Franciscan theologians who

---

author and Latin as the original language; the title *exercitia* is probably not authentic. See Hourlier and Schmitt, Introd., *Oeuvres* 1: *Exercices*, pp. 39–44.

25. I have used the edition of Pierre Doyère for books 1–3: Gertrude of Helfta, *Oeuvres spirituelles*, vols. 2 and 3: *Le Héraut*, SC 139 and 143, Sér. mon. 25 and 27 (Paris, 1968) [hereafter *Oeuvres* 2 and 3: *Héraut*]; and the older edition for books 4 and 5: *Legatus*. The prologue tells us that Christ himself gave to the second book the title *Memoriale abundantiae divinae suavitatis* and to the rest the title *Legatus divinae pietatis*. But Latin editions of the sixteenth century adopted the title *Insinuationum divinae pietatis libri V*. Dom Paquelin, in the 1875 edition, called the work *Legatus divinae pietatis*, the title which most editors since have used (see Doyère, Introd., *Oeuvres* 2: *Héraut*: 79–80). On Gertrude, see Doyère, "Gertrude d'Helfta (sainte)," cols. 331–39; idem, Introd., *Oeuvres* 2: *Héraut*; Vagaggini, *Initiation à la liturgie* 2: 190–93 and 206–39; W. Lampen, "De spiritu S. Francisci in operibus S. Gertrudis Magnae," *Archivum Franciscanum historicum* 19 (1926): 733–52; Sister Mary Jeremy, "'Similitudes' in the Writing of St. Gertrude of Helfta," *Mediaeval Studies* 19 (1957): 48–54; P. Doyère, "St. Gertrude et les sens spirituels," *RAM* 36 (1960): 429–46. None of the various collections of prayers attributed to Gertrude and Mechtild is authentic, although some contain authentic excerpts from the nuns' works.

26. Mechtild of Hackeborn's reputation quickly eclipsed Gertrude's in the fourteenth and fifteenth centuries, but in the long course of Catholic history it is Gertrude (because of her contribution to the cult of the sacred heart) who has been most influential and most revered, particularly in the seventeenth and nineteenth centuries.

had known her—a testimonial that became part of the manuscript tradition.[27] The revelations show that the mystics' experiences were discussed in small circles of spiritual friends (although Mechtild kept hers hidden for many years) and that the visions of one nun often confirmed the content of the visions of another or provided support for decisions made or practices adopted by the community. It is thus clear that the works of Mechtild of Hackeborn and Gertrude not only in fact reveal the spiritual orientation of the whole group of Helfta nuns but also were a conscious effort to establish and hand on to a next generation of sisters and to readers outside the cloister a spiritual teaching and a collective reputation. In this the Helfta mystics are like other thirteenth-century women mystics, especially in the Low Countries, who were more likely than their male counterparts to cluster together in a few well-known houses, to belong to spiritual networks, and to become subjects of admiring biographies that propagated a spirituality based in mysticism.[28]

Mechtild of Hackeborn—like the thirteenth-century abbesses of Helfta and most of the other nuns whose names have come down to us—came from the high nobility; Mechtild of Magdeburg and Gertrude, whose origins are unknown to us, probably did not, although their imagery suggests that they were familiar with wealth and with the etiquette of secular courts. None of the three nuns held an official position that involved any spiritual directing or administration. Mechtild of Hackeborn was chantress,[29]

27. See Appendix 1, *Oeuvres* 3: *Héraut*: 349–50; the text is reproduced in *Lib. spec. grat.*, pp. 724–25.

28. For example, the convent of Aywières (where we find Bertha of Marbais, Lutgard of Aywières, Elisabeth of Wans, and Sibylla of Gages), Ramey (which housed at some point in their lives Beatrice of Nazareth, Ida of Nivelles, and Ida of Léau), and Salzinnes in Namur (which housed Juliana and Agnes of Cornillon and Eva of St. Martin). See Michael Goodich, "Contours of Female Piety in Later Medieval Hagiography," *Church History* 50 (1981): 20–32, and Bolton, "*Vitae Matrum*." Clare of Assisi also gathered a circle at San Damiano. Roisin, *Hagiographie*, pp. 87–89 and 234 notes that in the thirteenth century female mystics were more apt than male mystics to be without sources of authority other than Christ's inspiration and that the lives of male saints are more apt to provide models for roles in the ecclesiastical or monastic hierarchy.

29. Preger, *Geschichte der Mystik* 1: 83–86, argues that Mechtild the

and Gertrude second chantress, serving beside her. Yet revelations and the enormous capacity to influence others that flowed from them came not primarily to leaders of the community at Helfta but to these three sisters, who were intellectually gifted but sickly, retiring, and without major administrative responsibilities. In the more than 1200 pages of visions that these four works present, we see that the two Mechtilds and Gertrude served as counselors and spiritual advisers not only to the sisters but also to laity, clergy, and friars who came from outside for advice. By their own account, these nuns were direct channels of God's power; they provided information about what practices Christ wished performed and about the state of souls in the afterlife. Christ himself guaranteed the efficacy of their prayers, particularly for removing souls from purgatory. The basis for their authority and for the utter serenity with which they exercised it lay in their mystical experiences.

The vision literature from Helfta has not been neglected by scholars. But because work on medieval religious movements and on thirteenth-century spirituality has tended to take two distinct directions, each unfertilized by the other, the Helfta visions and meditations, like other thirteenth-century mystical writing, have not been probed for what they might teach us about female piety and self-awareness. Scholarship on medieval religion has either focused on the theological content of texts without attempting to relate their doctrine to the authors' specific historical contexts or has studied the social and institutional background of those who peopled the movements without attention to the precise words in which their concerns were expressed.

Scholars who have focused on texts have noted the steady increase in spiritual writing by women in the thirteenth century and have frequently tried to assimilate this female piety to later, more highly schematized mystical theologies (e.g., those of St. Teresa or John of the Cross).[30] Insofar as they attribute any particular

---

chantress and Mechtild the sister of the abbess are two people but this opinion appears to be mistaken. See Halligan, Introd., *Gostlye Grace*, p. 36, n. 15.

30. See, for example, Evelyn Underhill, *Mysticism: A Study in the Nature and Development of Man's Spiritual Consciousness* (1911; reprint ed., Cleveland, 1970); and Conrad Pepler, *English Religious Heritage* (St. Louis, 1938).

characteristics to female mysticism, these scholars assume some kind of inherent affinity between women and affective spirituality and/or between women and female imagery.[31] Research on thirteenth-century mystical literature has often focused also on the origins in this period of later Catholic devotional practices.[32] Thus, accounts of the nuns of Helfta in the standard dictionaries of spirituality and textbooks of mysticism tend to concentrate on their role in the growth of the cult of the sacred heart and to mention as characteristics of their mysticism bridal imagery, devotion to Mary and to Christ's humanity, emotionalism, individualism, and an emphasis on liturgy. Such descriptions of mystical writing tend to leave the specific characteristics of female piety unexplained; nor do they even describe the full range of the piety itself, led as they frequently are by desire to trace the roots of later theologies or devotions or by unexamined assumptions about the nature of female religiosity.

Scholars who have emphasized the social context of religious movements have noted the swelling numbers of women attracted to both orthodox and heterodox movements in the twelfth to the fourteenth centuries.[33] Over the past century many explana-

31. See above n. 10.
32. See the works on the cult of the sacred heart cited in n. 12 above.
33. The basic works are still Joseph Greven, *Die Anfänge der Beginen: ein Beitrag zur Geschichte der Volksfrömmigkeit und des Ordenswesens im Hochmittelalter*, Vorreformationsgeschichtliche Forschungen 8 (Münster in Westphalia, 1912), and H. Grundmann, *Religiöse Bewegungen im Mittelalter* (1935, reprint ed., Hildesheim, 1961). R. W. Southern, *Western Society and the Church in the Middle Ages* (Harmondsworth, Middlesex, England, 1970), pp. 318–31, reproduces their interpretation (the "religious surplus" interpretation, which places the blame on male resistance to *cura monialium*) in a short, readable summary. In agreement also is the account in Brenda M. Bolton, *"Mulieres sanctae,"* Studies in Church History 10: *Sanctity and Secularity: The Church and the World*, ed. D. Baker (1973): 77–95. For earlier interpretations, which stress social and economic causation, see Greven's summary of the literature in *Anfänge*, pp. 1–27, and the often-cited study by Karl Bücher, *Die Frauenfrage im Mittelalter*, 2nd ed. (Tübingen, 1910); a more recent work that continues the older economic interpretation is Dayton Phillips, *The Beguines in Medieval Strasburg* (Stanford, 1941). For modifications in the Greven-Grundmann interpretation, see Freed, "Cura Monialium," pp. 311–27, and Frederick Stein, "The Religious Women of Cologne: 1120–1320" (Ph.D. disserta-

tions for this fact have been proposed. Demographic explanations (i.e., the increasing numbers of unmarried and/or unmarriageable women) show consistent popularity with historians.[34] Social scientists and religionists favor some form of deprivation theory, whether in the hostile formulation of William James, who saw in the Helfta nuns a "puerile" need for reassurance, or in the sympathetic analysis of I. M. Lewis, who sees the ecstatic experiences of women as a response to their social oppression.[35] But if ahistorical

---

tion, Yale, 1977). On nuns, see also Pontenay de Fontette, *Les religieuses*; Richard C. Trexler, "Le célibat à la fin du Moyen Âge: Les religieuses de Florence," *Annales: économies, sociétés, civilisations* 27 (1972): 1329–350; Hunt, "Notes on Benedictine and Cistercian Nuns," *Cistercian Studies* 8 (1973): 157–77; and Jean Verdon, "Les moniales dans la France de l'Ouest au XI᷎ et XII᷎ siècles: Étude d'histoire sociale," *Cahiers de civilisation médiévale* 29 (1976): 251–62.

Recent research suggests that, although the *vita apostolica* as an ideal probably originated with aristocratic clerics and never completely lacked adherents in the countryside, beguines and mendicant third orders and to some extent Cistercian nuns tended to be drawn from the new bourgeoisie or from a lower nobility associated with the towns. Thus women who joined the new types of religious life available in the thirteenth century often came from social groups that were rising and can be shown to have felt anxiety about their new wealth and status. Their ideal—as Grundmann pointed out years ago—was not simply poverty but rather *renunciation* of wealth. Women from the old nobility were apt to join traditional Benedictine houses or become secular canonesses; large dowries were required of entrants into such houses. See Ernst Werner and Martin Erbstösser, *Ideologische Probleme des mittelalterlichen Plebejertums. Die freigeistige Häresie und ihre sozialen Wurzeln* (Berlin, 1960); Eva G. Neumann, *Rheinisches Beginen- und Begardenwesen: Beitrag zur religiösen Bewegung am Rhein*, Mainzer Abhandlungen zur mittleren und neueren Geschichte 4 (Meisenheim am Glan, 1960); Freed, "Cura Monialium;" idem, *The Friars and German Society in the Thirteenth Century* (Cambridge, Mass., 1977); and Stein, "Religious Women of Cologne."
34. For example, David Herlihy comments: "The heretics, and equally the Beguines, offered particular support and solace to one of the most pitiful groups in the medieval world—unmarried and unmarriageable women." "Women in Medieval Society," p. 11, reprinted in *The Social History of Italy*.
35. William James, *Varieties*, p. 275; Lewis, *Ecstatic Religion*, especially pp. 85 and 88–99. See also Ronald A. Knox, *Enthusiasm: A Chapter in the History of Religion* . . . (New York, 1950), p. 20.

analyses of mystical texts tend to omit explanation for the increase of female piety, those scholars who have concentrated on the social context of women's religiosity have tended to explain only the fact of increasing female involvement without paying attention to its specific characteristics.

My purpose in studying the Helfta nuns is to unite the two emphases of earlier scholarship—theological content and historical context. Thus I wish not only to locate the spirituality of Helfta against the background of the nuns' communal experience; I also want to describe their piety more fully than has been done before, looking at religious imagery as well as at doctrine and delineating ideas, particularly the nuns' conceptions of evil and of God, which echo early medieval concerns as well as those that point to the future. The picture that emerges suggests answers to the two broad questions about thirteenth-century Christianity asked above: why were women so prominent in mysticism? and why did their piety have the particular characteristics that it did? Specifically, I want to argue five points about the religiosity of the nuns of Helfta. First, the mystical union these women achieved, which was sometimes expressed in visions of themselves as priests, enabled them to serve as counselors, mediators, and channels to the sacraments—roles which the thirteenth-century church in some ways increasingly denied to women and to laity. Second, the eucharistic piety that is so pronounced at Helfta, particularly in the form of the cult of the sacred heart, expressed the same need for direct contact with God and direct authorization to act as mediators to others. Third, although mystical union and reception of the eucharist were in some sense a substitute for clerical status, the spirituality of these women supported rather than undercut the power of the clergy. We can thus understand why the spread of their works was encouraged by their Dominican confessors; although we can also see the attraction that they, as alternatives to authority based on office, held for thirteenth-century clergy and laity who were ambivalent about the clericalization of the church. Fourth, the serenity with which these women exercised authority and guided their sisters was based not only in Christ's authorization of their role but also in a spirituality that saw Christ himself both as just judge of the universe and as an experience of sweet comfort. Fifth, the contrast between the more anxious quality of the writing of Mechtild of Magdeburg, who lived most of her life as a quasi religious or beguine and became one only as a young adult, and the positive sense of self found in Gertrude and Mechtild of Hackeborn who entered the convent as children, suggests that women who grew up in monasteries were less likely to be influenced by the contemporary stereotype of women as morally and intellectually inferior. Such women were more likely to see themselves as functioning with a full range of male and female, governing and comforting roles, paralleling the full range of the operations of God.

The piety of Helfta is a response to developments in the preceding two hundred years. By the 1280s and 1290s, opportunities for women to fill recognized religious roles in society had vastly increased. Yet religious women were more excluded than they had been a hundred years before from exercising clerical authority. The prestige of the clerical role for males—now much more clearly defined as control of the sacraments—had steadily grown. At the same time, religious writings had moved toward emphasizing the individual's likeness to God and the accessibility of that God in the humanness of Christ, without yet losing, as it sometimes did in the fourteenth century, a concomitant awareness of God's authority and power.[36] These basic shifts in mentality and institutions form the background to a poised, self-confident, lyrical female mysticism, which, as we shall see, found in direct authorization by a regal yet approachable God a substitute for clerical status.

In each of the Helfta texts, the conception of the nun's own authority mirrors in subtle ways her conception of the authority of

36. On the twelfth- and thirteenth-century sense of being created in God's image, see R. Javelet, *Image et ressemblance au douzième siècle de saint Anselme à Alain de Lille*, 2 vols. (Paris, 1967), and S. Ozment, "Luther and the Late Middle Ages," *Transition and Revolution*, ed. R. Kingdon (Minneapolis, 1974), pp. 109–29. Placing the emphasis in a different place from Ozment, I would say that we can see Luther, and much of Calvin, and some of Catholic Reformation spirituality as well as an attempt to recover the sense of God's glory that was characteristic of the early Middle Ages—i.e., as a reaction against the emotional piety of the late Middle Ages that made God human and comforting and accessible to those in all walks of life but thereby undercut in some sense man's ability to believe that salvation was done for him by a power infinitely other than himself.

God. But before we can understand the interrelationship of the various aspects of Helfta's piety, it is necessary to consider some specific examples from each of the late thirteenth-century mystics who have left us such voluminous records of ecstasy and devotion.[37]

Gertrude of Helfta: Images of God

To those whose picture of late-thirteenth-century piety derives from Huizinga's emphasis on its overblown emotionalism,[38] the spirituality of Gertrude of Helfta will come as a surprise. In many ways it harks back to earlier spirituality, sounding more like the eleventh-century prayers of Anselm or John of Fécamp than like the Cistercians and Franciscans who immediately preceded it. Not merely a hodge-podge of new and old elements, it can best be characterized as balanced.[39] Its God is judge as well as comforter; to question or circumvent his justice is as unthinkable as to question his love. Its Christ is divine and human. Its imagery is re-

37. I begin with Gertrude, the youngest of the mystics, for two reasons. First, we are most certain of having Gertrude's own words—in her *Exercises* and in book 2 of the *Herald*. Mechtild of Magdeburg's were arranged by her Dominican compiler; Mechtild of Hackeborn's were probably written down by Gertrude herself. Second, at least some of Gertrude's visions are, strictly speaking, the earliest Helfta literature. Mechtild of Magdeburg's revelations were written down much earlier, of course. But most of her mystical writing occurred before she reached Helfta and reflects her life as a beguine. Mechtild of Hackeborn was also in fact experiencing visions and mystical union years before Gertrude's first ecstasy in 1281, but she kept her experiences hidden until 1291. Book 2 of Gertrude's *Herald* (1289) is therefore our earliest account of the inner life of a nun who grew up at Helfta, although it is clear that Mechtild of Magdeburg's visions had begun to provide a spiritual center for the convent before Gertrude's or Mechtild of Hackeborn's were known and that both of the older women helped to shape Gertrude's piety. I begin by treating the three women separately because earlier scholars have done so, and I want it to be possible for readers to compare my conclusions with theirs.
38. Johan Huizinga, *Waning of the Middle Ages* (1921; English trans., London, 1924).
39. My characterization of Gertrude's piety as a combination of early and late medieval elements is not original. See Jacques Hourlier, "Humanité du Christ: Le 13ᵉ siècle," DS 7.1: col. 1061; and Hourlier and

gal and erotic and often taken from nature, but there is little of the Cistercian/Franciscan concentration on the details of Christ's earthly life. Its devotion requires both works (including vicarious worship) and affective response. Entirely at peace in the monastic role, Gertrude sees that role as including at its heart service of others by prayer, teaching, and advising—a definition that twelfth-century monks found attractive but disturbing. But not for her the new concern with apostolic poverty; to Gertrude the old monastic virtue of obedience is still central, and disobedience the gravest sin. Qualified neither by her gender nor by any official position in the monastery, Gertrude nevertheless felt almost no hesitation about her teaching and advising, and she was a tough rather than a tender counselor with her sisters. Her authority came from Christ, both in particular visions and in her entire mystical life. Despite the fact that her influence in the monastery came from her own inner gifts—despite the even more telling fact that her visions sometimes enabled her to bypass crucial structures or rituals of the church or assign to her an "inappropriate" priestly role—the basic impact of her spirituality is to enhance the importance of the eucharist and confession and thus of the clergy who are necessary for their operation.

Gertrude's God, like the God of the early Middle Ages, is the king of heaven. Her Christ, in images popular in the twelfth century, is a lover, friend, and bridegroom, but he is also ruler and judge. Even with Mary and the saints, power, glory and authority are at least as important as mercy and love. In a prayer, inserted in the *Herald* and typical of the *Exercises* also, we find the full sweep of Gertrude's images:

> You are the overflowing abyss of divinity.
> Oh king of all kings most worthy,
> Supreme emperor,
> Illustrious prince,
> Ruler of infinite sweetness,
> Faithful protector.

Schmitt, Introd., *Oeuvres* 1: *Exercices*, pp. 32–38. On the influence of Bernard on Gertrude, see Anselme Le Bail, "Bernard (saint)," DS 1 (Paris, 1932): col. 1496.

You are the vivifying gem of humanity's nobility.
Craftsman of great skill,
Teacher of infinite patience,
Counselor of great wisdom,
Most kind guardian,
Most faithful friend.

You are the delicate taste of intimate sweetness.
Oh most delicate caresser,
Gentlest passion,
Most ardent lover,
Sweetest spouse,
Most pure pursuer.

You are the burgeoning blossom of natural beauty.
Oh most lovable brother,
Most beautiful youth,
Happiest companion,
Most munificent host,
Most courteous administrator.[40]

Elsewhere she describes Christ as a prince who must imprison his favorite nobleman; she sees him as "grand king and sovereign of all emperors," raising Mary to a throne of glory and giving her "the power of a commander," which she uses to order angels to surround Gertrude's convent and defend it from the devil.[41] Even John the Evangelist, usually seen in the thirteenth century as the special lover of Jesus, is a kind of court recorder; he sits at the foot of Jesus's throne, writing down the good works done or not done by the convent, so that Christ may judge after their deaths.[42] In one of her visions, Gertrude herself brings a multitude of souls to Christ bound to her by a golden chain and he receives her and her

40. *Oeuvres* 3: *Héraut*, bk. 3, chap. 65, pp. 264–66. To take another example almost at random, *Oeuvres* 3: *Héraut*, bk. 3, chaps. 20–21, pp. 110–12, treats Christ as king on a royal throne and Mary as queen; ibid., chaps. 22–23, pp. 114–18, treats Christ as spouse and brother and Gertrude as God's little girl.
41. *Legatus*, bk. 5, chap. 18, p. 567, and bk. 4, chap. 9, p. 327.
42. *Legatus*, bk. 4, chap. 16, pp. 350–54. See also ibid., chap. 11, p. 332, on the two sides of Benedict's sceptre. In *Oeuvres* 2: *Héraut*, bk. 2, chap. 16, p. 294, the Virgin is both tender and severe.

captives "as a king would receive a beloved prince who brings all his adversaries captive to his feet to make peace and be enslaved to his pleasure."[43]

Unlike the God of fourteenth-century mystics (Julian of Norwich or Eckhart, for example), the God of these visions is tough. He punishes and damns. Although Gertrude worries occasionally about souls in hell and much about souls in purgatory, she accepts God's disposition of these matters without question. Indeed she is afraid of appearing to rebel against his justice if she intercedes for someone suffering hideously in purgatory.[44] When she kneels to atone for the negligence of the damned (which is not, it is important to note, a prayer for change in their status but an effort to make reparation to God for the damage they do), Christ appears and says: "It is mine to condemn with you, Father, because you made me judge; I have assigned them to eternal torment by the just judgment of my equitable truth."[45] When a fellow nun prays to God asking why Gertrude is never afraid of his anger, he replies: "If I never appear angry to her, it is because she judges that all I do is very just and very good, nor is she troubled by my deeds."[46]

Even where we find Gertrude using the idea of God our mother, which among twelfth-century Cistercians became a statement that God's justice and authority are tempered by love and comfort, the metaphor takes a harsher twist. Sometimes to Gertrude both "mother" and "father" express the loving and consol-

43. *Legatus*, bk. 4, chap. 35, p. 403. In *Oeuvres* 2: *Héraut*, bk. 1, chap. 12, p. 186, Christ praises Gertrude's willingness to criticize hypocrites when someone prays to him to moderate Gertrude's zeal; Christ himself draws the parallel to his own words during his earthly ministry. In ibid., bk. 2, chap. 8, pp. 264–66, she describes union with God as the raising of her baseness to participate in his majesty.

44. *Legatus*, bk. 5, chap. 16, pp. 563–64.

45. *Legatus*, bk. 4, chap. 24, p. 375; see also ibid., bk. 5, chap. 13, p. 559 for the stress on God's justice.

46. *Oeuvres* 2: *Héraut*, bk. 1, chap. 16, p. 216. And see *Oeuvres* 3: *Héraut*, bk. 3, chap. 9, pp. 40–42, where Gertrude says she dares not pray for the damned and will not pray especially for her relatives and friends; Christ assures her that he can save even sinners in a state of damnation; cf. *Lib. spec. grat.*, bk. 1, Prologue, pp. 5–7, and bk. 5, chap. 30, pp. 363–69.

ing aspects of God's operation;[47] but frequently God as mother means, in addition, discipline and testing. A mother sometimes uses frightening masks to alarm a child who has strayed too far from her arms or, for its own good, denies a child something it wants.[48]

The balance of justice and love, distance and intimacy, in Gertrude's view of God is paralleled by her insistence on the divinity as well as the humanity of Christ. The *Herald* includes one long meditation on the crucifixion and many references to blood and wounds.[49] There are several visions in which Gertrude takes the infant Jesus to her breast, although none dwells on the details of the nativity.[50] Christ frequently appears as a handsome young

47. *Legatus*, bk. 5, chap. 8, p. 546: God is a mother who covers with her robe the child too young for clothes; here mother is consoling; there is no mention of father. *Legatus*, bk. 5, chap. 26, p. 583: here the mother (God) protects her son during a storm at sea, and this is seen as an analogy to God's paternal affection. *Legatus*, bk. 4, chap. 5, p. 314: here God is a mother who teaches her daughter to work by guiding her hand; there is no pairing here of maternal and paternal and the mother is characterized as wise, but earlier in the passage God is seen as a schoolmaster with a pupil. There are also tender passages about resting on Jesus's breast and drinking from his side that may have overtones of nursing: see *Oeuvres 3: Héraut*, bk. 3, chap. 4, p. 24. Ibid., chap. 63, pp. 250–52: Christ is a tender mother kissing the child. *Oeuvres 2: Héraut*, bk. 2, chap. 18, p. 300: Christ is a tender father loving his children. There are feminine images for some of God's tender attributes in *Oeuvres 1: Exercises*, number 7, pp. 258–306 passim.

48. *Oeuvres 3: Héraut*, bk. 3, chap. 30, pp. 160–62: the mother (Christ) understands, embraces *and tests* the soul (by promising and denying what it wants). This passage is followed by descriptions of Christ as a good teacher explaining letters to a young pupil and as a king with his favorite courtier or courtesan. Ibid., chap. 42, p. 196: a mother (Christ) must sometimes deny a child certain ornaments because she knows which ones suit her most. Ibid., chap. 63, p. 250: Christ is a mother who frightens the child back into her arms with horrible masks. Ibid., chap. 71, pp. 288–90: Christ is a loving mother who knows better than the child where she should sit.

49. *Legatus*, bk. 4, chap. 5, pp. 346–50, especially p. 348: Christ appears to Gertrude at terce, scourged and crucified.

50. *Oeuvres 2: Héraut*, bk. 2, chap. 6, pp. 256–58; ibid., chap. 16, pp. 290–96 passim.

man and is loved and sought as a bridegroom.[51] The point of Christ's humanity in these visions is not, however, as it often is to Cistercians and Franciscans, that Christ had an actual, human, historical life that we can imitate, nor that that life moves us to effusions of tears and love. The point of Christ's humanity is that Christ *is* what we are: our humanity is in him and in him it is joined with divinity.[52] We encounter this humanity-divinity of Christ in the eucharist and in mystical union, each of which is an analogue for the other. It is symbolized especially in the sacred heart. We take refuge in it, drown in it, eat or drink it. It is a lake, a stream, an ocean, a chalice, a cave in the rocks, a nest.[53] The humanity of Christ means that the work of salvation is already accomplished; we need only to unite with (eat or drown in) a union of divine and human that already is. Gertrude addresses Christ in the *Exercises*:

> Now, O my beloved, in this triumphant love in which you sit at the right hand of the Father, keep me for yourself, written upon your hands and feet and upon your sweetest heart, that you may never forget for all eternity my soul, which you have bought so dearly. . . .[54]

In comparison to many thirteenth- and fourteenth-century mystics, Gertrude places little emphasis on suffering. Her *Exercises*, although they contain a section of penitential prayers, are permeated by a remarkable sense of God's glory and triumph, expressed not only in regal and nuptial imagery but also in lyrical

51. See, for example, *Oeuvres* 3: *Héraut*, bk. 3, chap. 15, p. 65. For examples of her erotic imagery, see *Oeuvres* 1: *Exercices*, number 5 passim, pp. 156–98.

52. We can see that the nuns who recorded her visions felt it important to make this theological point because they explicitly glossed visions of Christ as revealing both humanity and divinity. See *Oeuvres* 2: *Héraut*, bk. 1, chap. 14, p. 202. For other examples of this emphasis (coupled with a trinitarian emphasis) see *Oeuvres* 3: *Héraut*, bk. 3, chap. 18, pp. 82–86 passim.

53. See *Oeuvres* 3: *Héraut*, bk. 3 passim; and *Oeuvres* 1: *Exercices*, number 6 passim, pp. 199–256, especially p. 232. See also the works on the cult of the sacred heart cited in n. 12 above.

54. *Oeuvres* 1: *Exercices*, number 6, p. 214.

evocations of the beauty of creation. Almost never in the *Herald* is suffering primarily expiation (i.e., a sacrifice offered to assuage God's wrath or remove the fetters imposed by Satan). Although there are suggestions of affective identification with Christ's sufferings and suggestions that pain and illness are cleansing,[55] Gertrude's stress on heart and wounds is not primarily a stress on sacrifice; it is a stress on the blood that Christ feeds us in our most intimate union with him or a stress on the union itself.[56] In one of the *Herald*'s many visions of a soul drinking from Christ's heart through the wound in his side, Jesus says: "The union that you see between her heart and my side indicates that she is thus at every moment able to drink from the flood of my divinity."[57]

Gertrude's devotion to Christ's wounds and especially to his heart, which culminated in her receiving (inwardly, not visibly, we are told) the stigmata and the "wound of love," has certain precedents among twelfth-century Cistercians, especially Bernard, whom we know she read. But among the early Cistercians the heart—which is already the sweetness John tasted on Jesus' breast and the cleft in the rocks where the dove hides—is primarily God's love. Although feeding imagery and images of refuge surround it, it is not explicitly a symbol of the eucharist. Its function is to call forth our love in response to what Christ suffered and did for us. Between early writers (like William of St. Thierry and Bernard) and the Helfta of the 1290s, however, lies the thirteenth-century swell of eucharistic devotion, found especially in convents and beguinages in the area of Liège and in groups with ties to the Cistercian order. In figures like Baldwin of Ford (†1190), Gerard of

---

55. See especially *Oeuvres* 3: *Héraut*, bk. 3, chap. 41, p. 192, where Gertrude comments that meditations on the Passion have more value than other meditations for "just as it is not possible for anyone to handle flour without getting it on the hands," so it is not possible to meditate on the Passion without "deriving great fruit thereby." Throughout bk. 2 of the *Herald* there is a sense that Gertrude's own illnesses are cleansing.

56. On this point, see Doyère, "Gertrude d'Helfta (sainte)," col. 335; R. Daeschler, "Abnégation: tradition médiévale," DS 1: cols. 84–85; J. de Guibert, "Ascèse," DS 1: col. 978; Rayez, "Humanité du Christ," cols. 1068–76.

57. *Oeuvres* 2: *Héraut*, bk. 1, chap. 16, pp. 206–18, especially p. 208. And see also *Legatus*, bk. 4, chap. 4, and bk. 5, chap. 4, pp. 304–6 and 527.

Liège (†1254), Lutgard of Aywières (†1246), and Juliana of Cornillon (†1258), we find not only pressure toward more and more frequent communion but also increasing emphasis on the eucharist as the central moment of both union and affective response.[58] By Gertrude's day it seems to have been possible for the nuns of Helfta to receive the sacrament more frequently than every Sunday,[59] and Gertrude's devotion to the sacred heart is an explicitly eucharistic devotion. The mass is the most frequent occasion for her visions; it lies at the center of her piety.[60] Indeed the eucharist, the most intimate point of union, takes on in Gertrude's visions some of her sense of God; Christ's body and blood, in the hands of the priest, are awesome, powerful, and royal as well as comforting and accessible.[61]

Gertrude's sense of God, Christ, and eucharist is intimately related to her understanding of evil and sin—perhaps the aspect of her thought in which she is most clearly poised between early and late medieval spirituality. Like early medieval thinkers, she has a sense of sin as willed disobedience, of God as judge and as justice, of a universe whose basic structure includes damnation as well as salvation. Like later medieval thinkers, she concentrates on progress Godward rather than on sin as obstacle to that progress; her Christ is subjective experience as well as objective mediation; she focuses more on incarnation than on propitiation and atonement.

There is in Gertrude's writing no reference to a cosmic war between good and evil, little attention to the devil, and little sense of an ontological rift in the universe created by the fall and knit up

58. Roisin, *Hagiographie*, pp. 106–22; McDonnell, *Beguines and Beghards*, pp. 299–330; Greven, *Anfänge*, p. 69; Herbert Grundmann, "Zur Geschichte der Beginen im 13. Jahrhundert," *Archiv für Kulturgeschichte* 21 (1931): 314; E. G. Neumann, *Beginen- und Begardenwesen*, p. 91; Bolton, "*Vitae Matrum*," p. 267, all of whom mention the special attraction of the eucharist to women. See also Hontoir, "La dévotion," and C. N. L. Brooke, "Religious Sentiment and Church Design in the Later Middle Ages," *Bulletin of the John Rylands Library* 50 (Autumn, 1967): 13–33.

59. Hontoir, "La dévotion," pp. 146–47.

60. See the works on the cult of the sacred heart cited in n. 12 above; and Le Bail, "Bernard (saint)," col. 1496.

61. *Oeuvres 3: Héraut*, bk. 3, chap. 18, pp. 92–94; and see Rayez, "Humanité du Christ," cols. 1088–90.

in some way by the resurrection.[62] She stresses the goodness of matter.[63] Her own asceticism is harsh, but what must be removed is preference for self or disobedience and not the fact of physicality.[64] The visions are dominated by a sense, not of humankind bowed down by corruption or passively waiting for a champion, but rather of individuals on the move toward God—a motion made possible because God's image is already within each soul and humanity is already wedded to divinity.[65] Nevertheless there is no suggestion in Gertrude that sin is merely a psychological deprivation, an experience of lacking God; sin is objective, consciously chosen by evil wills and removed only by self-discipline and the grace of Christ. The paradigmatic sin is not lust or avarice (as it is to some later medieval writers) but disobedience, a deliberate turning away from the laws of the universe and the company of God.[66]

In the Godward progress of the human soul, works, particularly prayers, are seen as very important. They can be performed for one soul by another.[67] Indeed many of the visions in the *Herald* are devoted to explaining this: repeatedly Christ appears and tells Gertrude exactly how many souls are released from exactly how much purgatory by exactly which devotions of the community.[68]

62. On this point see Doyère, Introd., *Oeuvres* 2: *Hèraut*, p. 47.

63. The natural world and human physiology are the source of glorious images for Gertrude; for examples, see *Oeuvres* 3: *Héraut*, bk. 3, chap. 28, pp. 128–30. (For a catalogue of her images, see Jeremy, "Similitudes," pp. 48–54.) Gertrude points out that the eucharist redeems even that most horrible of natural objects, blood: *Oeuvres* 3: *Héraut*, bk. 3, chap. 30, p. 142.

64. *Oeuvres* 2: *Héraut*, bk. 2 passim, pp. 226–352; for a particularly intense passage see ibid., chap. 3, pp. 236–38.

65. Gertrude makes much use of the idea of our creation in God's image. She writes that divinity is imprinted in our hearts like a seal in wax: ibid., chap. 7, p. 260. And in a vision where Christ reassures her about her desire to introduce a special devotion, Gertrude is renewed with the words "God created man in his own image": *Legatus*, bk. 4, chap. 14, pp. 344–45.

66. Ibid., bk. 5, chap. 22, pp. 577–78: the terrible sin of disobedience to a superior. Note that in chap. 16, p. 564, Gertrude worries that interceding for a suffering soul would be disobedient to God's justice.

67. See, for example, *Oeuvres* 3: *Héraut*, bk. 3, chap. 9, pp. 34–42.

68. See *Legatus*, bk. 5 passim, pp. 496–613, and nn. 76 and 107 below.

There is, of course, nothing new in this: vicarious worship was one of the central functions of monasticism hundreds of years before the thirteenth century. And in these visions, prayers retain their objective efficacy despite passages in which routinized prayer is criticized, the external trappings of religion de-emphasized, and intention stressed.[69] Here again we find a combination of early and later medieval elements: ascetic discipline and the traditional monastic work of performing rituals are put in the service less of maintaining right order in the cosmos than of the busy progress of individual souls toward personal union with Christ. But this progress occurs in a highly structured universe in which there is an objective place for the damned and the tarnished as well as for the perfected.

To some extent Gertrude's concentration on disobedience is a reflection of the fact that her entire life (from age five on) was spent in a monastery, just as her images of God's power and glory and lavish wealth are in part a reflection of the lifestyle and values of the nobility from which the nuns of Helfta came. Gertrude had a strong sense of community,[70] and obedience is, of course, the primary insurer of community as well as the traditional monastic virtue. But one cannot help feeling in reading Gertrude that her stress on obedience is also part of an acceptance of divinity as an awesome order and justice beyond our comprehension. Gertrude expresses little of Julian of Norwich's need for a God of comfort and mercy beyond justice, a mother God who promises that "all shall be very, very well."[71]

Thus the God at the core of this theology is a combination of the early medieval God, who orders and judges the universe, and the later medieval God, with whom union is, so to speak, "in

69. See ibid., chap. 13, p. 560, where Gertrude says that the efficacy of prayers will last as long as the fervor with which they are said. In ibid., bk. 4, chap. 52, pp. 462–63, Christ tells Gertrude, who prays for a relic of the true cross, that the most valuable relics he left on earth were his words in Scripture. Gertrude is also, of course, worried about those who neglect the prescribed schedule of worship: ibid., chap. 4, pp. 470–71.

70. See, for example, ibid., chaps. 1–3, pp. 286–302.

71. See D. Hanshell, "A Crux in the Interpretation of Dame Julian," *Downside Review* 92 (1974): 77–91.

progress." If we are to understand Helfta's conception of what Christ effects through Gertrude, we must see it as based in this vision of what God is. The nuns' understanding of divine authority is reflected in their conception of Gertrude's role—both her role as nun and her role as spiritual adviser.

Gertrude's Role
and Sense of Self

In the *Herald of Divine Love*, Gertrude sees herself, and is seen by those who describe her, as a servant of others. The service includes: the intellectual work of translating Scripture and the Fathers, making *florilegia*, and composing prayers;[72] counseling and offering spiritual advice, which is explicitly called "the cure of souls" and "preaching";[73] being to others an example of virtue and a warning against vice;[74] praying for others in their individual spiritual journeys and for the practical needs of the convent;[75] serving as a channel of information directly from Christ about the fate of others in the afterlife and about which practices and devotions of the sisters he particularly values;[76] and serving herself as a mediator, a direct channel of grace and forgiveness that supplements and sometimes replaces the sacraments and the priesthood.[77]

Gertrude's own visions show no ambivalence whatsoever about the monastic life. There is no suggestion of desire for any other vocation; there is no evidence of struggle to renounce the world. The famous conversion she experienced at twenty-five was simply the beginning of her mystical life; the chapter that suggests that it was a conversion from love of profane letters may be a gloss by the

---

72. *Oeuvres* 2: *Héraut*, bk. 1, chap. 7, p. 152, and *Legatus*, bk. 4, chap. 23, pp. 373–74, for examples of Gertrude providing devotions for her community.

73. For example, *Oeuvres* 2: *Héraut*, bk. 1, chap. 7, p. 152–58, and ibid., chap. 12, pp. 184–88, especially p. 186.

74. Ibid., chap. 11, p. 174: Gertrude calls herself a scarecrow to frighten away the crows of temptation.

75. Many examples in *Legatus*, bks. 4 and 5, pp. 285–613.

76. Many examples, especially in ibid., bk. 5, pp. 497–613.

77. See below, pp. 204–7.

sixteenth-century editor.[78] Nor does Gertrude, unlike a number of twelfth-century figures, have any difficulty seeing service as the heart of the monastic vocation. She needs no theory to reconcile service and teaching, on the one hand, with ascetic discipline and contemplation, on the other; for to her the two are not in conflict. She is certain that her own extraordinary spiritual experiences are secondary to service of others. In discussing types of virginity she appears to prefer John the Evangelist's to John the Baptist's, because John the Evangelist did not withdraw from society, including (she says explicitly) women, who needed religious instruction and care.[79] In a vision at matins, God gives her the choice of having Christ serve her or serving Christ—that is, of being totally absorbed in rapture "so that she can explain for the utility of her neighbors only a very little of the truth she gains there" or conversing with God "familiarly, face to face, as a friend to a dear friend" and receiving the grace of instructing others. "Since she sought not her own things but the Lord Jesus', she chose rather to minister to his praise with the labor [of instructing her neighbor] than to repose in and taste the sweetness of the Lord to satisfy her own delight." And God appeared well pleased with her choice.[80] In a number of visions Gertrude and other nuns are explicitly enjoined to preach and serve. Once, upon praying for a certain sister, Gertrude received a rule of life for her: she should make a nest in Christ's side to suck his honey and should imitate Jesus especially in his nights of prayer, his preaching in villages by word and example, and his service of neighbor.[81] The absolute certainty about the priority of service that we find in Gertrude's own words and visions is underlined all the more by the fact that the compilers

78. Doyère, Introd., *Oeuvres* 2: *Héraut*, p. 32. On Gertrude's ease with the monastic role see Doyère, "Gertrude d'Helfta (sainte)," col. 336.

79. *Legatus*, bk. 4, chap. 4, pp. 307–10.

80. Ibid., chap. 2, p. 290. See also chap. 13, p. 339, on the importance of instructing others.

81. *Oeuvres* 3: *Héraut*, bk. 3, chap. 73, p. 302. This is not, of course, an injunction to preach literally: "Secundo, in hoc quod, sicut Dominus praedicando circuibat civitates et castella, sic ipse studeat non solum verbo, sed etiam in omni opere, gestu, vel quocumque motu corporis sui, proximum per bonum aedificare exemplum."

who interpret her experiences sometimes feel that they must give an explanation or justification of her combination of contemplation and service.[82] Gertrude herself, however, feels no need for such justification.

Gertrude held no official counseling or administrative position at Helfta. She stressed obedience to superiors as a virtue and was herself obedient. But she was absolutely convinced of her responsibility for others. Moreover, the nuns who compiled her visions saw her and Mechtild of Hackeborn, two sisters .with no functional qualifications, as the major spiritual advisers at Helfta, although they sometimes also referred to the abbess as a spiritual mother. In the account of Mechtild of Hackeborn's death in book 5, for example, Mechtild is said to gain Mary's crown because of her zeal for her spiritual children.[83] Thus Gertrude's own sense of the importance of service, and Helfta's recognition of it, do not derive from office. In part this emphasis on service is based on what appears to be a new conception of the monastic role—a conception that includes those elements of teaching and concern for souls that friars saw as components of their self-definition but in general monks did not. In part, however, the sisters' sense of Gertrude as pastor and mediator, and Gertrude's own self-conception, come from their belief that Christ communicated directly with her in ecstasy and visions.

The revelations in the *Herald of Divine Love* clearly justify Gertrude's ministering to others by showing that Christ commands it and, indeed, accomplishes it through her. In her biography (book 1) we are told that Gertrude sought out Mechtild, asking Mechtild to pray about Gertrude's visions, and Mechtild received a revelation of Gertrude joined to Christ.[84] In her autobiography we are told that Gertrude did not want to write, "thinking it would be difficult or even impossible to find the . . . words capable of expressing without scandal to the human understanding all that Christ had said," but Christ himself insisted.[85] Those who recorded the

82. *Oeuvres* 2: *Héraut*, bk. 1, chap. 16, p. 214.
83. *Legatus*, bk. 5, chap. 4, pp. 529–30. On abbess Gertrude, see ibid., chap. 1, pp. 497–517.
84. *Oeuvres* 2: *Héraut*, bk. 1, chap. 16, pp. 206–14.
85. Ibid., bk. 2, chap. 10, p. 274.

revelations also received direct confirmation from Christ of the value of their task.[86] In book 5 we find a long discussion of Gertrude being punished by God at Mechtild's deathbed for not revealing a vision, which is here treated as a kind of preaching.

> [Gertrude] knew all these things in spirit but wanted to keep them hidden in her heart lest it be suspected that she had received such revelations. But this was contrary to the Lord, whose glory it is to discover the truth [Tob. 12:11] and who commanded *that which you hear in the ear, preach ye upon the housetops* [Matt. 10:27].[87]

As might be expected, Gertrude's visions are presented to the reader in different ways in different portions of the *Herald*.[88] Sometimes the miraculous element is stressed, especially in the last books, where many of the revelations provide special information to the living about the state of the dead. But often the miraculous is downplayed by the compilers, who point out—sounding a traditional hagiographical theme—that the true test of sanctity is not miracles but love of neighbor.[89] The point is made explicitly in book 5 where Gertrude prays to Christ that a sister M. (Mechtild of Magdeburg) be given the power to work miracles after death and Christ replies that signs and wonders are unnecessary, for there are those who have tasted the kingdom and can talk about

86. *Legatus*, bk. 5, chaps. 33 and 34, pp. 609–11.

87. Ibid., chap. 4, pp. 528–29.

88. It seems pointless to worry, as many scholars have done, about exactly what the visions were; see F. Vernet, "Gertrude la Grande," DTC 6 (Paris, 1924): col. 1334.

89. *Oeuvres* 2: *Héraut*, bk. 1, chap. 13, p. 194: "Sed cum Beatus Gregorius testetur [*Dialogi*, bk. 1, chap. 12, PL 77: col. 213B–C] proborum sanctitatis non esse signa facere, sed proximum sicut seipsum diligere, de quo superius satis dictum est, sufficiant etiam haec dicta ad comprobandum quod vere istam Dominus elegerit ad inhabitandum, cum non defuerint emissiones fulgurantium miraculorum ut vel sic obstruatur os loquentium iniqua contra gratuitam Dei dignationem et etiam ut erigatur confidentia humilium, qui sperant sibi omnia prodesse quae cuilibet electorum, Deo donante, gaudent inesse." In ibid., bk. 2, chap. 20, p. 318, Gertrude accuses herself of having sought "signs, in the manner of the Jews." The few miracles that are attributed to Gertrude in bk. 1, chap. 13, pp. 190–96, are unspectacular: she finds an object lost in straw; her prayers for rain, or sun, or a thaw are answered.

it.[90] Mystical union is thus sometimes seen as a substitute for miracles—another, more inner, and higher way of making direct contact with the divine. Indeed Gertrude's visions are sometimes explicitly depicted by the compilers as simply elaborate metaphors for the inexpressible,[91] and there are passages that report Gertrude's own doubts about visions or suggest that reason must test inspiration.[92] The authors themselves state that Gertrude needed visions less and less as she progressed in the spiritual life and that particularly those visions that authenticate her role as spiritual leader are included largely for the sake of the reader.[93] Nonetheless, whether seen with the eyes of the body or the eyes of the mind, Gertrude's visions and the inexpressible union that lay behind them authenticated her reaching out to her neighbors. In the view of those who recorded them, these visions brought God's words directly to Gertrude's followers.[94]

In Helfta then we have a monastery staffed from the upper ranks of society, drawing on long-established Benedictine and Cis-

90. *Legatus*, bk. 5, chap. 7, p. 543.

91. Ibid., bk. 4, chap. 12, p. 334: here Gertrude reflects on why Christ teaches by visions and learns that Christ uses sensible things to express what surpasses the senses. In ibid., chap. 55, p. 471, the compilers say that Gertrude could not explain what she beheld in the mirror of divinity and so had to resort to images and comparisons. In chap. 26, p. 382, they quote Bernard to the effect that things come from God without images.

92. On one occasion Gertrude doubted "as is the human fashion" whether a vision came from God or from her imagination and Christ reassured her: *Legatus*, bk. 4, chap. 2, p. 297. In another vision Christ urged her to let her reason convince her of the validity of his words if his inspiration failed to persuade her: ibid., chap. 52, p. 462. In chap. 14, pp. 343–44, Gertrude worries that if she introduces devotions on the authority of visions alone, then the community will have no protection against false sisters who claim similar inspiration.

93. *Oeuvres* 2: *Héraut*, Prologue, p. 114.

94. Some of the visions are written up in such a way as to make complex doctrinal points or convey intellectual insights: for example, much of *Oeuvres* 3: *Héraut*, bk. 3, is designed to show the proper attitude toward the eucharist; in *Oeuvres* 2: *Héraut*, bk. 2, chap. 15, p. 288, Christ teaches Gertrude that the brain is the seat of the soul. In the portions written by the compilers—but not those by Gertrude herself—explicit morals are often drawn. In Gertrude's own book 2, we see a life

tercian traditions, supplied with and presumably to some extent scrutinized by Dominican confessors, and working to propagate devotion to the eucharist—a devotion that in itself helped to combat both of the major forms of heresy threatening the church: dualism and antisacerdotalism.[95] Yet, at the heart of Gertrude's spirituality are direct communications from God that bypass all ordinary channels of grace in the church. To what extent were the nuns aware of this conflict? Did the threat to the institutional church posed in the visions actually surface?

The revelations reported in the *Herald of Divine Love* do not in any sense undermine the importance of the sacraments. They not only occur primarily in the context of the liturgy, they also clearly reinforce its centrality. Their message is usually that prayer (especially the prayer of monastic communities) is effective and that Christ is met in the mass. Sometimes specific devotions or monastic regulations are introduced or supported in visions. In one, Christ tells Gertrude of a new position for praying;[96] in another, sisters who move toward God holding the hands of others (i.e., trusting in others' prayers for them) reach first the splendors of light from his heart.[97] And in book 4 we are told that Gertrude knew Christ was present in person at the monastic chapter meet-

dominated less by paramystical experiences than by an ultimately inexpressible union. (See, for example, ibid., chap. 1, pp. 226–32.) It is not surprising that the visions should show different faces, sometimes didactic, sometimes miraculous, sometimes merely metaphorical. In general, thirteenth-century saints' lives directed toward the laity contain more miraculous elements, whereas those written for the cloistered stress inner spiritual development and mystical union; see Roisin, *Hagiographie*.

95. Administration of the eucharist was the preserve of the clergy, and the required preparation for communion—i.e., confession—was that point at which the priest exercised most control over the morals of the ordinary believer. Moreover, the doctrine of God's presence in bread and wine reaffirmed the goodness of matter and the Incarnation. See McDonnell, *Beguines and Beghards*, p. 4 and passim.

96. *Legatus*, bk. 4, chap. 16, p. 353.

97. Ibid., chap. 1, p. 286. We should also note the individualism of this spirituality: we are assured that each sister who reposed on Christ's breast enjoyed him so fully that he might have been given to her alone (ibid., p. 287). See also ibid., chaps. 6, 13, 35 and 58, pp. 315–19, 339–41, 403 and 477, for a stress on shared prayers.

ing because it had been revealed to Mechtild—a remark that shows us how the experiences of the visionaries reinforced not only monastic practice but also each other.[98]

There is in these visions some criticism of reliance on externals and occasionally a tension between mystical union and the eucharist, almost a suggestion that union is preferable or that abstention from communion is rewarded by an even more direct and pleasant feeding.[99] In book 3, chapter 10, we are told that on the day of St. Matthias, Gertrude resolved "for several reasons" to abstain from holy communion, but during the mass she concentrated her attention on God, and the Lord presented himself to her "with a friendship of so great tenderness that a friend can have no greater for a friend."[100] On another occasion, when Gertrude was preparing for confession, Christ appeared and said:

> Why are you troubled, my love? For as often as you desire it of me I, the sovereign priest and true pontiff, will enter you and will renew in your soul all the seven sacraments in one operation more efficaciously than any other priest or pontiff can do by seven separate acts. For I baptize you in my precious blood; I confirm you in the power of my victory; I take you for my spouse in the pledge of my love; I consecrate you in the perfection of my most holy life; I absolve you from all chain of sin in the piety of my mercy; I feed you with myself in the superfluity of my charity, and satisfy you with delights; and I penetrate your entire being like ointment by the sweetness of my spirit . . . that you may grow in sanctity and aptitude for eternal life.[101]

Occasionally there is the suggestion that Gertrude may at Christ's explicit authorization and for love of him ignore the monastic rule.[102]

---

98. Ibid., chap. 2, p. 293; see Mechtild, *Lib. spec. grat.*, bk. 1, chap. 5, pp. 14–15.

99. See *Oeuvres* 2: *Héraut*, bk. 1, chap. 10, p. 168, where, while emphasizing the importance of the eucharist and of preparation for it, she stresses even more the providence of God: "Ego quidem ex corde desidero saluberrimis sacramentis praemuniri, sed tamen voluntas et praeordinatio Domini mei videtur esse optima et saluberrima praeparatio . . ."

100. *Oeuvres* 3: *Héraut*, bk. 3, chap. 10, p. 42.

101. Ibid., chap. 60, pp. 244–46.

102. Ibid., chap. 44, p. 200.

But there are in the *Herald* no passages that suggest that the mystic should regularly ignore either the details of monastic life or the sacraments. Christ tells Gertrude:

> I, the Creator and Framer of the universe, take infinitely more pleasure in loving souls than in labors and corporeal exercises performed without love and pure intention. . . . But if any person is clearly not called by my spirit to the quiet of contemplation and yet neglects the observance of his order in an effort to attain contemplation, he is like one who places himself at the table with the king when his assigned task is to serve before the table.[103]

And in another vision:

> . . . it is equally the same to me whether you repose in spiritual things or sweat in exterior labors, provided you refer your will in free intention to me. For if I only took pleasure in spiritual exercises I should have so reformed human nature after the fall that it would no longer have needed food or clothing or the other things for which human industry exerts itself. . . .[104]

Many of the visions are intended to underline the fact that Christ himself is the priest at mass and the eucharist indeed his body. Visions that substitute for the eucharist usually occur when Gertrude is prevented by illness (not by choice) from attending church.[105] And in one of the homiest tales in book 5, Gertrude sees a nun suffering in purgatory because she often pretended to be asleep when the confessor came to hear confessions.[106]

Gertrude's piety is thus profoundly centered in the sacraments. Yet, in a number of visions, she herself serves as a direct channel of grace to the sisters, acting with authority reserved to the priesthood and explicitly identified as priestly. At Christ's command, she binds and looses the souls of others.

Sometimes visions that appear to give Gertrude extraordinary powers to remove souls from purgatory actually make a very traditional theological point: the power of prayer and of the eucha-

---

103. Ibid.
104. Ibid., chap. 68, p. 274.
105. For example, *Legatus*, bk. 4, chap. 59, pp. 482–93; *Oeuvres* 3: *Héraut*, bk. 3, chap. 38, pp. 180–84.
106. *Legatus*, bk. 5, chap. 9, p. 547.

rist. In one revelation (which comes characteristically at mass), Christ says to Gertrude: "In the reception of the sacrament, I will draw you into me in such a way that you will draw with you all those to whom the odor of your desires spreads. . . ." Gertrude, thinking that he will remove from purgatory as many souls as she can make crumbs of eucharistic bread in her mouth, tries to divide the bread as much as possible. And Christ says: "So that you may understand that my pity is greater than all my works and because the depths of my pity can be exhausted by no one, behold through the price of this living sacrament I shall protect many more than your prayer can imagine."[107] Sometimes visions in which Gertrude has almost priestly authority are toned down in the interpretation with which the authors gloss them. When (in a vision which accompanies the gospel story of the loaves and fishes) Christ gives Gertrude bread to distribute to the church, the authors say simply: "By the loaves . . . she understood that whenever anyone performs any good work for the praise of God, however small, . . . the Son of God receives it as if it were a fruit of his sweetest humanity, . . . blesses it and distributes it multiplied to the whole church, for the perfecting of eternal salvation."[108] But sometimes we actually see Gertrude functioning as a kind of priest. She is herself a mediator, and imagery of binding and loosing (chains tying other souls to her, etc.) is used to describe her relationship to her sisters.

On one occasion Christ forgave Gertrude's sins and told her he would accept for their remission in the future any act offered in memory of his mercy; Gertrude then asked the same benefit for her friends, and Christ granted that the sisters might "share with you in the satisfaction I have imposed on you." Gertrude advised the sisters of this. On that particular day, the sisters were unable to approach the sacrament of penance because their confessor was

107. *Oeuvres* 3: *Héraut*, bk. 3, chap. 18, pp. 102–4.
108. *Legatus*, bk. 4, chap. 21, pp. 361–64. Cf. ibid., chap. 49, pp. 445–48, where Gertrude at mass prays for those of whom she has charge and especially for those who are devoted to Bernard. Those devoted to Bernard are said to acquire his merits. Thus the message of the story appears to be the efficacy of Bernard's and Gertrude's intercession, but the explicit moral drawn by the compilers is that we should act with good intentions.

absent. But the next day, some of the sisters went to communion, trusting in Gertrude's assurance that they were forgiven and should communicate. About all this, Gertrude then had another vision in which Christ clothed with white robes of innocence those who took her advice but also clothed (with rose-colored robes) those who "in humility and compunction" abstained because they could not confess and those who communicated without confessing and without asking Gertrude's advice, "confident in the goodness and grace of God." Those who followed Gertrude's words, however, sat closest to Christ "that it may be known that it is not by accident, but on purpose, that the first place is kept for them; because from all eternity it has been ordained that those who have followed your [Gertrude's] advice shall receive extraordinary favors from me [Christ] today." [109] In the plethora of penitential theories available in the thirteenth century, some theologians argued that genuine contrition was enough, but most saw absolution by a priest as necessary—either because it bestowed grace or because it announced the forgiveness already guaranteed by genuine sorrow. [110] Gertrude's revelation does not undercut the necessity of confession or support any heterodox theorizing, but it does allow her to serve on this occasion in the way in which a priest would: she provides that announcement of forgiveness without which it is dangerous to approach the eucharist.

In an even more explicit vision, given on the Sunday after Easter, Christ breathed upon Gertrude and said: "*Receive the Holy Spirit. Whosesoever sins you remit shall be remitted*" (John 20:22–23). And Gertrude said: "How can this be since the power of binding and loosing belongs only to priests?" Christ said to her: "Those whom you, discerning through my spirit, judge to be not guilty will surely be accounted innocent before me, and those whose case you judge to be guilty, will appear such to me, for I will speak through your mouth." Gertrude said: "Oh God of mercy, since your dignity has assured me of this gift so many times, what profit is it to give it to me again?" Christ replied (and the analogy is surely no accident): "When anyone is consecrated into the diaco-

---

109. Ibid., chap. 7, pp. 319–21.
110. See Thomas Tentler, *Sin and Confession on the Eve of the Reformation* (Princeton, 1977).

nate and then into the priesthood, far from losing his office as deacon he just acquires a greater honor from the priesthood; so when I give a gift several times to a soul, truly it is established in it more firmly by repetition and its blessedness is thereby increased." [111]

Such assurances are frequent in the *Herald*. We find a series of them in book 1, chapter 14:

> For when many people consulted her about their scruples, and especially to know if they should abstain from communion for such or such a reason, she counseled those whom she thought to be in a correct intention to approach the Lord's sacrament confidently and even constrained them to do so. . . . [One day she began to fear her presumption and Christ said:] "Do not fear; be consoled, comforted and reassured; for I, the Lord God your lover, who created and chose you by love to dwell within and fill with delights, indubitably give a sure response through you to all who devoutly and humbly seek me, and this you may hold as a promise from me that never will I let anyone whom I judge unworthy of the vivifying sacrament of my body and blood ask this of you. . . ."

> And another time when she prayed for someone . . . the Lord replied: "Whatever anyone hopes to be able to obtain through you, so much without a doubt she will receive from me. Moreover whatever you promise to someone in my name, I will certainly supply. . . ."

> After several days, remembering this promise of the Lord without forgetting her own unworthiness, she asked how it was possible . . . and the Lord replied: "Is not the faith of the universal church that promise once made to Peter: *Whatever you bind on earth will be bound in heaven* [Matt. 16:19], and firmly she believes this to be carried out by all ecclesiastical ministers. Therefore why do you not equally believe because of this that I can and will perfect that which, moved by love, I promise to you by my divine mouth?" And touching her tongue he said, "Behold, I give my words into your mouth. . . ." [112]

Both Gertrude and those who record her visions clearly see her

111. *Legatus*, bk. 4, chap. 32, pp. 394–95.
112. *Oeuvres* 2: *Héraut*, bk. 1, chap. 14, pp. 196–98.

powers as analogous to those of the priest and make no apology for the similarity.

The cumulative impact of Gertrude's visions is not to undermine the structures and rituals of monasticism or the church but rather to project women into one of those structures, the pastoral and mediating role, which is otherwise denied to them. That the basis for Gertrude's "clerical role" is not the traditional one (office) but rather a direct commissioning by Christ leads not to anxiety and defensiveness but to firmness and serenity. Christ himself praises Gertrude's zeal in castigating hypocrites and draws an analogy to his own thundering words during his earthly ministry.[113]

By the late thirteenth century, canonists and theologians had spoken again and again on the ineligibility of women for priesthood and university education—for preaching and teaching.[114] Gertrude was surely aware of the prohibition. Moreover, her writings make clear her awareness of her subordination, as a nun, to superiors and confessor.[115] Vainglory, anger, and hypocrisy are the sins she fears most in herself.[116] She envies priests their daily contact with the sacrament.[117] And yet I have found only one reference in which she refers to "weak women."[118] Her worries about being revered or about calling attention to herself are remarkably infre-

113. See above n. 43.
114. V. L. Bullough, "Medieval Medical and Scientific Views of Women," *Viator* 4 (1973): 487–93; K. E. Børresen, *Subordination et equivalence* (Oslo, 1968); E. McLaughlin, "Equality of Souls, Inequality of Sexes: Women in Medieval Theology," *Religion and Sexism*, ed. R. Ruether, (New York, 1974), pp. 213–66; and M.-T. d'Alverny, "Comment les théologiens . . . voient la femme?" *Cahiers de civilisation médiévale* 20 (1977): 105–29. And see above pp. 135–36.
115. For Gertrude's obedience to her spiritual mother, see *Legatus*, bk. 4, chap. 13, p. 338. See also n. 66 above.
116. *Oeuvres* 2: *Héraut*, bk. 2, chap. 23, p. 346.
117. *Oeuvres* 3: *Héraut*, bk. 3, chap. 36, p. 176. Christ assures her that priests gain nothing by mechanical contact with Christ's body or routinized repetition of the office: they who perform the eucharist worthily will shine with great glory, but delight and joy in Christ last longer than any appearance of glory.
118. Ibid., chap. 15, p. 64. In chap. 23, p. 116, the angel of God presents her as a baby to God the Father and says, "Lord, God, Father, bless your little daughter."

quent.[119] She identifies with female saints or Old Testament figures who taught or were characterized by wisdom; she also identifies with male saints.[120] Unlike many female mystics (for example Elisabeth of Schönau in the twelfth century and Julian of Norwich in the fourteenth) who mention female incapacity, although they dismiss it as unimportant, Gertrude never even raises the issue of her own gender.[121] The *Herald* shows her as not only a wise but also a stern counselor and leader. She is severe with those she advises and instructs, and Christ in several revelations supports this severity.[122] The kind of authority her compilers attribute to her—an authority she herself accepts with ease and confidence—is analogous to the kind of authority her theology ascribes to God.

Gertrude clearly has maternal visions. She cradles the baby Jesus at her breast and has revelations in which all the sisters share in this mothering.[123] And she connects such motherhood with care and service of others. But motherhood to her is stern as well as comforting. In one vision, in which Christ has to remind her how a mother behaves with a child because she cannot remember having seen it, mothers are said to issue commands and to test children (by offering them a choice between two things and then giving them neither) as well as to understand when no one else does.[124] Moreover, Benedict appears to Gertrude offering both

119. *Oeuvres* 2: *Héraut*, bk. 1, chap. 15, pp. 204–6, and ibid., bk. 2, chap. 10, pp. 27?–76.
120. Especially St. Catherine and Esther; Bernard, Augustine, Francis, and Dominic are also important to her. See ibid., p. 204; *Oeuvres* 3: *Héraut*, bk. 3, chap. 81, p. 332; *Legatus*, bk. 4, chaps. 49–50, pp. 445–55; and especially ibid., chaps. 56–58, pp. 474–80.
121. See n. 199 below and above, chapter 4, n. 87.
122. *Oeuvres* 2: *Héraut*, bk. 1, chap. 12, pp. 184–88, and ibid., chap. 14, p. 200; see also *Oeuvres* 3: *Héraut*, bk. 3, chap. 18, p. 92.
123. *Oeuvres* 2: *Héraut*, bk. 2, chap. 16, pp. 290–300; ibid., chap. 6, pp. 256–58; *Legatus*, bk. 4, chap. 3, pp. 300–1.
124. *Oeuvres* 3: *Héraut*, bk. 3, chap. 30, pp. 160–62. The passage is a fascinating bit of information about Gertrude's own life: "Dominus respondit: 'Sicut mater consolatur filios suos, et ego, consolabor te.' Et adjecit Dominus: 'Num vidisti aliquam matrem blandientem filio suo?' Ad quod cum illa reticeret, non recordans, Dominus proposuit illi quod pene ante dimidium annum viderat matrem quamdam blandientem parvulo suo, et specialiter trium commonefecit eam, quae tunc videndo non adverterat. Primo quod mater saepius osculum a parvulo postulavit;

happiness and condemnation; the picture of abbess Gertrude in the *Herald* emphasizes her possession of Aaron's staff and the tables of the law as well as of the manna of tenderness.[125] When the nuns of Helfta describe rule they see it as both forceful and compassionate. Thus the image, found in the *Herald*, of leaders as the mothers of souls is not merely a description of nurturing but a summation of a wide range of counseling and teaching activities.

Although writing in what might, broadly speaking, be characterized as a Cistercian tradition, Gertrude and those who record her spirituality differ from many earlier Cistercian usages. Whereas male Cistercian writers tend to romanticize motherhood, to worry about authority, and to feel uncertain about combining teaching with contemplation, Gertrude sees the monastic role as having service of others at its very heart. She exercises a serene and stern authority, despite her lack of qualification to do so either by gender or by position. She sees mystical union as more delightful than priesthood and as permitting a kind of "apostolate."[126] She sees the motherhood of God and Christ and Mary as a testing of the soul. Gertrude and her compilers see her authority, irrefutably grounded in Christ's commands, as part of a universe whose ultimate governor is also stern and just.

Mechtild of Hackeborn: Images of God

Like her younger friend Gertrude the Great, who entered Helfta at age five, Mechtild of Hackeborn was a child when she entered the convent in 1248. At age seven she accompanied her mother on

ad quod parvulus propter teneritudinem membrorum surgere est conatus. . . Secundo, quod mater tentavit voluntatem parvuli, dicens: 'Vis hoc et vis illud,' et neutrum perfecit. . . Tertio, quod omnium praesentium nullus intellexit loquelam pueri nondum verba formare valentis, excepta sola genitrice."

125. See above n. 42 and *Legatus*, bk. 5, chap. 1, pp. 502–3.

126. See n. 117 above. There are cases of Cistercian nuns, like Cistercian monks, wishing to avoid abbatial responsibility: for example, Lutgard of St. Trond and Aywières prayed to the Virgin to make her unable to learn French and thereby discourage her election (McDonnell, *Beguines and Beghards*, p. 383).

a visit to the monastery (still at Rodarsdorf) to see her older sister Gertrude, who would later become abbess; crying, she begged to stay. But she waited until 1291, when she was gravely ill and her sister was dead, to reveal not only to friends in the monastery but also to the monastery's supervisors and to those outside the visions of Christ that dominated her inner life.[127] Two nuns received these confidences and wrote them down. Scholars have usually assumed that one author was Gertrude the Great herself, and certainly there are in the *Book of Special Grace* characterizations and visions of Mechtild on her deathbed and after that are, in the *Herald*, reported as Gertrude's visions and descriptions.[128]

Mechtild's *Book of Special Grace* presents the same basic spirituality that we find in Gertrude's *Herald* and *Exercises*—the same sense of the universe, of self and of God, with the same theological emphasis on God's glory and on the centrality of the eucharist. We find in the very first vision of the book many of the central Helfta themes: God's sovereignty and accessibility; Christ as mediator who incorporates us into himself and restores his resemblance in our "self," which is created in his image; the eucharist as the occasion for this union or incorporation, symbolized especially by the heart of Jesus; the visionary herself as mediator to others. In this vision Mechtild sees herself covered with ashes before a God girded with justice and Christ shining on his throne; the ash disappears, and Mechtild, shining now with Christ's merits, rests on Jesus's breast in all security, accepting God's invitation to offer him praise. Christ places his hands on hers to give her the "work and works of his holy humanity" and she is entirely "incorporated in Christ and liquified in divine love" and "receives the imprint of resemblance like a seal in wax." Then in the hour of communion as Mechtild is receiving "her beloved" she hears the words "I in you and you in me" and Christ gives his heart in the form of a cup marvelously chiseled and says: "By my heart you will praise me always; go, offer to all the saints the drink of life from my heart that they may be happily inebriated with it."[129]

127. See nn. 13 and 23 above; and *Lib. spec. grat.*, bk. 1, Prologue, pp. 5–7, and bk. 5, chap. 30, pp. 363–69.
128. *Legatus*, bk. 5, chap. 4, pp. 523–36.
129. *Lib. spec. grat.*, bk. 1, chap. 1, pp. 7–10.

Mechtild's role at Helfta was fundamentally the same as Gertrude's: she provided some intellectual leadership through the composition of prayers; she served as spiritual adviser and comforter to the nuns and to many from the outside world, both friars and laity; she was a "bridge," a "door," a mediator, whose prayers were effective at removing sin and its punishment, and she was also a channel of information from God, including occasionally prophecies of future events. In a typical, fairly brief description, we are told that she once suffered for a month from a headache and at the beginning lost all sense of God's consolation. But when consolation came, she remained from prime to none "with her eyes closed like death, absorbed in the joy of the Lord."

> And during this the Lord revealed to her his marvelous secrets and she rejoiced in the sweetness of his presence so that she could not hide it, although she had hidden it within her for so many years, and she showed it even to guests and strangers; and because of this many committed to her petitions they sought to bring before God, and she revealed to them, as God revealed to her, the desires of their hearts, and they, rejoicing, gave thanks to God.[130]

There are nonetheless differences of emphasis and tone between the *Herald* and the *Book of Special Grace*. Some of this is simply owing to the greater coherence of the *Special Grace*.[131] But some of the differences appear to reflect two very different personalities living in the same milieu. Since Gertrude was probably one of the authors of Mechtild's visions and Gertrude's visions were for the most part not recorded by her own hand, it is likely that differences in sensitivity and imagery that survive this filtering through the minds and words of others reflect the personalities of the visionaries themselves.[132]

130. Ibid., bk. 2, chap. 26, pp. 168–69.
131. There is one inserted letter of Mechtild's own composition (ibid., bk. 4, chap. 59, pp. 310–15) and some of the visions are clearly closer to her words than others. The purpose of the entire work is didactic: see ibid., bk. 1, Prologue, p. 6, and bk. 2, chap. 43, pp. 192–93, where the authors claim to have chosen to report those visions and instructions that are useful. In bk. 2, chap. 31, p. 177, we are told that the authors omit visions that were interrupted or that Mechtild herself suppressed.
132. For example, Gertrude's conception of mothering in the *Herald*,

Mechtild's visions are much more vivid, poetic, and affective than Gertrude's and, to some tastes therefore, more beautiful.[133] Mechtild shows slightly more interest in the details of Christ's earthly life and a somewhat greater emphasis on God as comforter. She has a keener sense of emotional identification with Christ's suffering and of the theological significance of the crucifixion. Her personal asceticism appears (at least in this account) to have been somewhat harsher.[134] She seems to have been a more tender counselor to others than Gertrude. Her visions are much more consistently a reinforcement of the sacraments and the power of the clergy; there is no suggestion of a substitution of personal mystical experience for the church's ritual. Moreover, there is more sense in the *Special Grace* of the nuns seeking approbation and discipline from outside ecclesiastical authorities and of the recipient's hesitation to reveal her visions. But in the final analysis Mechtild shares

---

both her own and God's, has a strong component of testing and discipline (see above nn. 47 and 48); Mechtild's use of "mother" in the one insertion in the *Special Grace* known to be from her own pen is as a metaphor for tenderness (*Lib. spec. grat.*, bk. 4, chap. 59, p. 311). This use of "mother" as equal to "tender" (which does not exclude a concern for discipline expressed in other images) is found almost consistently throughout the *Lib. Spec. grat.*: bk. 2, chap. 2, p. 137 and chap. 16, pp. 149–50; bk. 3, chap. 9, p. 208; bk. 4, chap. 7, p. 264. Cf. bk. 4, chap. 32, pp. 290–91, where Christ is a father and spouse who is both tender and severe, and bk. 7, chap. 21, pp. 418–19, where Christ is a loving father embracing a tiny child. The one exception is a final vision—a vision of Mechtild after her death that came to one of the authors. See ibid., chap. 19, pp. 414–15: Christ is ". . . sicut matris ad unicum suum, quem eximio affectu semper vult ut in sinu suo sedeat . . . sicut fidelis mater, quae puerum, dum a se discedit et cadit, verberibus corripit, ut per hoc discat quod a se ulterius non recedat. Et sicut mater in hoc delectatur, ut puer amicabilibus sibi blandiatur verbis, ita et multo amplius amabilis Sponsus vester a vobis audire desiderat verba, in tantum ut divini Cordis sui medullam penetrent." In this vision, which cannot, of course, be Mechtild's own words but may be Gertrude's, we find mother God testing and disciplining her children, which is Gertrude's characteristic use of the image.
133. See, for example, ibid., bk. 1, chap. 1–3, pp. 7–44; here we find Christ's heart as cup and pipe, Christ as beautiful young man, priest, king, lamp, stream, baby, ray of light, door, fountain, and cord.
134. See below, n. 152.

Gertrude's sense of God as just, of evil as objective (i.e., a defect that appears in us because of our deliberate rebellion against God and not merely an inner experience of the absence of God's sustenance), of the Incarnation as the fundamental fact in the redemption of all creation, and of the eucharist as the point of union with divinity. She rests as securely in her role as nun, mediator, and counselor; and that role is described as a kind of apostolate. Although she uses the image of the soul as bride to express her lowliness as well as the extraordinary personal favors she receives,[135] she makes no reference to the weakness of women, nor does she underline certain religious activities as female, certain as male.

Mechtild's God is lord, father, judge. He is described as soothing with fatherly affection;[136] he is king and pope.[137] Her Christ, like Gertrude's, reigns. The Virgin is, to her, a queen as well as a comforter and mediator. "Mother of God and of men," "queen of the angels," "joy of the saints," "consolation of the unhappy," "refuge of all sinners," she appears to Mechtild as a "royal mother" on a throne beside Jesus.[138] And when Jesus addresses her, "Stand up, make a place for [Mechtild]," Mary picks up Mechtild's terrified soul and gives it into Jesus' embrace.[139] Even on Good Friday, Mechtild's visions of Jesus (which come during the mass that was in the thirteenth century still celebrated on Good Friday) are not of sacrifice and pain but of Christ in flowers and jewels, Christ in a crown giving shields and bucklers to each of the nuns, Christ as a

135. Ibid., bk. 4, chap. 33, p. 292: Christ is a spouse vastly superior in rank to the young girl he marries; she should fear to make the least mistake in etiquette. But God is also her refuge in all her needs.
136. Ibid., bk. 1, chap. 19, p. 68: "Cui Dominus: 'Ego tecum manebo, quasi pater cum filio, dividendo tecum coelestem haereditatem quam tibe mercatus sum meo pretioso sanguine. . . . Secundo ero tecum quasi amicus cum amico. . . . Tertio tecum ero sicut sponsus cum sponsa . . . Sed si tu infirmaveris, ego sum medicus peritissimus. . . . Quarto, tecum manebo, velut socius cum socio. . ." Ibid., bk. 3, chap. 24, pp. 227–28: Christ inclines toward our misery from his infinite majesty; he is also creator, redeemer, brother, lover, faithful minister, and advocate.
137. Ibid., bk. 1, chap. 31, p. 105: royal imagery for Christ and Mary; chap. 8, pp. 26–27: Christ's feet are the just judge, his heart love and delight; chap. 10, p. 33: God is pope; p. 34: Christ is king of glory.
138. Ibid., bk. 1, chap. 38, p. 122.
139. Ibid., chap. 46, pp. 131–32.

fragrant odor, Christ as a transparent crystal into whom Mechtild runs like pure water.[140]

Like Gertrude, Mechtild stresses Christ's divinity as well as his humanity. She sees in the beats of Christ's heart both divine power (the strong beats) and his example as a man (the weak beats); she tells us that John the Evangelist is loved especially by Christ because his gospel speaks of Christ's divinity.[141] And in a charming passage, which shows that the revelations came in Latin, Mechtild sees a dove on its nest and asks Christ: "What is this egg [*ovum*] on which I meditate?" Christ replies: "Egg is a two-syllable word. The O-syllable symbolizes my majesty and divinity, the *vum* the depths of your baseness. Unite these and rest like a bird on its egg."[142] The eucharist is not primarily a symbol of Christ's physical humanity or suffering; Mechtild's visions are not primarily of the host as bleeding flesh or as an infant. The eucharist is the point at which our humanity meets divinity and is united with it; her visions are primarily of Christ as priest administering his divine self.[143] In book 5, chapter 3, for example, Mechtild sees a departed sister as a beautiful virgin who has to wait to enter glory until someone on earth makes the oblation of the host at mass for her because she has missed communion so often through illness. Then during the offertory, when no one comes to make the offering "for this poor little one," Mechtild sees "the king of glory, the spouse of virtue," approaching God the father and offering "the most holy passion of his humanity with the glory of his excellent divinity," and Mary offering all her gifts and graces and virtues "to augment the glory of the spouse of her son."

> [Then] at the oblation of the host, there appeared in the East a marvelous and ineffable light that signified the glory of divinity into which that blessed soul was ravished, and she received then

140. Ibid., chap. 18, pp. 51–60.
141. Ibid., chaps. 5 and 6, pp. 19 and 22.
142. Ibid., bk. 3, chap. 42, p. 245.
143. For example, ibid., bk. 1, chap. 4, pp. 13–14: Christ, a magnificent king, replaces the priest at mass; he is also the oil that fuels the lamps of the sisters. See also ibid., chap. 27, pp. 95–97. In chap. 5, pp. 14–21, where she does receive Christ at mass as a baby, the point is not Christ's humanity but the deliciousness of his love; he is described as doctor, defender, and consoler.

the society and joy of God . . . and superabundant remuneration more than the human heart can believe or speak or think of.[144]

To Mechtild, as to Gertrude, it is the union of humanity and divinity in Christ that is our salvation. We are saved not because there is a spark of divinity in us (as many different kinds of fourteenth-century mystics held) but because our humanity is incorporated in Christ's, which is joined to divinity.[145] Christ's humanity is the "door" through which we enter.[146] For Mechtild, as for Gertrude, entry is possible because we are created in God's image.[147] But, more explicitly than in Gertrude, Christ's humanity is seen as the redemption of the whole creation. In a stunning vision, which comes characteristically during the eucharist and culminates in Christ covering the priest with his mantle and becoming the host, Mechtild sees the Lord on the altar clothed in a garment made of the hairs of men and the blades of grass and the skins of animals. As she looks in surprise, she sees that "the smallest details of creation are reflected in the Holy Trinity by means of the humanity of Christ, because it is from the same earth that produced them that Christ drew his humanity."[148] In another vision, Mechtild sees Mary and the prophets and patriarchs standing above the apostles and virgins. She is surprised "because [the prophets and patriarchs] had women and goods of the world." But John the Evangelist tells her that they are not further from Christ "because the word is made flesh."[149]

We see in these two visions the particular way in which the piety of Helfta affirmed the goodness of matter. To underline this is not, however, to underestimate the asceticism of the Helfta mystics. The Lord tells Mechtild that those who fall from virginity can

144. Ibid., bk. 5, chap. 3, pp. 320–21.
145. There is one passage in Mechtild where we find a hint (but only a hint) of the kind of antinomianism that is implicit in much fourteenth-century mysticism (see nn. 253 and 297 below). In ibid., bk. 2, chap. 42, p. 190, she writes that the soul lifted into contemplation ought to put into oblivion her own person and even her sins in order to rest in the joy of God.
146. Ibid., bk. 1, chap. 8, pp. 26–27.
147. Ibid., bk. 3, chap. 5, p. 201.
148. Ibid., bk. 4, chap. 3, p. 260.
149. Ibid., chap. 8, p. 265, but cf. n. 150 below.

be purified by confession but that "the delicious intimacies of my divinity" are reserved for virgins.[150] She speaks of the flesh weighing down the soul.[151] And in a vignette more vivid than anything in Gertrude we are told of Mechtild rolling on bits of glass to punish her flesh for the self-indulgence of others.[152] The humanity, the creation, which is caught up in Christ's humanity and thereby joined to divinity, is clearly *other than* divinity; a lifetime of purification is necessary to tame the otherness and prepare for incorporation into Christ. But because it is our humanity that is God's image and caught up into Christ's humanity, our human works are efficacious—for ourselves and others—and the physical world is redeemed.

Despite the prominence of regal imagery in her visions, Mechtild's God is more comforting and tender than Gertrude's, her Christ more loving.[153] Mechtild sees Mary more frequently as mother. Moreover, Mechtild has more interest in Christ's life; her response to Christ and to his mother is more affective; she has a greater sense of Christ's humanity as example.[154] There appears to be a greater emphasis on Christ's suffering for us, which is sometimes (although infrequently) treated as expiation or propitiation.[155] But basically Christ's mediation is the union with God that he offers us. We see this clearly in book 3, chapter 36, where Mechtild, groaning with sadness because illness prevents her from keeping the observances of her order, hears Christ say: "Come to me, that I may refresh in you the ardor of my divine heart." She then understands that Christ's passion saved the world, that his sufferings "contributed to the merits of the just [and] the pardon of sinners," and that the soul that has been refreshed on earth by the heart of Christ, when it enters the sky, "flies straight to God's

150. Ibid., bk. 2, chap. 37, p. 186.
151. Ibid., bk. 3, chap. 21, p. 224; ibid., bk. 5, chap. 11, p. 338.
152. Ibid., bk. 5, chap. 30, pp. 365–66; and see also chap. 30, p. 364: she was so absorbed in Christ that she used her senses little and sometimes (as is told of St. Bernard) she ate rotten eggs without knowing it.
153. See, for example, ibid., bk. 3, chaps. 5 and 9, pp. 201–3 and 207–8, where Christ is lover, tender father, and mother.
154. See, for example, ibid., bk. 1, chaps. 4–12, pp. 13–40.
155. See ibid., bk. 3, chap. 29, p. 233–34; ibid., chap. 36, pp. 240–41; ibid., bk. 4, chap. 5, p. 261.

heart, and, impregnated with divinity like a sweet unguent, is consumed in love." [156]

Mechtild, like Gertrude, has a clear sense that God is just. Therefore damnation and hell are just. Although she is more inclined than Gertrude to pray for the conversion of all sinners, [157] she never prays for the relief of the damned. Sin is, to her, a conscious choosing of self over God. ". . . the treasure of [God's] inexhaustible tenderness . . . never wishes anyone to perish. Only those are excepted who voluntarily choose their own damnation." [158] ". . . God, on the day of profession, takes each religious to his fatherly breast and never rejects him from it unless man, God forbid, rebels against obedience. But whoever withdraws himself from the hand of God will not be able to seize it again until he prostrates himself humbly before God in true penitence and worthy satisfaction." [159] Sin is not simply loneliness or estrangement from God; it is an objective defect, a corruption that must be removed by Christ. Christ is not simply an example of good behavior; he is the bridge or door through which we are able to return whence we chose to leave. A vision of a virgin who carries a stone and knocks on the heart of God is explained thus: ". . . she [the virgin] replied: 'I am divine love and the stone is the sin of Adam; just as steel cannot be broken without blood, so the fault of Adam could not be dissolved without the holy humanity and blood of Jesus Christ.'" [160] Mechtild is more inclined than Gertrude to stress Christ's blood and wounds and the crucifixion, but to her also it is union with a regal God and not sacrifice that is the fundamental fact in salvation. [161]

Mechtild of Hackeborn: Role and Sense of Self

When we turn to consider Mechtild's sense of herself and the picture of her conveyed by her compilers, we find that her concep-

156. Ibid., bk. 3, chap. 36, p. 241.
157. Ibid., bk. 4, chap. 57, p. 308.
158. Ibid., chap. 59, pp. 313–14.
159. Ibid., chap. 18, p. 275.
160. Ibid., bk. 2, chap. 17, p. 151.
161. Ibid., bk. 4, chap. 56, pp. 307–8.

tion of the monastic role is slightly more conventional than Gertrude's. Anxious, as was Gertrude, to stress nuns' service of others, Mechtild sees this service less as instruction, teaching, and preaching, than as prayer and offering an example. In her universe, filled as it is with mediators (Christ, the Virgin, the saints, priests) it is not surprising to find that the special role of monks and nuns is mediation—to pray, and to bind together all other orders and link them to God. In a vision on the feast of St. Bernard, Christ says to Mechtild:

> The order of Benedict stands in the middle of the church, holding up the church like a column on which the whole house rests; for it is in relation not only with the whole church but also with all the other orders. It is tied to its superiors—i.e, the pope and prelates—by the respect and obedience it renders them; it is tied to religious by its teaching and the informing offered by its good life, since all other orders imitate that of Benedict on this point. The good and just find aid and counsel in it; sinners find there, through compassion, correction and the means to confess; souls in purgatory find the aid of holy prayers. Finally it offers hospitality to travelers, sustenance to the poor, renewal to the sick, nourishment to the hungry and thirsty, consolation to the sorrowing, and liberation for the souls of the faithful.[162]

Many of Mechtild's visions and the authors' glosses upon them are guarantees of the efficacy of nuns' prayers. Over and over the message is: the system works. Prayer really does remove sin, protect the vulnerable, hasten the end of suffering in purgatory. When Mechtild saw Christ "like a munificent king, give, through the ministry of the celestial principalities, a royal gift to each one of the congregation," she knew "that this gift affirmed what the Lord had certified to another devout soul on this same feast; because by this pledge of special friendship he promised that a thousand souls would be given to any member of the community to deliver by their prayers from the ties of their sins and to help to enter

---

162. Ibid., bk. 1, chap. 28, p. 97; cf. bk. 4, chap. 8, p. 266. In ibid., bk. 1, chap. 30, pp. 102–4, where she discusses nine steps to heaven and ranks of angels, she alternates contemplating with teaching and consoling.

heaven."[163] Thus, some of Mechtild's sense of her own efficacy is simply the nun's sense of the importance of prayer. But Mechtild is an especially effective mediator. Like Gertrude, she is a channel of grace and information from Christ, and a counselor of remarkable perspicacity, and in these roles her authority comes not from her monastic status but from her mystical life and visions.

Throughout the *Special Grace* we see very clearly the author's belief and the belief of the other nuns that Helfta benefited in a special way from Mechtild's prayers. Mechtild is frequently asked by other sisters to pray for them;[164] there are visions in which Christ frees from sin at her behest a specified number of souls;[165] in times of war Christ's protection of the monastery from rape and pillage is seen to come in response to Mechtild's petitions;[166] after her death her merits remove souls from purgatory.[167] In book 4, chapter 11, the authors write:

> Another time, when we dreaded very much the presence of the king [Adolph of Nassau, who was warring against the son of Albert of Saxony in 1294] who found himself not far from the monastery, she prayed to the Lord who is the king of all kings to protect us with fatherly kindness lest we suffer anything evil from the army of the prince. The Lord replied to her: "You will not see a single soldier of his army." But she thought that even if no one saw them, nonetheless the cloister could be harmed by them. And the Lord said to her: "Not a one will approach your monastery, and I will defend you with tenderness against all these things." And it happened thus; for the Lord protected us with all mercy so that we suffered no evil from them, although many other monasteries suffered great harm.[168]

Moreover, Mechtild's mediation links her with other mediators.

163. Ibid., bk. 1, chap. 31, p. 108; see also ibid., bk. 4, chap. 57, pp. 308–9. The reference in the quoted passage is probably to Gertrude's vision in *Oeuvres* 3: *Héraut*, bk. 3, chap. 9, pp. 34–42.

164. *Lib. spec. grat.*, bk. 4, chaps. 22, 23, 32, 34, 38, 39, and 40, pp. 279–80, 290–92, 293, 296–97, and 298–99.

165. See the passages cited in n. 163 above.

166. Ibid., bk. 4, chaps. 12 and 22, pp. 268 and 279.

167. Ibid., bk. 7, chaps. 1 and 14, pp. 391–92 and 408–9.

168. Ibid., bk. 4, chap. 11, p. 268; see also chap. 13, p. 270.

When the convent, "in a time of pressing necessity," recites the whole psalter to beseech God's protection, the sisters confide this gift to Mechtild and she confides it to her angel, who receives the prayers "in the form of a living lark" and gives them to God.[169] And, on her deathbed, Mechtild, who "had shown herself while she lived, as far as she was able, a benevolent and learned advocate for all," asked that after her death "the mother of mercy show herself the perpetual mediator and advocate for the congregation." The Virgin heard this plea, and, "with remarkable tenderness, spreading her most delicate hands over the hands of the sick one, she received the care of the congregation committed to her as if from these hands."[170] Not the least remarkable thing about this vision is its implication that Mechtild (and not the abbess) was the mother of the cloister.

Not simply a channel of grace from Christ, Mechtild is also a source of information. She communicates Christ's wishes and his guarantees of safety to the sisters. She conveys information about the state of souls in the afterlife and about what virtues are rewarded. (It is not surprising that lay supporters of the monastery of Helfta are seen as richly recompensed in heaven.)[171] Sometimes she actually predicts the future.[172] In a fascinating incident she is requested by the abbess "as if she [the abbess] were commanding," to find out from God the state of the soul of the abbess's deceased father. Mechtild wished to be rid of this order for she never solicited any revelation but rather placed her will in God's, receiving whatever he wished her to have. Then Christ appeared to her and, relieving a potential conflict between the monastic vow of obedience and the necessity to submit to rather than manipulate the will of God, he told her to "accomplish your obedience" and granted her a vision of the abbess's father in the green robe of eternity girded with the belt of the catholic faith.[173]

In Mechtild's visions, more than in Gertrude's, we see friars and laity having recourse to Helfta for information and counsel-

169. Ibid., chap. 22, p. 279.
170. Ibid., bk. 7, chap. 6, p. 397, cf. n. 195 below.
171. Ibid., bk. 5, chap. 10, pp. 334–36. See also Gertrude, *Legatus*, bk. 5, chap. 21, p. 576.
172. *Lib. spec. grat.*, bk. 5, chap. 30, pp. 366–67.
173. Ibid., chap. 15, pp. 342–43.

ing.[174] In the most revealing of the many visions concerning friars, Mechtild sees a certain brother N., "faithful friend and intimate of [Helfta]," eight days after his death, wearing elegant boots. "And these boots symbolized the exhausting journeys of the friars preacher." And he said: "Now I know what you hid from me." Mechtild asked Christ what merit brother N. had acquired by appreciating the gift of God in sister Mechtild [perhaps Mechtild of Magdeburg]. Then she saw a current flowing from the divine heart of brother N. and "she learned that the current runs equally to all those who love in others the gift of God even if they do not receive it in themselves."[175] The suggestion is clear not only that one may participate, through reverencing and love, in the mystical accomplishments of others but also that the friars, more involved in practical affairs, do well to have recourse, as they do in these pages, to women mystics who live in greater isolation from the busyness of the world.

In addition to her role as mediator of grace and conveyor of information, Mechtild was a counselor of great skill and tenderness. We find all these gifts described in book 4, chapter 38, where Mechtild consoles and prays for someone who cannot cease weeping. The sister is so quickly relieved that she asks Christ how this can be and he replies: "From my goodness." Then the authors comment:

> You who read or hear these consolations given by God to men through his lover [Mechtild], I counsel you that you take them as if they were made for you, for God reveals to her that it pleases him much to see you reclaim the favor he accords to another. And many people received from her [Mechtild] spiritual consolations but most often she gave them as instructions or as if she had learned them from another. And let God be blessed, who gave us such a mediator with himself, who shows herself the tender mother of the unfortunate by her continual prayers, her zealous instruction and her consolations.[176]

Throughout book 4 especially, there are incidents in which we see how people, both in the cloister and outside, were drawn to

174. Ibid., bk. 4 passim, pp. 257–316.
175. Ibid., bk. 5, chap. 7, pp. 329–30.
176. Ibid., bk. 4, chap. 39, pp. 296–97.

Mechtild. Her sensitivity to the unspoken needs of suffering souls seems to have been far greater than that of Gertrude or Mechtild of Magdeburg, and the descriptions we are given of her consoling advice provide a glimpse of what bothered nuns and friars in the late thirteenth century. She comforts a sinner who had unsuccessfully sought consolation from friars and clergy;[177] she supports a friar who is chastising his brothers for laxity;[178] she worries lest her assiduousness for a troubled sister go too far, and Christ, to reassure her, appears as a seamstress sewing the sister's garments;[179] Christ, speaking through her, reassures a sister who is afraid of communicating too often;[180] she makes reparation for the negligences of others and comforts those who "fear having made a bad confession without having . . . kept anything back."[181]

The overwhelming impact of Mechtild's visions is to reinforce the monastic practice of her day, the power of the clergy, and the centrality of eucharist and confession in Christian life. There is no hint, as there is in Gertrude, that mystical union might substitute for and surpass communion. Christ says he will give her visions if she is unable to attend mass;[182] perhaps her most magnificent eucharistic vision comes while the community is suffering under interdict.[183] When Christ tells her to communicate without confession he stresses that she must confess later.

> Wanting one day to confess but not having a confessor, she was very sad because she did not dare receive the body of the Lord unconfessed. Then in prayer she began to deplore bitterly her negligences and faults to God the highest priest, and he gave

177. Ibid., chap. 39, p. 298.
178. Ibid., chap. 40, pp. 298–99.
179. Ibid., chap. 49, p. 303.
180. Ibid., bk. 3, chap. 26, pp. 229–30.
181. Ibid., chap. 6, p. 204; see also chap. 18, pp. 219–21.
182. Ibid., chap. 19, p. 221; she asks Christ if one loses something by hearing mass from a distance and Christ replies: "Bonum est ut homo praesens sit, ut verba valeat audire; quia secundum quod Apostolus dicit: *Sermo Dei vivus est et efficax et penetrabilis* [Heb. 4:12]. Verbum enim Dei animam vivificat. . . . Sed cum infirmitate vel obedientia, vel alia rationabili de causa praepeditur, ubicumque tunc homo est, ibi eidem praesens et cum illo sum."
183. Ibid., bk. 1, chap. 27, pp. 95–97.

her assurance of the remission of all sin . . . and she asked: "O sweetest God, what will become of my sins now?" He replied: "If a powerful king is coming to a place for lodging, that house is quickly cleaned so nothing will appear there to offend his eye; but if he is already so close by that it is not possible to throw away all the trash, one hides it in a corner to throw away later; so when you have the sincere will and desire to confess your sins and never repeat them, they are all effaced before me so that I no longer recall them. But afterwards you should retract them through confession. For the will and desire that you have . . . is like a tight cord binding you to me. . . ." But she still hesitated . . . , thinking herself unworthy to come to the imperial banquet with the king of the angels. . . . The Lord said: "Think that every desire that anyone ever has for me is inspired by me in him. . . ." And she knew that this desire that she had to consume the body of Christ was inspired in her by the Holy Spirit. . . .

And when she was thus confirmed she heard a chorus of angels in the sky . . . and she drew near to the meal of the most excellent body and blood of Christ.[184]

Mechtild sees disobedience (to monastic superiors or to clergy or to God) as the paradigmatic sin, explicitly emphasizes frequent communion and tells us that it was abbess Gertrude's policy to do so also,[185] and stresses respect for priests and tells us that they gain merit simply from distributing communion—that is, from handling God.[186]

Yet we also find in Mechtild greater doubts than in Gertrude about the wisdom of revealing her visions both to individual sisters and to those outside.[187] For all the strong sense in the visions of a community bound together and incorporated in Mechtild as a link to God there is also a hesitation about community, about turning to the sisters and sharing confidences with them. Christ warns her to turn to him *rather than* to her companions.[188] Mechtild wor-

184. Ibid., bk. 2, chap. 14, pp. 147–48.
185. Ibid., bk. 5, chap. 2, p. 319.
186. Ibid., bk. 4, chap. 15, pp. 272–73; bk. 5, chap. 2, p. 319, and chap. 10, pp. 334–36, for respect for priests.
187. Ibid., bk. 2, chap. 53, pp. 192–93; bk. 4, chap. 7, pp. 263–64; bk. 5, chaps. 22–24, pp. 53–58, and chap. 31, pp. 369–72.
188. Ibid., bk. 4, chap. 7, pp. 263–64: "Si quis etiam acceptabile mihi munus offerre voluerit, in his tribus se studeat exercere. Primum est, ut

ries when the abbess commands her to seek a revelation.[189] Even within the cloister Mechtild seems to have feared exploitation of her visions, despite (or perhaps because of) her sisters' enthusiastic endorsement of them. And we find hints in the *Special Grace* of both supervision and suspicion from ecclesiastical authorities. References to the prelate of the monastery forbidding Mechtild to make her revelations known are quickly followed by assurances that the authors of the *Special Grace* write with the consent of both abbess and prelate.[190] But the incidents that tell of recourse to Mechtild by friars and laity clearly suggest competition with the local clergy and criticism by the nuns of the friars' worldly involvement.[191] We thus find in Mechtild's book a precarious balance between support of and (totally unintentional) threat to ecclesiastical hierarchy. And in Mechtild's visions, as in Gertrude's, we find that the imagery powerfully and explicitly assimilates the mystic's role to that of the priest.

As the very first vision in the *Special Grace* makes clear, Mechtild's sense of herself as mediator is sometimes expressed by images of feeding others or distributing a chalice to them.[192] She is a bridge, a chain, an incorporation of others in God, just as are Christ, the Virgin, the saints, and priests; she sees nothing odd in visions of the Virgin Mary or of herself as a kind of deacon.[193] She

---

proximo suo fidelis sit in omni sua necessitate. . . . Secundum est, ut homo in omni tribulatione sua ad me solum habeat confugium, nullique molestiam suam conqueratur, sed mihi soli omne gravamen cordis sui cum fiducia pandat: hunc ego in suis necessitatibus numquam derelinquam. Tertium est ut mecum in veritate ambulet. . . ."

189. See above. n. 173.

190. Ibid., bk. 5, chap. 18, p. 347: "Cum Praelatus interdictum fecisset huic ancillae Christi devotae, ne quid de animabus, quod eidem revelaretur, ediceret, quia timebat publicari, et ex hoc gravamen coenobium incurrere, ista compatiens animabus dixit ad Dominum: 'Eia dulcissime consolator et tribulatorum adjutor, quid modo faciemus pro animabus, specialiter cum eleemosynam pro ipsis accepimus, ut citius absolvantur?' Cui Dominus benigne respondit: 'Legite orationem illam quae dicitur *Fons vivus.* . . .'" See also chap. 31, p. 369.

191. See above nn. 176–181.

192. See above, n. 129.

193. Ibid., bk. 1, chap. 27, p. 96.

is explicitly called "preacher" and "apostle" and identified as the "governor" of the monastery along with the abbess.[194]

> She gave teaching with such abundance that such a one has never been seen in the monastery and we fear, alas, will never be seen again. The sisters gathered around her as around a preacher to hear the word of God. She was the refuge and consoler of all and by a singular gift had the ability to make others open to her in trust the secrets of their hearts; how many not only in the monastery but also from outside, religious and seculars, came from afar and were rescued by her from their troubles; and they said that they had discovered such consolation nowhere except with her. She dictated and taught so many prayers that if they were all collected together they would surpass the number of the psalter. . . . Just as the men chosen in olden times, i.e., the apostles, who clung to Christ day and night heard daily his sweet eloquence and enjoyed his presence, so did this devout disciple of Christ enjoy his eloquence, seeing him face to face . . . and, like a disciple and cherished daughter, was instructed by him concerning all things she desired and lacked. . . . She merits a place with [the thrones and principalities] because, like the prince of an army, she with her sister the abbess governed the monastery well and with good order in both interior and exterior things. . . .[195]

Gertrude's God is a tougher counselor than Mechtild's; Gertrude herself seems to have been more the disciplinarian, Mechtild the perceptive consoler of hearts. But the important point is that both women see the Lord of the universe, the Virgin, the saints, priests, *and themselves* as characterized by a very wide range of modes of operation. Mechtild, like any Christian, has a sense of herself as other than God, and the image of the bride seeking the bridegroom or the child the parent expresses this difference from divinity. But she has no sense of teaching and governing activities as inappropriate to herself and little sense of certain characteristics as male and certain as female. Christ and Mary are each regal and

---

194. Ibid., bk. 5, chap. 30, pp. 363–69.
195. Ibid., pp. 366–68. See also bk. 4, chap. 38, p. 297: "Benedictus igitur per omnia Deus, qui talem interventricem apud ipsum nobis contulit, quae orationibus continuis, et sedulis instructionibus aut consolationibus benigna mater exstitit miserorum!"

each tender, each a suppliant to God for mercy, each a ruler of heaven. Mothering is a more tender image to Mechtild than to Gertrude but so is paternity. Fathers feed and console, as do mothers; mothers teach, as do fathers: the full range of such images applies both to God and to self.[196] God is mother, emperor and pope; Mary is mother and queen; Mechtild herself is a prince leading an army, a preacher, a conduit for grace, a parent to her children.[197]

Mechtild and Gertrude use little inverted imagery for themselves and for nuns in general; they do not describe themselves as fools or paupers (although they do see themselves as children). In contrast to twelfth-century Cistercian monks who used much inverted imagery for themselves and included references to weak women as a way of speaking of their abasement and renunciation as monks, these nuns do not refer to the inferiority of women. In contrast to twelfth- and thirteenth-century exegetical convention, they do not use woman as a symbol of flesh, or lust, or of the irrational.[198] In contrast to their female German predecessors, they do not fear clerical ridicule, like Elisabeth of Schönau, or express the sense of woman as matter, man as spirit, that Hildegard espoused while reinterpreting it in a positive vein.[199] Insofar as they

196. Ibid., bk. 2, chap. 2, p. 137: the soul enters the heart of mother Christ; ibid., chap. 16, pp. 149–50: Christ gives the soul love for a mother; bk. 3, chap. 5, p. 202: Christ as tender father; ibid., chap. 9, p. 208: Christ as tender mother; ibid., chap. 24, p. 228: Christ as tender father, brother, and advocate; bk. 4, chap. 7, p. 264: Christ as loving mother; bk. 5, chap. 8, p. 332: the soul as a child weaned from breast of mother Christ. In bk. 7, chap. 22, pp. 420–21, the Virgin says: God took your mother—i.e., the abbess—and commended you to me as mother; now he has taken your consoler—i.e., Mechtild—and he will give himself to you for consolation.
197. On Mechtild, see nn. 194 and 195 above. In ibid., bk. 5, chap. 30, p. 364, she is compared to the Fathers.
198. D'Alverny, "Les théologiens . . . voient la femme."
199. On Hildegard see ibid., pp. 122–24, and above chapter 3, nn. 22 and 26. Hildegard insists that women are weaker than men: Scivias, pt. 2, vision 6, chap. 76, ed. A. Führkötter and A. Carlevaris, CCCM 43, 2 vols. (Turnhout, 1978), 1:290. In a letter to Hildegard, Elisabeth of Schönau complained of disapproval from those in religious orders: letter 45: Elisabeth Magistrae in Schonaugia ad Hildegardem, PL 197: cols. 214–16. In the Liber viarum Dei, Elisabeth defends her visions: "Do not

find power in any female image, it is the loved bride sought by the bridegroom.[200] Moreover, motherhood does not to Gertrude and Mechtild refer to a set of characteristics different from fatherhood.

The visions of the nuns of Helfta projected them into the priestly role from which they were clearly by canon law excluded. Despite an increasing effort in the thirteenth century to curtail clerical activities by women and a clear understanding in theology of women's inferiority in the natural order, these women did not perceive their gender either as a disqualification for service or as an image to express the soul's incapacity or baseness. Their teaching, counseling, and consoling was done with power and serenity. They do not seem to have viewed it as in any way circumscribed or ineffective, or as "male" or "female." Mechtild was seen by her contemporaries as a teacher comparable to the Fathers of religion and as a mother of souls. Because Christ acted through them, the mystics of Helfta functioned with the full range of his operations—royal and parental, judgmental and loving.

---

think these the imaginings of a woman, because they are not, but they are from God. . . ." Elisabeth, *Die Visionen der hl. Elisabeth . . . von Schönau*, ed. F. W. E. Roth, (Brünn, 1884) p. 122.

200. V. Bullough, "Transvestites in the Middle Ages," *American Journal of Sociology* 79 (1974): 1381–94, shows that, whereas female cross-dressing or transvestism is common in medieval legends and is approved of, male cross-dressing is very rare and is condemned; this is, he argues, because masquerading as a woman was a status loss for males. J. Anson, "The Female Transvestite in Early Monasticism," *Viator* 5 (1974): 1–32, gives a more psychological interpretation of legends of female cross-dressing, seeing in them reflections of male fears of erotic impulses. Whichever specific interpretation one prefers, these studies clearly show that for a woman to become a man was seen by medieval religious writers as spiritual growth; for a man to become a woman was a descent to sin or to irrationality (see above chapter 4, nn. 63 and 98). Thus males who wished to use the inverted imagery so popular in Christianity (e.g., 1 Cor. 1:20, Mark 10:31) had available to them the image of woman (who was seen as of lower status or of an inferior type of humanity) as a metaphor for their own sinfulness. Women were in a more complex situation: to use inverted imagery (i.e., call themselves male) was to claim spiritual growth or improved status; to embrace their own femininity might provide a statement of unworthiness but not an image of inversion or renunciation. Because woman was already lower than man she lacked an image of renunciation and an act of renunciation: she

Mechtild of Magdeburg:
Images of God

Scholars have frequently emphasized the similarities between the beguine Mechtild of Magdeburg and the two Helfta nuns, Mechtild of Hackeborn and Gertrude, stressing particularly the hints in Mechtild of Magdeburg that become in the two younger nuns a passionate attachment to the sacred heart of Jesus. But Mechtild of Magdeburg (1207/10–ca. 1282 or 1297) was more than a full generation older than Gertrude the Great, and although the Holy Spirit began to visit her daily when she was twelve, she did not leave her family and friends for the life of a beguine in Magdeburg until she was twenty-three. It was only in about 1270, after much of her mystical writing was done and she was an old woman, that she entered Helfta.[201] Thus Mechtild of Magdeburg, unlike Gertrude and Mechtild of Hackeborn, grew up in the world, for all her intense adolescent experience of being apart from it; she spent her adult life as a quasi religious, a beguine, set off from others by lifestyle but not protected by a rule, long-established traditions, or the physical walls of a convent.[202] Although there is much in her experience of God as accessible, loving, and personal that is similar to the experiences of Gertrude and Mechtild of Hackeborn, we find, when we look at her sense of authority and of herself, differences that appear to reflect in part the different lives of beguines and nuns, in part the different sensibilities of adult converts and child oblates. Mechtild of Magdeburg is far more aware of herself as female and of femaleness as a positive and negative fact and image. She is less secure with God's justice, more worried about hell and sin; Christ's suffering is far more central to

---

could not prove humility or advance spiritually by renouncing a status she did not possess.

It is interesting that Hildegard of Bingen vigorously condemns cross-dressing by *both* sexes: *Scivias*, pt. 2, vision 6, chap. 77, 1:291.

201. See works cited in nn. 21 and 22 above.

202. Some beguines lived alone; many lived in beguine communities. See E. G. Neumann, *Beginen- und Begardenwesen*, p. 122, and Stein, "Religious Women of Cologne," p. 64. It is difficult to tell much about how Mechtild lived from her work. The opening pages of bk. 6 (*Licht*, pp. 171–78) are about cloistered life but are fairly general in tone.

her, and her own need to suffer with him through loneliness, illness, and persecution far more intense; she is more afraid of the implications of her own mysticism and more aware (and afraid) of the dangers of power. These differences are certainly related to her greater involvement in and awareness of the world. But it is impossible to say whether she chose a life of insecurity and persecution because of the kind of young girl she was or came to a more anguished sense of her self and those around her and her God because of her life as a beguine.

The most obvious contrast between Mechtild of Magdeburg and the two Helfta nuns studied above is in imagery. Mechtild of Magdeburg comes far closer to what the textbooks lead us to expect of a thirteenth-century woman mystic. Obviously influenced by vernacular love poetry as well as by some earlier mystical writing, Mechtild produced lyrical love poems to God, filled with erotic and nuptial imagery. The soul is God's bride. Mary, both as queen and as beautiful young maiden, is sometimes mother and mediator, but frequently she is also a symbol for the soul.[203] Bashful, submissive, weak, hesitant, a maiden who finds courting (i.e., asserting herself) difficult,[204] this soul is nonetheless passionately joined with God in a union that transcends awareness of self or sin and is frequently described in images of light and heat.[205] Mechtild's God is also a king and a judge; her heaven, like Gertrude's and Mechtild of Hackeborn's, is a wealthy and lavish court. But far more than to the younger nuns at Helfta, God is a lover and a spouse.[206] And far more than to the younger nuns, Christ is an example of suffering and expiation.

---

203. Mary as mother and nurse of the soul: *Licht*, bk. 1, chap. 22, pp. 12–13. Mary as mediator (her breasts flowing with milk parallel Christ's bleeding wounds): ibid., bk. 2, chap. 3, p. 29. Mary as mediator (goddess and granter of grace): ibid., bk. 3, chap. 1, p. 58. Mary as our soul: ibid., bk. 1, chap. 22, p. 11, and see n. 224 below. For Mechtild's views of Mary, see also Ancelet-Hustache, *Mechtilde de Magdeburg*, pp. 169–96, and Franklin, *Mystical Transformations*, pp. 47–52 and 137–45.

204. *Licht*, bk. 2, chap. 19, p. 39; ibid., bk. 3, chap. 23, p. 88.

205. On the prominence of these images, see Ancelet-Hustache, *Mechtilde de Magdeburg*, pp. 309ff.

206. Ibid.

Like Gertrude and Mechtild of Hackeborn, Mechtild of Magdeburg stresses Christ's humanity and divinity. In a dialogue of the soul with God, the soul asks where it should lay its heart's desire, "withdrawn . . . from the world, . . . myself and all creatures." God replies:

> Thy heart's desire shalt thou lay nowhere
> But in mine own Divine Heart
> And on My human breast.[207]

We are saved by the fact that humanity is joined with divinity in Christ. The fact that Christ was fully human guarantees that sin is not intrinsic to human nature. (Mechtild also tried to guarantee this by a strange theory of a preexistent Mary, to which I shall return below.)[208] But to Mechtild of Magdeburg it is not so much the fact of Christ's humanity as the fact of Christ's suffering that is crucial for us.[209] We must join with Christ, not only as encounter with divinity but also as expiation. Mary, who is our protector and nurturer, is also a symbol of our suffering as well as our searching self; we do and should suffer as she suffered at the foot of the cross.[210] Mechtild's devotion to Christ's sacred heart is not so much a sense of incorporation in God as an identification with Christ's bleeding and pain.[211] Mechtild's work is clearly dominated by the idea that away from (i.e., deprived of the experience of) God we suffer a suffering that is cleansing and expiation; with God we are ravished in delight. Her own mystical experience (of a throbbing alternation of ecstasy and alienation) thus provides the structure of her perceptions and of her universe far more clearly than is true in Mechtild of Hackeborn and Gertrude. This probably reflects in part the fact that the writing we have, however rearranged, is in her own words and not those of her confidantes. In part, however, Mechtild's greater sense of suffering and deprivation—Christ's and

207. *Licht*, bk. 1, chaps. 42 and 43, p. 18, tr. Menzies, *Light*, pp. 19–20.
208. *Licht*, bk. 5, chap. 16, pp. 141–42, and see below, n. 226. On Mechtild's sense of sin and evil, see also Ancelet-Hustache, *Mechtilde de Magdeburg*, pp. 106–255 passim.
209. *Licht*, bk. 1, chaps. 25 and 29–34, pp. 13–16.
210. *Licht*, bk. 1, chap. 22, p. 12.
211. On this, see Ancelet-Hustache, *Mechtilde de Magdeburg*, pp. 344–50.

ours—seems to be related to a more vivid and agonized sense of sin.

Throughout the seven books of the *Flowing Light* there is more stress on penitence and less on praise than in Gertrude's prayers and ecstasies or Mechtild of Hackeborn's visions. There is more sense not only that Christ suffered but also that each soul on earth must suffer—in cleansing, in preparation, in expiation.[212] And the suffering with which each of us should identify is, to Mechtild, less the chastising of the flesh (although she does refer to scourging oneself—a practice she borrowed from the Dominicans, who influenced her deeply)[213] than being alone, persecuted, falsely accused, misunderstood, isolated from spiritual comfort and even from the sacraments.[214] In contrast to Gertrude's serene glorifying of God and acceptance of his decisions, Mechtild appears to feel tenuous, at home only (when she is not in ecstasy) in an acute suffering that mirrors in her psyche and body the fact that she is apart from God. And along with this tenuousness goes an intense fear of sin and a feeling of personal responsibility for sinners.

Mechtild, as many earlier scholars have pointed out, displays an agonized awareness of the corruption of the church of her own day. Her intemperate language in chastising her clerical contemporaries finds no parallel in Gertrude or Mechtild of Hackeborn, nor does her feeling of being threatened, persecuted, and misperceived by the powerful in return for her criticism of them.[215] Yet for all her sense of being the victim of evil, deliberately chosen by evil men, for all her theological statements about sin as freely espoused by Adam, she appears more worried than Gertrude and Mechtild of Hackeborn about a universe in which some remain forever in

212. See, for example, *Licht*, bk. 3, chap. 5, pp. 66–67, and chap. 16, p. 78; bk. 4, chap. 2, pp. 90–95. On Mechtild's asceticism and sense of suffering, see Franklin, *Transformations*, pp. 52–58.

213. *Licht*, bk. 3, chap. 17, p. 79; cf. bk. 2, chap. 1, p. 26, where she argues against extreme asceticism.

214. *Licht*, bk. 3, chap. 5, p. 66: here we see Mechtild's sense that the beguine has chosen the ultimate earthly suffering (and cleansing): the possibility of being cut off even from regular pastoral care and the sacraments.

215. *Licht*, bk. 3, chap. 21, p. 85, and chap. 24, pp. 88–89; bk. 4, chaps. 3 and 4, pp. 97–100; bk. 6, chap. 21, pp. 198–99.

hell. For all her sense of Christ and crucifixion as expiation, she feels a need for a guarantee that humanity in some sense never sinned. Although she does not say so (and she defends herself vigorously against the charge that she taught that we share God's divine nature),[216] it is almost as if she needs to remove sin and punishment for it from her picture of the universe because both are inconceivable to her.

Mechtild of Magdeburg shares with Mechtild of Hackeborn and Gertrude an intense belief in the efficacy of the prayers of religious people; we find in her writings very close parallels to those visions of Mechtild of Hackeborn and Gertrude in which specific numbers of souls are released from sin or purgatory in response to the visionary's intercession.[217] But Mechtild of Magdeburg's sense of responsibility is more agonized than that of her younger contemporaries; she tries to bear all Christians on her shoulders to Christ.[218] And, unlike Mechtild of Hackeborn and Gertrude, she has trouble accepting a dispensation that includes damnation. She volunteers to go to hell if it will bring God praise;[219] she describes souls in hell as suffering from the painful loss of their lover.[220] Both opinions imply that hell is not really rejection of God but simply the farthest point of distance from him— a kind of extreme case of the deprivation we suffer at every moment we are not in ecstasy and therefore in some sense an alienation that might, like other sufferings, be cleansing. She actually asks Christ how he can let souls languish eternally.[221] And, in contrast to Mechtild of Hackeborn and Gertrude, she repeatedly prays for souls in hell and wonders whether alms and prayers might help them.[222]

216. *Licht*, bk. 6, chap. 31, pp. 205–6; cf. bk. 1, chap. 44, p. 22.
217. *Licht*, bk. 3, chap. 15, p. 76–78.
218. *Licht*, bk. 5, chap. 34, p. 166.
219. *Licht*, bk. 1, chap. 5, p. 7.
220. *Licht*, bk. 3, chap. 10, p. 72. Cf. bk. 3, chap. 21, p. 84, where she has a vision of hell and doubts whether a pure soul among the wretched creatures there could bring comfort.
221. *Licht*, bk. 3, chaps. 21–22, pp. 86–87.
222. See n. 220 above, and *Licht*, bk. 3, chap. 10, p. 72, and chap. 21, pp. 85–86; bk. 5, chap. 8, pp. 135–36. On prayers for those in purgatory, see bk. 3, chap. 15, pp. 76–78, and chap. 17, pp. 79–80; bk. 7, chap. 2, pp. 221–22.

We also find clearly articulated in the writing of Mechtild of Magdeburg a sense that sin is something outside human beings, inflicted on them by the devil as a kind of persecution. Occasionally she speaks as if sin were another hardship suffered by the soul, which could itself be offered as sacrifice to God. She thinks that, even after the fall, sin is not a taint intrinsic to humanness.

> Some learned people say that it is human to sin. In all tempta-tions of my sinful body, all feelings of my heart, all understand-ing of my senses and all nobility of my soul, I could find none other but that it is devilish that man sins. . . . More than that, wickedness acquired of our own free will is always more harm-ful to us than all the rest of our weaknesses such as hunger, thirst, heat, frost, pain, sorrow, longing, sleep, weariness. These are all things which Christ too suffered who became true man for and with us. Moreover, if sins were only human then He too had sinned, for He was true man in the flesh. . . .[223]

Going beyond Mechtild of Hackeborn's and Gertrude's sense that we are saved because our sinful humanity is joined in the Incarna-tion to the sinless humanity of Christ and thereby to divinity, she almost seems to hold that there has been throughout time a *de facto* sinless humanity.[224] She writes that Christ was the Son (i.e., ours) from the beginning but was given to us only in Ga-briel's mission; he became one nature with Adam before Adam soiled himself through sin. Therefore, she says, what broke Adam was not of God; God preserved Adam's noble nature; we can still return to God. Lucifer had only one nature; once fallen, he could not return. But God draws us back to him, joins with us; "the divine nature now has bone, flesh, body and soul"; our soul like a humble housewife (and the homey, female metaphor is typical of Mechtild) sits with Christ in heaven. Mechtild is suggesting here that we have two natures, a sinful and a sinless one.[225] And else-where she seems to suggest that this sinless humanity resided in Mary between Adam's fall and the Incarnation, almost as if Mary were a preexistent humanity of Christ as the Logos is a preexistent

223. *Licht*, bk. 5, chap. 16, pp. 141–42; tr. Menzies, *Light*, pp. 136–67.
224. *Licht*, bk. 1, chap. 22, p. 12; cf. bk. 4, chap. 14, pp. 107–9.
225. Ibid.

divinity.[226] Mechtild writes that God made the soul because he did not want to remain alone; the soul commingles in the Trinity, soaring high over all creatures and yet remaining itself. But God was angry when Adam fell; in order to have something to love he chose the Virgin as a bride when his bride the soul (i.e., Adam) died. This view of Mary does not, to Mechtild, imply the Immaculate Conception, nor does it imply that Mary by her nature could not sin. Indeed the Holy Spirit told Mechtild that Mary could sin, that she was created by God "a complete human being in womanly nature."[227] But, Mechtild continues, Mary was held by the Trinity in bonds so that she never wished to move against God; she was "divinely noble," "above all human beings," and therefore she could not sin.[228] And Mechtild thinks that we also can be held so tightly by God that we do not sin.[229]

There is certainly nothing heterodox here in a technical sense. Mechtild holds that hell is "eternal hatred,"[230] that sin is rebellion against God, that we are not one in nature with God. Her views on Adam and the fall have a Thomistic ring, and her idea of a sinless humanity has close parallels with the twelfth-century ideas of image and likeness that so influenced her younger contemporaries and find occasional echoes here.[231] But Mechtild, like the great fourteenth-century recluse and mystic Julian of Norwich, is nonetheless uncomfortable with ideas of sin and damnation in a way Gertrude and Mechtild of Hackeborn are not.[232] She usually writes as if the greatest possible distance from love of God is absence (not rejection) of him; it is as if she cannot imagine anyone who does not yearn for him. And she sometimes seems so afraid of (or uncomprehending of) sin that she implies that there must be a continuous sinless humanity; it is as if humanity must in some sense always be free from sin if it is ever to be saved.

---

226. *Licht*, bk. 1, chap. 22, p. 12.
227. *Licht*, bk. 3, chap. 4, pp. 65–66; see also bk. 5, chap. 23, p. 147.
228. *Licht*, bk. 3, chap. 4, pp. 65–66.
229. *Licht*, bk. 2, chap. 24, p. 49.
230. *Licht*, bk. 3, chap. 21, p. 82.
231. See above, pp. 17–18, 101–2, and 185, and below, n. 243.
232. See above, chapter 4, n. 146.

Mechtild of Magdeburg:
Role and Sense of Self

When we turn to Mechtild's sense of herself, we find both similarities and differences from the younger Helfta mystics. In most of her writing, Mechtild's identification is not, of course, with nuns but with the Dominicans, who were her counselors, confessors and defenders in Magdeburg.[233] Although toward the end of her book there are a few sensitive passages on the nature of the cloistered community that stress the obligation of a convent or beguine group to serve others,[234] Mechtild's writing is infused with no sense of being part of a community. Whether or not she actually lived in a beguine group, her picture of herself is of someone alone and persecuted. Yet she is more aware of the world outside the cloister than Gertrude and Mechtild of Hackeborn. She writes explicitly, as they do not, of the devotional practices of the laity,[235] of clerical corruption, of the threat of heretics.[236] Like the younger Helfta nuns, she has a clear sense that Christ speaks through her, although she goes less far than they in seeing her own authority in priestly images; but she has a far greater sense of the potentially dangerous implications of her direct communication with God.

Mechtild of Magdeburg sees herself as a teacher, counselor, and mediator. While we do not get the impression, as we do with Mechtild of Hackeborn, of an adviser and director of souls of extraordinary sensitivity, we do find in Mechtild of Magdeburg's visions clear evidence that she counseled others and felt a heavy responsibility to do this well.[237] And her writing expresses a much

233. See Ancelet-Hustache, *Mechtilde de Magdeburg*, pp. 54–59. Ancelet-Hustache thinks Mechtild was a Dominican tertiary but this is unlikely; see Grundmann, *Religiöse Bewegungen*, p. 330, n. 22.
234. *Licht*, bk. 6, chap. 1, pp. 171–76; in bk. 4, chap. 21, p. 116, she stresses the service of the Dominicans.
235. *Licht*, bk. 5, chap. 23, pp. 151–52, and bk. 7, chap. 1, p. 217.
236. *Licht*, bk. 7, chap. 47, p. 260; this seems to be a reference to a kind of Free Spirit or antinomian heresy.
237. *Licht*, bk. 1, chap. 35, p. 17, and bk. 4, chap. 18, p. 113, gives her sense of a good person as one who teaches. See also n. 239 below.

greater sense of responsibility for the whole church, down to the lowliest peasant.[238] In one vision, in which she dies on the cross with Christ and visits hell to comfort the sorrowing souls there, she describes her own side as pierced and calls what pours out "holy teaching."[239] In a number of visions she saves souls from purgatory—in one case 70,000 of them.[240] Her three children are, she says, souls in everlasting death, souls in purgatory, and spiritual people who have not yet achieved perfection; she carries each child to the feet of the father, praying that he change its illness; of those in purgatory she writes:

> I must give them my heart's blood to drink. If I pray for them because of their great need and see the bitter fate they must suffer for every sin, then I suffer as a mother. Yet it pleases me that for real sin they should suffer pain to honor God.
>
> If this child is soon to recover
> Its mother must be faithful and compassionate.[241]

She writes of herself as in the desert, fleeing the bondage of things, loving "the naughting" of self God gives; yet even in the desert she thinks one should

> . . . loose those who are bound
> And exhort the free.
> Thou shalt care for the sick
> Yet dwell alone.[242]

There are in this hints that Mechtild is a teacher and direct mediator of the grace of Christ. But there are no images of her binding and loosing, or delivering chalices to others; there are no clerical allusions or metaphors. And yet it was Mechtild of Magdeburg, not Mechtild of Hackeborn or Gertrude, who received criticism for heterodox or anticlerical ideas. In one of her most powerful visions, Christ provided a church and a mass for a "poor

---

238. *Licht*, bk. 7, chap. 1, p. 217.
239. *Licht*, bk. 3, chap. 10, p. 72.
240. *Licht*, bk. 2, chap. 8, p. 35, and bk. 3, chap. 15, pp. 76–78.
241. *Licht*, bk. 5, chap. 8, p. 136; tr. Menzies, *Light*, p. 133.
242. *Licht*, bk. 1, chap. 35, p. 17; tr. Menzies, *Light*, p. 18.

maid" (i.e., Mechtild herself) who prayed: "Lord! Must I be without mass this day?" The maid then confessed to John the Evangelist; John the Baptist, whom she calls "that same priest who had been dedicated by the Holy Spirit while he dwelt in his mother," celebrated.

> Then the maid went up to the altar with great love and widely opened soul. John the Baptist took the white Lamb with the red wounds and laid it on the mouth of the maid. Thus the pure Lamb laid itself on its own image in the stall of her body and sucked her heart with its tender lips.[243]

Later Mechtild had to defend herself for this vision; the criticism seems to have been that it implied that a layman could say mass. She argues in reply that it must be understood in a spiritual sense and that in that sense John the Baptist is not a layman, because he touched God, as priests do.

> My Pharisee says of my account, "John the Baptist was a layman!" Now the holiest of holies in the mass is the Body of God. John the Baptist touched the Son of the same God with humble, trembling fear in the great merit of his holy life, so that the Baptist heard the voice of the heavenly Father. . . . John the Baptist also openly preached the holy Christian Faith . . . and pointed with his finger to the true Son of God there present. . . .
>
> No Pope nor Bishop nor Priest could speak the Word of God as John the Baptist spoke it. . . . Was he then a layman? Instruct me ye blind! Your lies and hatred will not be forgiven without suffering![244]

The important thing about these passages is the evidence they provide that some members of the hierarchy were extremely sensitive to possible anticlericalism, and that Mechtild was sensitive to this too, enough so that she defended herself not by justifying John the Baptist as an extraordinary layman but by claiming for him priestly status in a metaphorical sense.

Mechtild of Magdeburg's mysticism, like Mechtild of Hackeborn's and Gertrude's, explicitly reinforces rather than undercuts

---

243. *Licht*, bk. 2, chap. 4, pp. 30–33; tr. Menzies, *Light*, p. 32–36.
244. *Licht*, bk. 6, chap. 36, p. 210; tr. Menzies, *Light*, p. 199.

church, clergy, and sacraments.[245] We find hints throughout her visions of a fear of making communion—so powerful is God and so unworthy the soul.[246] But Christ repeatedly urges her to go to mass and offers an intimacy so profound that "no bride may tell what happens to her."[247] In the eucharist, God gives to the soul power over himself.

> Yet I, least of all souls,
> Take Him in my hand
> Eat Him and drink Him,
> And do with Him what I will!
>
> Why then should I trouble myself
> As to what the angels experience?[248]

Although Mechtild once suggests that mystical experience goes beyond the mass—that mass is for a lower stage (when one is in the senses) whereas one would not be aware of communicating at the moment of ecstasy[249]—the eucharist is nonetheless central to her. Feeding images (either we eat God or he eats us) are a very frequent way of expressing God's closeness to the soul.[250] Moreover, although there are hints in Mechtild that we should reject external practices and rules,[251] that in ultimate union we pass beyond awareness of self or love or sin, Mechtild is very anxious to avoid any implication of antinomianism or rebellion against the church's ordinary prescriptions. No words fill her with greater dread, she tells us, than the claim: "I am beyond human guidance! I will live only according to the will of God." She writes of a woman who ruined her health for Christ and after death was imprisoned in great darkness because she exercised "self-will without guidance."[252] It is probably because she was in far greater danger of

245. *Licht,* bk. 2, chap. 4, pp. 30–33, chap. 7, pp. 34–35, and chap. 22, p. 43; bk. 3, chap. 15, pp. 76–77; bk. 7, chap. 39, p. 254.

246. *Licht,* bk. 2, chap. 4, p. 32; bk. 3, chap. 15, pp. 76–77.

247. *Licht,* bk. 2, chap. 19, p. 39.

248. *Licht,* bk. 2, chap. 22, p. 43; tr. Menzies, *Light,* p. 48.

249. *Licht,* bk. 3, chap. 3, p. 63.

250. See above nn. 243 and 248 for examples.

251. *Licht,* bk. 2, chap. 23, p. 44; see also bk. 1, chap. 44, pp. 18–22.

252. *Licht,* bk. 5, chap. 5, p. 134; see also bk. 7, chap. 47, p. 260.

suffering such accusations herself that Mechtild feels more need than the Helfta nuns to reject these temptations explicitly.[253]

To Mechtild of Magdeburg, as to Mechtild of Hackeborn and Gertrude, disobedience is the ultimate sin and subordination to confessors and prelates absolutely necessary.[254] In part 4, chapter 2, she tells us of her first vision in Magdeburg: the devil appeared to her and offered to worship her, showed her five wounds and told her to live by his counsel and teach it to others. To this Mechtild replied, underlining her sense of Christ as particularly present in priest and eucharist: "Thou dost tell me thou art the son of God. . . . Then tell me, Who is He who now here as the Son of the living God lies in the hands of the true priest?"[255] And in another, similar vision, on an occasion when she could not go to mass, the devil appeared and offered her the pax; she refused the devil's substitute. Then the devil asked her assistance, asserting "to do good . . . is not against the will of God." To which argument Mechtild replied: "If thou wouldst be healed thou must go and show thyself to a Priest or Archbishop or the Pope."[256] Thus, obedience to the clerical hierarchy becomes to Mechtild, in her exposed and persecuted position, a final test of religious intention in a much more explicit way than to Mechtild of Hackeborn or Gertrude, protected as they were by membership in a very established house. Holy Church (always a female image) must have male priests. Of the three gifts of wisdom from God, the first is "priestly wisdom";[257] of the three arches of the eternal crown (God's wisdom), the second (the prophets) is all male—"the Popes and spiritual Fa-

253. Some of Mechtild's statements are, of course, very similar to those of contemporary heretics. See Robert E. Lerner, *The Heresy of the Free Spirit in the Later Middle Ages* (Berkeley, 1972), pp. 17–19 and 63–65, drawing on Grundmann, *Religiöse Bewegungen*, pp. 402–13. Kurt Ruh, "Beginenmystik: Hadewijch, Mechtild von Magdeburg, Marguerite Porete," *Zeitschrift für deutsches Altertum und deutsche Literatur* 106 (1977): 265–77, points out her differences from the "heretical" Marguerite.

254. *Licht,* bk. 5, chap. 5, pp. 134–35; bk. 4, chap. 26, pp. 120–21; bk. 3, chap. 17, pp. 79–80.

255. *Licht,* bk. 4, chap. 2, pp. 90–95; tr. Menzies, *Light,* p. 96.

256. *Licht,* bk. 2, chap. 24, pp. 47–48; tr. Menzies, *Light,* p. 53.

257. *Licht,* bk. 4, chap. 3, pp. 95–96.

thers to whom God entrusted His flock."[258] Mechtild writes that she saw "with the eyes of my eternity" a maid (i.e., church) in whose heart a spring of living water welled up.

> To it were carried heathen children
> Leprous and blind.
> Above the spring stood a very holy man;
> None but he might draw water from it.
> He was John the Baptist.
> He washed the children in the spring. . . .

And the maid tells her:

> I am Holy Church.
> We have each a bridegroom;
> He is the priest of the blessed maids
> Who looks so lovingly on them.[259]

In contrast to Mechtild of Hackeborn and Gertrude, Mechtild of Magdeburg is intensely aware of lacking priestly status and learning. When "many" warned her that her book was dangerous and should be burned, she addressed God, never doubting his inspiration but slightly irritated at the lack of protection she experienced: ". . . Must I walk uncomforted for thy glory?! Thou hast misled me . . . were I a learned priest . . . then hadst Thou endless honor therefrom."[260] And yet Mechtild is acutely aware of the temptations and hazards of power (both secular power and clerical power). Her criticism of clerical corruption and her sense of the burdens of office go much further than the hints of such attitudes we find in Mechtild of Hackeborn. She writes of a woman tempted by desire for rank at court;[261] she writes of the friars, special sons of the church, tempted by "earthly honor" and "the reverence with which they are regarded";[262] she pities a certain brother Baldwin, held "under obedience" to high office, which

258. *Licht*, bk. 7, chap. 1, p. 217.
259. *Licht*, bk. 4, chap. 3, pp. 95–98; tr. Menzies, *Light*, pp. 100–1.
260. *Licht*, bk. 2, chap. 26, pp. 52–53; tr. Menzies, *Light*, pp. 58–59.
261. *Licht*, bk. 4, chap. 17, pp. 110–11.
262. *Licht*, bk. 5, chap. 24, p. 156.

drains from him all his "youthful strength and manly power;"[263] her sixth book begins: "Great danger lies in power."[264]

Thus Gertrude and Mechtild of Hackeborn actually mediate grace and information to souls in their community and outside and think of their authority in priestly images, whereas Mechtild of Magdeburg, although she shares her sisters' utter confidence that Christ speaks and acts through them, gives less prominence to both the service of others and the conception of this as clerical or pastoral. Yet it is Mechtild of Magdeburg, whose visions claim less priestly authority, who is explicitly aware of her own lack of clerical status and of the benefits and liabilities accorded by such status. And it is Mechtild of Magdeburg who, in striking contrast to Gertrude and Mechtild of Hackeborn, is explicitly aware of being female and of the benefits and liabilities of the gender. She speaks of herself frequently as a "poor maid," an "unlearned" or "despised" or "weak" woman.[265] Not only priestly authority but also writing itself is unsuitable for women.[266] The female is submissive, humble, lowly, without power and learning.

Since Mechtild desires to emphasize the fact that every moment apart from God is suffering and inadequacy, it is not surprising that she uses for herself many inverted metaphors (fool, beggar, etc.) nor that, in her general effort to underline not only her rejection of the values of the world but also her total worthlessness apart from God, she embraces her own femaleness as a sign of her baseness. But there is another side to her awareness of her gender. For, to Mechtild, power is dangerous, arrogance and disobedience damning. Thus she embraces her femaleness as a sign of her freedom from power. And exactly this freedom makes her a channel

263. *Licht*, bk. 4, chap. 26, pp. 120–21.

264. *Licht*, bk. 6, chap. 1, p. 171.

265. *Licht*, bk. 2, chap. 24, pp. 48–49, and chap. 26, pp. 52–53; bk. 5, chap. 12, p. 140; bk. 6, chap. 1, pp. 175–76; bk. 7, chaps. 47, 48, and 64, pp. 260–61 and 279. And see Franklin, *Transformations*, pp. 77–78, and 144–45.

266. Mechtild comments that a brother is surprised and unhappy with her masculine way of writing: *Licht*, bk. 5, chap. 12, p. 140. Christ tells her that she has special grace because she is lowly and unlearned: *Licht*, bk. 2, chap. 26, pp. 52–53. See also above n. 260.

through which God acts. God, who has not given her masculine or clerical authority, has chosen her to write.[267] God sends female saints to teach and bring messages especially to women.[268] Mechtild tells us that there are no women in hell except princesses (clearly implying both that rank and power damn and that princely status is the only form of this temptation available to women).[269] Her list of the powerful who are tortured in the lowest part of purgatory includes only men.[270] She speaks of herself not only as a "beggar woman" and "bride" but also as "mother" to needy souls, bearing them to heaven.[271] Once, when she was making reparation for a friar who had disobeyed his superior, he appeared to her and beseeched: "Have women and priests pray for me."[272] The vision implies that those especially endowed with clerical authority and those especially prohibited from it are equally effective in mediating remission of the suffering brought by sin. The disqualification of gender becomes itself a qualification. Exactly because she lacks masculine and clerical authority, Mechtild sees herself as denuded, base, suffering in union with the suffering Christ, and yet also as a purged channel by which God may speak to others.

Connected to Mechtild of Magdeburg's awareness of herself as female is a much more consistent use of male and female images than we find in Mechtild of Hackeborn or Gertrude. Although the two younger Helfta mystics make use of the nuptial imagery that had begun to flower in the twelfth century and show a devotion to Mary common in thirteenth-century writers, neither of these themes is as prominent in their writings as in Mechtild of Magdeburg's. In Gertrude and Mechtild of Hackeborn, all figures (self, Christ, God, Mary, priests, saints) tend to be seen in male and female metaphors (as mothers, fathers, queens, princes, servants, priests) and as having a broad range of modes of operation (judging, loving, disciplining, comforting, teaching, feeding, mediating). It is hard to find any very clear stereotypes of roles appropriate to one gender or the other: sons are submissive, as are maidens;

267. *Licht*, bk. 2, chap. 26, pp. 52–53.
268. *Licht*, bk. 2, chap. 24, pp. 46–49; bk. 5, chap. 34, pp. 166–68.
269. *Licht*, bk. 3, chap. 21, p. 86.
270. Ibid., p. 85.
271. *Licht*, bk. 5, chap. 8, pp. 135–37.
272. *Licht*, bk. 3, chap. 17, p. 79.

fathers, like mothers, feed, cherish, and reprimand. Mechtild of Magdeburg, however, is much more consistent in her use of male images for God, female images for ourselves. With two exceptions, she speaks of God and Christ in male images, although she frequently sees God and Christ as comforting and feeding. Unlike Gertrude and Mechtild of Hackeborn, she does not explicitly take the maternal or the female into God: her two allusions to God as mother are slight, unextended metaphors.[273] In her lovely dialogue of the soul with the senses, the senses urge her to be refreshed at Mary's knee, watching the angels drink Mary's milk. But the soul tells her this is childish: the adult is a lover, not a nursing baby. "I must [hasten] to God—My Father through nature, My Brother through humanity, My Bridegroom through love. . . ."[274] And just as consistently as God is male, so the soul, the church, and Christendom are female. The soul is a courting maiden who finds it hard to assert herself, a humble housewife.[275] These images are

273. *Licht*, bk. 4, chap. 22, p. 117: Mechtild sees a brother who has died, lying on God's breast:

> Und also snelleklich
> We er do ane pine komen
> Als ein mûter ir liebes kint
> Vs der eschen in ir schosse hat genomen.

(And thus quickly he came there without pain as a mother takes her dear child from the ground into her lap.)
Licht, bk. 6, chap. 7, p. 183: "Hievon wart min sele also snell zû gotte, de si sich rehte vfhûp ane arbeit ir selbes, und bewant sich rehte in die heilige drivaltekeit, als ein kint sich bewindet in den mantel siner mûter und leit sich rehte an ir brust." (At this went my soul so quickly to God that it rose without effort and found itself truly in the Holy Trinity, as a child finds itself under its mother's cloak and lays itself truly on her breast.)
In contrast, Mechtild uses much nursing imagery for Mary and for the church. See *Licht*, bk. 5, chap. 22, pp. 12–13, chap. 23, pp. 149–50, and chap. 24, p. 155.
274. *Licht*, bk. 1, chap. 44, pp. 21–22.
275. *Licht*, bk. 2, chap. 22, p. 43: "Die minste sele ist tohter des vatters und swester des sunes und vrúndíñe des heligen geistes und werliche ein brut der heligen drivaltekeit." (The smallest soul is the daughter of the father and the sister of the son and the friend of the Holy Spirit and indeed the bride of the Holy Trinity.) Ibid., bk. 3, chap. 23, p. 88; see n. 204 above. Ibid., bk. 4, chap. 14, p. 109; see n. 225 above.

not simply poetic substitutions for a feminine noun, *anima*. Mechtild of Magdeburg, to a greater extent than Mechtild of Hackeborn and Gertrude, chooses specific female images that stress lowliness, submission, and an inadequacy that must be complemented by a male image—bridegroom or husband. There is even a suggestion in Mechtild's writing that the female is matter and the male spirit, an idea that has roots in exegetical tradition, where Adam and Eve were often seen as spirit and flesh.[276] What is striking here is the centrality of femaleness as a symbol of our lowliness and otherness from God—an otherness that cries out for complementing by the bridegroom and therefore makes intimate union possible.

Nor is Mary, for all her importance to Mechtild, a female image of God's operation. Sometimes Mechtild writes of Mary and Jesus as parallel figures, each a nurturer of the soul.[277] Mary feeds with milk, Christ with blood. In her discussion of Mary as a kind of preexistent humanity of Christ, Mary takes on a mediating role; Mechtild refers to her as a goddess and as granting grace.[278] But Mary's humanity is not by its nature sinless as Christ's is; and Mary's feeding is a lower kind of succor, inferior to the erotic union offered by Jesus.[279] Moreover Mary is at least as often a symbol of our suffering and lowly soul as she is a mediator, above us and below divinity.[280]

Therefore, in a sense not true for Gertrude and Mechtild of Hackeborn, God, for Mechtild of Magdeburg, is male (although to these mystics, as to all mystics, no language, no metaphor, ever captures the divine essence). It is not surprising that Mechtild of Magdeburg, who grew up in the world and fled from it into a quasi-religious role that left her open to misunderstanding, should

276. *Licht*, bk. 4, chap. 18, p. 111; see d'Alverny, "Les théologiens . . . voient la femme."

277. *Licht*, bk. 1, chap. 22, pp. 11–13; bk. 2, chap. 3, pp. 29–30.

278. *Licht*, bk. 3, chap. 1, p. 58.

279. *Licht*, bk. 1, chap. 44, p. 21.

280. See above, n. 203. Mechtild also has a more extensive interest in the details of Christ's life and Mary's than do Gertrude or Mechtild of Hackeborn; see *Licht*, bk. 5, chap. 23, pp. 147–54. Franklin, *Transformations*, pp. 137–45, gives a very sensitive exposition of Mechtild's use of nursing imagery for Mary.

show in her religious imagery an awareness of the world's opinion that females are lowly, powerless, without learning or authority, and in need of complementation. Nor is it surprising that she found in Christ, who makes wise the foolish and powerful the powerless, an authorization for transcending the world's opinion and for allowing him to speak through her.

Mechtild of Magdeburg, like the other mystical women studied here, has a strong sense of her counseling, mediating, pedagogical, and prophetic role as authorized by Christ. Indeed in her harsh prophecies, which have occasionally a political and a Joachite content, she continues, in a way the Helfta nuns do not, the prophetic strain found in the great twelfth-century German visionaries Hildegard of Bingen and Elisabeth of Schönau.[281] Like the Helfta nuns whose experiences are recounted in the *Herald* and the *Special Grace*, Mechtild is secure in her role as Christ's mouthpiece. She never falters in her angry accusations of clerical corruption, calling the canons of Magdeburg "goats" and various other uncomplimentary epithets.[282] When she points out to Christ her lack of education and of the authorization of office, he suggests to her that he chooses her for mediating and instructing exactly because of her powerlessness and ignorance. There is clear evidence in her visions that the friars who advised her also listened to her. For lay people who could find no release from guilt through consulting local clergy and friars and for the clergy themselves who were burdened by and ambivalent over the exercise of clerical authority because of its inevitable trappings of money and influence, Mechtild of Magdeburg, like Mechtild of Hackeborn and Gertrude, provided both the spiritual comfort and the prod to amend-

---

281. See *Licht*, bk. 4, chap. 27, pp. 121–27; and Ancelet-Hustache, *Mechtild de Magdeburg*, pp. 272–85. A number of contemporary women had visions concerning political affairs, especially the church's war against heresy: see, for example, Mary of Oignies (James of Vitry, *Vita B. Mariae Oigniacensis*, AASS: June, vol. 5 [Paris, 1867]: 560) and Margaret of Hungary (Garin of Guy-l'Evêque, *Vita B. Margaritae Ungaricae virginis*, AASS: January, vol. 3 [Paris, 1866]: 520).

282. *Licht*, bk. 6, chap. 3, pp. 178–79. She even puts criticism of the clergy into the mouth of the pope himself: ibid., chap. 21, pp. 198–99, amplified in the Latin version, *Revelationes*, ed. the monks of Solesmes, 2:524.

ment of life that came most persuasively in direct visions of Christ himself disposing of and saving souls.[283]

But Mechtild does not see herself as priest or pastor or apostle. Like Hildegard of Bingen in this as in her political prophecies, she sees women as unsuited for priesthood. The special religious role of woman is as God's spouse. Like Hildegard, she has a clear sense of male/female differences. Although she gives prominence to both church and Mary, she does not take the female into Christ. Her own mystical vocation is based in a sense of otherness from God's authority, an otherness that is, to her, a condition for the gift of union.

Mechtild was in fact in greater danger than the younger Helfta nuns for the mystical authority she claimed. Her own words show her to be quite aware of the antinomian or Free Spirit implications that can be found in mystical ideas unless they are very precisely formulated; she explicitly rejects and guards against such implications—something Mechtild of Hackeborn and Gertrude feel no need to do or comment on. She was accused of anticlerical and quietist ideas; in the visions we read her spirited defense.[284] It seems reasonable to suggest that Mechtild's greater awareness of her femaleness as both inferiority and superiority, of the implications of the presence or absence of clerical status and the dangers of implying it to exist (even metaphorically) where it has not been bestowed, of the struggle involved in renouncing the world, owes a great deal, first, to her protracted adolescent effort to withdraw from what she says was a circle of loving family and friends and, second, to her adult life as a quasi religious, which, she tells us, she chose exactly so that she would continue to be exposed and persecuted and lonely.[285]

But it is not simply lack of support from a long-established female community and of socialization within that community that we sense in Mechtild. Her theology and her understanding of the universe also seem to provide for her less support. Although all contrasts between the Helfta nuns and Mechtild of Magdeburg

283. For example, *Licht*, bk. 6, chap. 17, pp. 110–11; bk. 4, chap. 22, pp. 116–18, and chap. 26, pp. 120–21.

284. See above, nn. 216, 243, 244, 252, and 253.

285. *Licht*, bk. 4, chap. 2, pp. 90–95, and see n. 296 below.

are matters of degree, it seems safe to say that Mechtild rests less easily with the justice of God.[285] Although she agrees that sin is objective evil, objectively removed by the Incarnation, which restores humanity to saving union with divinity, she usually talks of sin as subjective experience, as loneliness and absence of comfort. She feels therefore a personal responsibility to remove all of Christendom from this experience of deprivation of God, to get all creation back to God. She petitions for the damned; she finds in Christian history a sinless humanity between the fall and the Incarnation. Mediation to her is more the removing of suffering than a single link in a vast chain of prayer for others that objectively binds them to heaven. She shows less awareness in her imagery than do Gertrude and Mechtild of Hackeborn that her own role as scourge and comforter, prophet, teacher, and mediator parallels the operations of God himself, who is judge as well as comforter. Thus, although Mechtild of Hackeborn and Gertrude make a place for suffering as cleansing, and Mechtild of Magdeburg has a vivid sense of the utter glory of God's power, it is nonetheless possible to draw a contrast between them. Mechtild of Hackeborn and Gertrude see themselves as queens and princes, conduits to others of divine food and drink, brides reigning beside their bridegroom, in a universe that is irradiated by splendor and praise at least partly because its rules, and its structure, are so explicit and unquestionable. Mechtild of Magdeburg sees herself as the courting maiden for whom moments outside the ecstasy of union are secure only if they are experienced as alienation and deprivation; to her the structure of the universe *is* the rhythm of oneness and loss.

Conclusions: Women Mystics and the Clericalization of the Church

Before it is possible to determine whether the picture of Helfta I have sketched above describes any general pattern of thirteenth-century spirituality we need much more study that carefully ana-

286. This attitude has been noted by scholars particularly in Julian of Norwich. See Hanshell, "Crux"; Colledge, *The Medieval Mystics of En-*

lyzes the religious imagery and theological emphases (not just the doctrine) of religious writing against the background of the authors' social origins and types of institutionalized religious life. But the work that has been done for the beguines and for Dominican and Cistercian nuns in the Low Countries and in Germany suggests that the salient characteristics of Helfta's spirituality were widespread among women in these areas in the late thirteenth century.[287] The saints' lives, *Nonnenbücher*, and mystical treatises that have been studied show the range of these characteristics: a balance of regal and erotic imagery, with much less nuptial imagery in some of the vision literature than textbook accounts lead one to suppose;[288] a sharp decline in the role of the devil and in any sense of cosmic warfare; a growing anxiety about one's own access to heaven and a growing fear of purgatory, yet a continuing confidence in Christ's objective mediation; a devotion to Christ's humanity that reflects, on the one hand, the fact that Christ is mediator and, on the other hand, a desire to identify with his suffering and model oneself on his example; a flowering of eucharistic piety among all types of women religious, coupled with devotion to Christ's body, blood, wounds, and sacred heart;[289] a tremendous growth in mystical and paramystical experiences, especially among women and among individuals of both sexes who do not have other sources of religious authority;[290] a very careful retaining of mystical experiences in the context of the sacraments and obedience to the hierarchy, so that for the thirteenth century it seems difficult to argue that quasi religious and/or women·were any more inclined than others to deliberately expand the antinomian or anti-

gland (New York, 1961), p. 87. Pepler, *English Religious Heritage*, pp. 321–27, discusses this with reference to a number of mystics, including Mechtild of Magdeburg. See also Louis Cognet, *Introduction aux mystiques rhéno-flamands* (Paris, 1968).

287. See Lerner, *Free Spirit*; Eleanor C. McLaughlin, "The Heresy of the Free Spirit and Late Medieval Mysticism," *Medievalia et Humanistica*, n.s. 4 (1973): 37–54; and the works cited in n.9 above.

288. This is Stein's conclusion about the late thirteenth- early fourteenth-century vision literature from Engelthal. See above n. 9.

289. For authors who discuss the particular attraction of women to the eucharist, see n. 58 above.

290. Roisin, *Hagiographie*, pp. 87–89.

clerical implications of their experiences; a much greater vulnerability nonetheless on the part of women and quasi religious to attack for heterodox tendencies, because they were less under ecclesiastical control and more cut off from theological training.[291] Although conclusions must remain tentative, it nonetheless seems possible to extrapolate from my analysis of the vision literature produced at Helfta to suggest certain general answers to the two questions posed at the outset of this essay: why were women so prominent in thirteenth-century mysticism? and why did their spirituality have the particular characteristics that it did?

The nuns who are presented in the vision literature of Helfta as the central figures in the spiritual life of the house were counselors, teachers and mediators of the grace and will of God to their fellow nuns and to the monastery's admirers. With the exception of the abbess Gertrude of Hackeborn, who receives a few of the revelations, these nuns derive their authority vis-à-vis others not from office but from their mystical union with Christ and the accompanying visions. They are seen by those who wrote down the visions not primarily as models for imitation or as vicarious expiation of the sins of others; rather they are chains linking others to

---

291. The question whether women were generally represented in medieval heresies more frequently than men (an argument put forth by Gottfried Koch, *Frauenfrage und Ketzertum im Mittelalter: die Frauenbewegung im Rahmen des Katharismus und des Waldensertums und ihre sozialen Wurzeln: 12.–14. Jahrhundert*, Forschungen zur mittelalterlichen Geschichte 9 [Berlin, 1962], and frequently cited) has yet to be answered; it should be considered in light of the prominence of women in the development of certain orthodox devotions. See Eleanor McLaughlin, "Les femmes et l'hérésie médiévale. Un problème dans l'histoire de la spiritualité," *Concilium* 111 (1976): 73–90; and Richard Abels and Ellen Harrison, "The Position of Women in Languedocian Catharism," *Mediaeval Studies* 41 (1979): 215–51. The position I take here on the thirteenth century seems justified by the recent work on the Free Spirit: Lerner, *Free Spirit*; Bolton, "*Mulieres sanctae*"; E. McLaughlin, "Free Spirit," all of whom reject the opinion that the Free Spirit was actually an organized sect. By the late thirteenth and early fourteenth centuries, churchmen were beginning to be anxious about some of the implications of mysticism, particularly in the hands of lay people to whom it was increasingly available in vernacular treatises: see Grundmann, "Die Frauen und die Literatur," and M. Lambert, *Medieval Heresy* (New York, 1976), p. 176.

God, mediators in whose merits others may participate. They are called preachers and teachers. Their impact on others is described as a cure of souls. In some of the visions, they see themselves or are seen by others in priestly trappings or stances; occasionally they are given by Christ explicitly sacerdotal powers. Moreover, they are convinced of the necessity of teaching others the truths revealed to them in visions and of bringing souls in suffering and sin into Christ's presence by their prayers. Although the sisters who write about these visionaries sometimes worry about how to reconcile action and contemplation, the mystics themselves are secure in their view that consoling and teaching are more pressing (although less delightful) obligations than resting in the arms of Christ.

In the Christendom of the twelfth and thirteenth centuries, clerical authority and mediation grew steadily in importance through the elaboration of canon law, the growth of the penitential system, and the elaboration of ecclesiastical bureaucracy. Clerical status—an amorphous concept in the early twelfth century—was increasingly defined as including the right to preach and practice the cure of souls (within which hearing confessions and the counseling that might attend it became ever more important). The role of the priest in consecrating the eucharist was increasingly emphasized and held in awe. Moreover, in a fundamental shift in Christian mentality, the "imitation of Christ," the "following of the Gospel," came to mean "evangelism" in the modern sense of the word—that is, preaching the gospel by life (poverty and chastity) as well as word. Thousands upon thousands of men and women from all social groups determined to follow Christ in this sense, and the creation of the friars was an institutionalization of this new ideal. But women, who were caught up in this religious fervor as often as men, could not become priests (or even by the end of the twelfth century marry them); they could not become friars (and the tertiaries were not at all the same thing); they could not remain wandering evangelists for long without threat of ecclesiastical censure. Double monasteries in which abbesses ruled, which were popular in the twelfth century, were mostly eliminated by the thirteenth century; other clerical roles of abbesses were generally curtailed. Thus men and women were coming to value more and more certain religious roles and activities that women were more and more unable to fill. For the nuns of Helfta, Christ himself solved the dilemma. He gave them an authorization to do and be much of what contemporaries understood by evangelism, and his authorization was far more direct and final than any office or tradition could be.

By Christ' own command, the nuns of Helfta were mediators with powers to bind and loose; teachers who spoke Christ's own words and provided irrefutable evidence on that haunting concern, the afterlife; counselors and advisers to whom the convent's neighbors turned when local clergy and friars failed. Indeed under the impact of Christ's authority what had traditionally been the central aspect of the monastic role—vicarious worship—became newly important: by belief in (and thus sharing in) the mystical attainments of a Mechtild or a Gertrude those who were busy in mundane affairs or lacking in spiritual accomplishments might take steps forward, out of purgatory and toward bliss. Also under Christ's authorization the old conflict between service and withdrawal, action and contemplation, love of neighbor and love of God, which lay at the heart of twelfth-century monastic self-doubts, was quietly resolved in the direction of service and teaching. Mechtild, Gertrude, and some of the other nuns we meet in the pages of the visions are concerned lest their power be exploited by others and resist revealing the inspiration they have received from Christ, but they are self-confident and effective in their actual counseling and teaching. They see themselves as mothers consoling children and as princes leading armies; Christ speaks words of encouragement when they are stern with their sisters as well as when they are tender. Although they frequently worry about prelates and friars (and occasionally about convent officials) who are exhausted by the demands of office, they themselves worry neither about the quality of the particular advising they do nor about possessing the role. Christ has commanded them to speak and has through them released souls from punishment for sin.[292] Like a

292. It is fascinating to note that Aquinas and Bonaventure agree in listing as major arguments *for* the ordination of women the fact that women have been prophets and prophecy is higher than priesthood. They both, of course, decide against the ordination of women but for different reasons: woman's natural state of subjection (Aquinas); the fact that the male Christ can only be signified by the male sex (Bonaven-

number of other thirteenth-century women mystics (for example, Christina called *Mirabilis*, Lutgard of Aywières, and Mary of Oignies), the nuns of Helfta never explicitly challenge the exclusive claims of the priesthood, but unlike Christina, Lutgard, and Mary they make no special point of their ignorance of the fine points of scriptural interpretation.[293] In contrast to twelfth-century women and to many of their thirteenth-century predecessors (including Mechtild of Magdeburg), Gertrude and Mechtild of Hackeborn are serene about the implications of both their learning and their contact with Christ.

The nuns of Helfta were recruited from among the privileged in the German society of their day; their monastery was well respected and established. If it was subject to attack from local lords and harrassment from local ecclesiastical authorities, this was exactly because of its ties to powerful families. Those nuns who were blessed with visions and mystical authorization for leadership grew up within its walls, free from the pressures young women in medieval society experienced at puberty, when the failure or success of parents at procuring husbands might equally be occasions for a daughter's consternation and awareness of vulnerability.

The nobility to which these nuns remained tied provided many of their images of heaven, which they see as a royal court or lavish banquet over which Christ and Mary preside as emperor and empress. Their imagery of gender is, however, less tied to the world. Gertrude and Mechtild of Hackeborn have little sense of stereotypical behavior for the two sexes: they are no more likely to see tenderness as maternal than as paternal, no more likely to see harsh discipline as paternal than as maternal. They have little awareness of themselves as female in a negative sense: they do not use weak women or unclean women as symbols of their own sinfulness, although they do see the bride or the little girl as a symbol of God's love toward and search for the soul. Their lack of a negative sense

---

ture). See Francine Cardman, "The Medieval Question of Women and Orders," *The Thomist* 42 (October, 1978): 582–99, and J. Rézette, "Le sacerdoce et la femme chez saint Bonaventure," *Antonianum* 51 (1976): 520–27.

293. Bolton, "*Vitae Matrum*," pp. 269–70.

of the female and of the equation of male with authority is probably a result of their socialization in a secure, established female
community. Furthermore, there is a slighter emphasis on erotic
and nuptial imagery in the writings of Mechtild of Hackeborn and
Gertrude than in those of Mechtild of Magdeburg, whose bride is
more languishing and insecure than the beloved queen of Gertrude
and Mechtild of Hackeborn. Perhaps this reflects the fact that
Mechtild of Hackeborn and Gertrude escaped the experience of
going through puberty in the world (and the crucial decision—
whether made by others or by oneself—to marry or not to
marry).[294]

Thus, while deprivation of opportunities for evangelism may
be one reason for the mystical authorization these nuns received
for teaching and mediating, a relative lack of deprivation in other
areas (social status, self-awareness associated with gender) helps to
explain the strength and self-confidence with which they viewed
their authority.[295] Moreover, the contrast with Mechtild of Magdeburg, who was criticized for doctrinal aberration despite a mys-

294. This should not be taken to imply that women in the cloister were
cut off from family ties (note the number of blood sisters or of mothers
and daughters in thirteenth-century convents) or unaware of the dynas-
tic concerns of noble families. In some cases, of course, young women
who were raised in convents left, or were constrained to leave, at
puberty to marry; St. Hedwig (+1243) is an example. On the feminine
images discussed here see n. 200 above.

295. Scholars have speculated about the significance of the fact that
the *Herald*, bk. 1, remains silent about Gertrude's background (see Doyère, "Gertrude d'Helfta [sainte]," col. 331). Gertrude herself had, it
seems, no memories of a mother (*Oeuvres* 3: *Héraut*, bk. 3, chap. 30, pp.
160–62; see n. 124 above) and reveals in her visions a certain pride in not
putting relatives first in her prayers or being hindered by family ties
(ibid., chap. 18, p. 82). It may be that her lack of a family was a personal
deprivation that was important in the formation of her personality. We
should also note the importance of physical illness (particularly acute
headaches) in the experience of all three women. But it is impossible to
know, first, how much of this was induced by fasting and staying awake
long hours praying and, second, to what extent headaches and weakness were common to all women in the convent. Illness is a prominent
motif in female mystical writing (e.g., Julian of Norwich's *Showings*);
see Benz, *Die Vision*, pp. 17–34.

ticism that was orthodox, suggests that mystical authorization for teaching and mediating, which might come to women anywhere, could be seen in far more priestly images and acted upon with greater equanimity in established convents. It also suggests that the particular ways in which beguines were vulnerable to and set apart from ecclesiastical authority (lack of prescribed schedule of worship, of complex institutional links between groups, of large endowments and prestigious founders and protectors) suited better those, like Mechtild of Magdeburg, who needed to function as voices crying in the wilderness—needed, as she herself puts it, "to be despised through no fault of [their] own." [296]

The equanimity and power of the mysticism of Gertrude and Mechtild of Hackeborn cannot of course be explained as a direct reflection of aspects of the social structure that produced the convent of Helfta. It found its major support in their theology. The nuns of Helfta see God as regal and just. They see evil as objective. They see Christ as objective mediation, bringing humanity to divinity. Although their visions are awash with blood, it is a symbol less of pain and expiation than of nurture and comfort. The dominant note throughout is praise, joy, and awareness of glory.

Within such a theology there is clearly a place for individuals, like Mechtild of Hackeborn and Gertrude, who are themselves mediators and counselors/leaders/teachers; a sense of security, serenity, confidence, and effectiveness seems a natural response to the inspiration of such a God. In many fourteenth-century mystics (and there are hints of this in Mechtild of Magdeburg) the immediacy of personal union overwhelms a sense of objective order in the universe; damnation becomes hard to accept and evil to comprehend; brooding on suffering seems to accompany an inability to explain it. [297] None of this is true at Helfta. For if the structure of the universe is just, authority in general is trustworthy. A nun through whom Christ speaks will herself speak with sternness and wisdom as well as compassion. If evil is objective, there is really

296. Mechtild of Magdeburg, *Licht*, bk. 4, chap. 2, p. 91.
297. See nn. 253 and 286 above. On the ways in which mysticism could slide over into antinomian ideas, see Lerner, *Free Spirit*; and E. McLaughlin, "Free Spirit."

something to remove by one's own asceticism or by sharing in the virtues of others. If the Incarnation, mystical union, and the eucharist are all moments in a bringing of humanity to divinity that is salvation, then mediation is effective; mediation is how the universe is bound together. Female visionaries will not be merely models for imitation, prophets, or workers of miracles; they will also be able to incorporate others in their own mystical union and bind others to Christ.

There appears to have been a moment in the thirteenth century at which the growing sense of man's likeness to God—expressed not only in the later medieval emphasis on Christ's humanness and the rich variety of homey and natural metaphors for the divine but also in the new confidence about man's capacity for intimate union with God—was still balanced by older images of an awesome God, totally unlike man, who rules a universe of the good and the evil. This thirteenth-century combination of likeness and unlikeness underlay the optimism and strength of the piety of Helfta. The sense of likeness to God made possible the nuns' confidence in mystical union; their sense of unlikeness made equally possible their confidence in the justice and glory of the universe and in the justice and glory of the deeds that Christ accomplished through them.

The spirituality that we find in Mechtild of Magdeburg and the younger nuns of Helfta does not undercut the church. Although it provides women with opportunities to participate in certain aspects of the priestly role that theologians denied them—and sometimes even suggests that the combination of mystical authorization and a peculiarly female freedom from the power of office is a superior role—it functions in its deepest implications to enhance doctrinal orthodoxy and the authority of the priesthood. The vision literature of Helfta emphasizes the need for obedience and recourse to clergy, especially through confession and communion. Those whose progress in the afterlife is delayed are usually those who have been delinquent in receiving the sacraments often enough. All three visionaries see priests as having a special advantage in the clerical status that enables them to consecrate the elements, although only Mechtild of Magdeburg perceives her own lack of such status as a liability. (Gertrude, characteristically, points out that the priest's special proximity to Christ is an irrelevancy or a danger unless coupled with spiritual attainments).[298]

The eucharistic devotion that is central in the spirituality of Helfta is itself an undergirding of clerical power, directed against both dualist denials of the goodness of creation and antisacerdotal attacks on the properly constituted rituals of the church. In a late thirteenth-century world that still feared Catharism and was coming to fear the Free Spirit, it is not hard to see why the nuns' Dominican advisers approved of these overwhelmingly eucharistic visions and soon after Gertrude's death gave her *Herald* a testament of orthodoxy. Indeed it is quite possible that the male confessors the women consulted about their visions encouraged the eucharistic content. Increasingly in the twelfth and thirteenth centuries reverence for the clergy, as expressed by both priests and non-priests, centered on the priest's ability to consecrate the elements, which was seen as a kind of momentary divinization.[299] Moreover, frequent confession and communion provided a guarantee of clerical supervision of convents at a time when female heterodoxy was an increasing worry to the church. But the eucharistic piety of Helfta was not imposed by male supervisers. We know that it was abbess Gertrude who took the lead in stressing frequent communion, and one of the purposes of the nuns who wrote down the vision literature was clearly to propagate eucharistic piety.

The emphasis of thirteenth-century devotion on reception of and adoration of the eucharist seems to have been a particularly female emphasis. The feast of *Corpus Christi* was championed by Juliana of Cornillon.[300] Mary of Oignies (†1213), Margaret of Ypres (†1237), and Christina *Mirabilis* (†1224) could not bear to be without the eucharist. Lutgard of Aywières (†1246) took such pleasure in it that her abbess once compelled her to omit it as a

---

298. Gertrude, *Oeuvres*, 3: *Héraut*, bk. 3, chap. 36, p. 176; Mechtild of Magdeburg, *Licht*, bk. 2, chap. 26, pp. 52–53, and bk. 5, chap. 12, p. 140; Mechtild of Hackeborn, *Lib. spec. grat.*, bk. 4, chap. 15, pp. 272–73, bk. 5, chap. 2, p. 319, and bk. 5, chap. 10, pp. 334–36.

299. Congar, "Modèle monastique et modèle sacerdotal en Occident de Grégoire VII (1073–1085) à Innocent III (1198)," *Études de civilisation médiévale (IXᵉ–XIIᵉ siècles)* (Poitiers, 1973). And see above, p. 11.

300. McDonnell, *Beguines and Beghards*, pp. 305–15.

penance.[301] Early in the thirteenth century, Francis of Assisi seems to have turned to the mystical women of the Low Countries in a desire to partake of their eucharistic piety.[302] Agnes Blannbekin (†1315) chose to become a beguine in Vienna so that she could communicate more frequently; Ida of Nivelles (†1231) moved from the beguines to the Cistercians for the same reason. The biography of Ida of Louvain (†ca. 1300) gives many examples of obsessive devotion to the eucharist, which led, as it frequently did among thirteenth-century women, to the appearance of stigmata.[303] The psychological and spiritual reasons for this female concentration on the eucharist seem to have been fundamentally the same as the reasons for the flowering of women's mysticism— that is, the need for a substitute for clerical experience. If Christ was incarnated in the hands of the celebrating priest as in the Virgin's womb, might he not also be incarnated within the communicating nun or beguine, and might not each of these types of spiritual maternity bear fruit in spiritual children?

There are, of course, other factors that may help to explain this female eucharistic piety. The experience of menstruation may have made blood a particularly potent symbol to women. Gertrude calls it the most horrible of natural objects,[304] and it was central in the Helfta nuns' visions of the eucharist. It is also likely that there are sexual reasons why the stress on the physicality of Christ's humanity, which was very much part of thirteenth-century eucharistic devotion, appealed to women and was spoken of in highly erotic imagery. It is only, theologically speaking, in his humanity that Christ is male, and only in the eucharist that that male humanity (united with divinity) is handled and consumed. But I would argue that there are far more important reasons than sublimated affectivity or sexuality for the eucharistic emphasis of many thirteenth-century women.

To the nuns of Helfta, the eucharist was the equivalent of and the occasion for ecstasy. Ecstasy gave them religious power as well

301. Bolton, "*Vitae Matrum*," pp. 266–68.
302. McDonnell, *Beguines and Beghards*, p. 313.
303. Ibid., 302–20. And see above, n. 9.
304. See above n. 63.

as delight—authorization for at least some elements of the most highly valued male religious role without the anxieties that accompanied that role. (It was office that brought the worldly power and wealth that contradicted renunciation, and the evangelism of these women was not based on office.) Yet ecstasy—mystical union—could not be compelled, although it could be prepared for; it was, to many, beyond their spiritual capabilities. The eucharist was therefore the only repeatable and controllable moment of union with God. It was theologically guaranteed to be union quite objectively whether or not ecstasy occurred. It was also for these women the most frequent setting for ecstasies. In the mass they made the physical contact with God that they envied priests; there they achieved union with the central moment of mediation and thereby became mediators themselves. Their images for the eucharist (images of incorporation—I "eat" or "drown in" God's heart) make clear what was crucial about the eucharist to them: it was union from which flowed joy and power; it was controllable, repeatable, coercible union; it was union with Christ's humanity and therefore a moment at which the mediating role to which the woman was called by Christ was reinforced through incorporation in that ultimate mediation, the Incarnation. There is nothing inconsistent in seeing the piety of these nuns both as a support to the church's emphasis on the priest's sacerdotal powers and as an effort by nuns to be themselves what was crucial about priesthood—mediators, preachers, touchers of God, vessels within which God happened.[305]

My interpretation of the vision literature of Helfta thus suggests that deprivation of the opportunity to fill certain roles and express certain deeply held religious values lies behind the greater incidence of mysticism and of intense eucharistic devotion in thirteenth-century women. Social scientists who have seen the ecstatic experiences of women as a response to deprivation have

305. Nicolas Huyghebaert, "Les femmes laïques dans la vie religieuse des XIᵉ et XIIᵉ siècles dans la province ecclésiastique de Reims," *I laici nella "societas christiana" dei secoli XI e XII: Atti della terzia Settimana Internazionale di Studio: Mendola, 21–27 agosto, 1965* (Milan, 1968), p. 347, suggests that there is an "undeniable complementarity" between woman and priest in the early twelfth century but does not elaborate this idea as I have done here.

sometimes argued that these responses are an attempt to manipulate males, an oblique attack on male privilege, and are permitted by males because of their guilt about social oppression of women or because of ignorance of the true nature of women's experience.[306] My interpretation, however, stresses other factors. First, emphasis on a particular religious role (in this case the priesthood) may vary from period to period; deprivation of a particular role therefore may or may not be an acute problem for those deprived. Because clerical status—and desire to perform certain kinds of service that that status permits—was more important in the thirteenth century and women's incapacity for it more clearly defined, women's need for a substitute was stronger than in the earlier Middle Ages. Second, the presence of institutions within which women could be socialized by women and the privileges that many women enjoyed as members of the nobility made it possible for them to develop genuinely positive images of their substitute religious role despite a prevalent theological conception of their gender as naturally inferior. Third, because Christianity, like all great religions, encompasses contradictory and paradoxical values, it is too simple to see the mystical role of late medieval Christian women as an oblique attack on dominant values or statuses, or as permitted by males out of ignorance of its true nature. The Helfta literature supports the morality, theology, and spirituality preached by the male clergy; it also, both directly and implicitly, supports the power of the clergy. Moreover it was read in other houses and was urged on men and women alike by their confessors.[307] Indeed, in the thirteenth century, the reputations of female mystics appear to have had more influence outside their cloisters than the reputations of male mystics; their *Lives* were frequently read in male houses.[308] The female mysticism that we find at Helfta was permit-

306. Lewis, *Ecstatic Religion*, pp. 85 and 88–99. On p. 177, Lewis remarks that, where there is a male priesthood not dependent on "possession" for its authority, women and subordinate males are sometimes allowed a limited role as inspired "auxiliaries"; this would appear to be an accurate description of the thirteenth-century situation, but Lewis has no good explanation of why the limited role is not only allowed but also admired.

307. See above n. 27.

308. Roisin, *Hagiographie*, pp. 113 and 129.

ted and admired not because it was misunderstood but because it was understood.[309]

In any religious tradition that denounces as well as affirms the values of the world, an ambivalence will be attached to both the powerful and the powerless. Men who have power will feel ambivalent about its significance for religious reasons (in Christianity the injunction to "flee the world"); therefore they will be ambivalent also—that is, at least partly positive—about those who do not have power and may be purer for the lack. Thus women will be, in their self-perception and in the view males have of them, of great religious significance because they do not have certain functions that men have, value, and feel confused about. In the twelfth and thirteenth centuries, male ambivalence about wealth and the exercise of power contributed both to the rise of the friars and to the flood of criticism directed against them as they departed from their early image under the inexorable pressure of clericalization. It was probably such ambivalence that led men to seek out mystical women whose lives could be interpreted as expressing both the positive and the negative valuation of power. (They surpassed the clerical role they were disqualified from exercising.) Such respect for prophetic and mystical women was expressed in the twelfth century in Bernard of Clairvaux's letter to Hildegard of Bingen: "Therefore we beg and entreat you to remember us before God and also those who are joined to us in spiritual union. For since the spirit in you is joined to God, we have confidence that you can in

309. The analysis I present in this essay would seem to support the theory of Philip Carl Salzman, "Ideology and Change in Middle Eastern Tribal Societies," *Man: The Journal of the Royal Anthropological Institute*, n.s. 13 (1978): 618–37, except that I take quite seriously the possibility that subgroups of a religion may not merely preserve subordinate ideologies that will emerge into new usefulness at times of change but may also embody for a culture a variety of genuinely contradictory values that are simultaneously necessary. I should also point out that women mystics, as I describe them, are characterized by what Victor Turner means by "liminality"; many of their images express what Turner calls "anti-structure." See Victor Turner, "Passages, Margins and Poverty" and "Metaphors of Anti-Structure in Religious Culture," *Dramas, Fields, and Metaphors: Symbolic Action in Human Society* (Ithaca, 1974), pp. 231–99, especially pp. 246, 270, and 272–75.

great measure help and sustain us."[310] In the thirteenth century such diverse individuals as Robert Grosseteste and James of Vitry saw a special sanctity in women.[311] This adulation flowered in a much more exotic form in the heterodox cult of the Guglielmites, some of whose members proposed substituting women for men as leaders of the church.[312] Ambivalence about wealth and authority, which lies at the heart of Christianity, also helps to explain why the mystical authorization that, for women, substitutes for clerical status is never seen as second best, why the sense of self of the nuns of Helfta is, if anything, stronger than that of the great male and female mystics of the previous century. Both the suggestion that an ecstatic alternative to clerical power can be permitted only out of ignorance of the nature of the alternative as well as the standard interpretation of the later Middle Ages as a period in which a mystical alternative undercuts the institutional church seem to be based on an understanding of medieval religion that ignores the extent to which its fundamental values are not only complex but also truly paradoxical.

The mysticism of thirteenth-century women is therefore an alternative to the authority of office. It is an alternative that is fostered by the presence of institutions within which a female religious culture can develop. It is fostered also by a theology that emphasizes God as accessible in intimate union and comprehensi-

310. Bernard, letter 366 *Ad Hildegardem abbatissam*, PL 182: col. 572B–C.

311. Bolton, "*Vitae Matrum*," and Southern, *Western Society and the Church*, pp. 320–21.

312. Stephen E. Wessley, "The Thirteenth-Century Guglielmites: Salvation Through Women," in *Medieval Women*, ed. Baker, pp. 289–303. It would, of course, go too far to suggest that religious women were always admired. One is reminded of the often-cited and unkind remark of the saintly Richard Caister to the saintly, effusive Margery Kempe: "God bless my soul—what could a woman find to say about our Lord's love that would take an hour or two?" *The Book of Margery Kempe*, ed. S. B. Meech and Hope Emily Allen, Early English Text Society 212 (London, 1940), pp. 38–40. In the early thirteenth century in the area of Liège, holy women were called some very unholy names, and an old Cistercian monk from the Abbey of Aulne, who doubted their sanctity, received an answer justifying their activities directly from the Holy Spirit: James of Vitry, *Vita B. Mariae Oigniacensis*, p. 548.

ble in human images, yet just, powerful, infinitely more glorious and complicated than any particular human vision of him. Moreover, the mystical alternative flourished as a complement to, not a contradiction of, the clerical role—and this in two senses: first, the visions mystical women received from Christ show admiration for the priest's authority; second, the mystical alternative to the authority of the priest gave Christians of both sexes an opportunity to express an ambivalence about power that was part of the Christian tradition. Despite the new prominence given to priest and eucharist and the fears of lay heterodoxy and antinomian or anti-sacerdotal challenges, the values of religious people in the thirteenth century were varied enough to affirm as well as to question many kinds of religious power. But the uneasiness of Mechtild of Magdeburg with the doctrines of sin and damnation and her awareness of the possibly heterodox implications of mysticism show that the varieties of thirteenth-century religious experience were not unlimited nor was the mystical role of women totally serene. In the nuns and beguines associated with the convent of Helfta in the 1270s, 1280s, and 1290s, we thus have in full view the strength and grandeur of female piety; we also find hints of the insecurity religious women could experience when not protected by wealth, rank, and long-established monastic traditions.

Epilogue

THE INTRODUCTION to a collection of essays is, in the nature of things, a conclusion. There is then no need for a conclusion here. Moreover, the method I have followed of beginning with images and then moving back into the experience of those individuals or groups that produce them makes generalization from one group to another unwarranted. But a perceptive reader, applying my own method to my prose, may notice certain images and figures of speech that occur repeatedly in my account. Perhaps therefore I should close by considering these and whatever more general interpretation they may imply.

In describing twelfth- and thirteenth-century spirituality I have spoken again and again of tension, ambivalence, paradox, but also (another way of saying the same thing) of balance and equilibrium. Underlying my analysis is the conviction that Christianity, like most religions, is fundamentally paradoxical: all medieval spiritualities therefore express both affirmation and rejection of the world, the flesh, and the institutions and rules they necessitate. These essays, however, argue something more. They see the period from 1050 to 1250 as, in a specific and special sense, a period of equilibrium or balance in spirituality.

In the mid-twelfth century, Herrad of Hohenbourg (or Landsberg) replaced the older equation of "religious person" with "monk" by a new depiction of human virtue. The figures in her illustration of the path toward God (see frontispiece) are not a series of monks, as they were in the iconographic tradition she inherited; they are the various statuses within the church: soldiers, lay women, clerics, nuns, monks, recluses, and hermits. Some twelfth-century writers pictured the variety of Christian roles more statically than Herrad, as rooms in a building or parts of a body; others made the steps toward God more psychological, seeing them as aspects of a developing person rather than as separate roles. But, taken together, these analyses and representations reflect the genius of twelfth- and thirteenth-century religiosity. For the most striking characteristic of Christianity between 1050 and 1250 is its ability to express new spiritual concerns and goals in new rules, institutions, and styles of life. This creativity was predicated upon optimism about the human being, created in God's image and therefore capable, by nature, of moving Godward. And because the God whom the individual dimly mirrored was both judge and lover, creator of rules as well as inspirer of hearts, the men and women moving toward him expressed their progress not just in personal outpourings but also in leadership, in the creation of institutions, in service of neighbor.

The twelfth-century ability to complement individual with community, personal growth with service of others, affectivity with authority, gave birth to the friars—a new role that solved many earlier ambivalences by explicitly combining renunciation of the world, through extreme personal poverty and penitence, with evangelism by example (or life) as well as by word. The creation of new orders, forbidden by the church at the Fourth Lateran Council (although ways were found around the prohibition), then slowed as the thirteenth century wore on. But the mysticism that continued to flourish as institutional creativity abated was not a rejection of church or community; its eucharistic emphasis, for example, contributed to the clericalization of the church already underway. Moreover, the growing affectivity in spirituality was not, at least in the thirteenth century, a replacement of God's power with a sense of his accessibility. Even the increasing feminization of religious language can be seen as arising at least in part from male and female responses to the charismatic alternative to clerical authority, an alternative that women especially embodied. The ultimate equilibrium that undergirded twelfth-century spirituality—a sense of a God of might and tenderness, who creates in his image human beings to serve and lead, as well as to love, each other—outlasted the equilibrium between group and self.

By the early fourteenth century, however, the balance was gone. Personal religious visions remained personal. What new groups there were existed on the fringes, rejecting vows, rules, and structures. Mystics began to speak of a freedom that bypassed church and sacraments, even if it did not reject them. Anthropomorphic descriptions of God stressed his mercy and humanity; the alternative to such descriptions stressed not might but unknowability.

The affectivity of the Cistercians, the regular canons' concern for edification, and the serene mysticism of the nuns of Helfta are thus products of a period of Christian history in which men's and women's conceptions of self and God combined, however ambivalently, authority with humility, leadership and service with love.

Appendix:
Monastic and Canonical
Treatises of Practical
Spiritual Advice

———

UNLESS OTHERWISE noted, the treatises are from the twelfth century and are listed in chronological order within each category (see chapter 1, n. 44 above).

Commentaries on the Benedictine Rule: Rupert of Deutz, *Super quaedam capitula regulae divi Benedicti abbatis*, PL 170: cols. 447–538. Peter the Deacon of Monte Cassino, *Expositio super regulam sancti Benedicti*, 3 books, in the monks of Monte Cassino, *Bibliotheca Casinensis* 5 (Monte Cassino, 1894), *Florilegium:* 82–165; and idem, *Explanatio brevis*, in ibid., pp. 165–74. Hildegard of Bingen, *Explanatio regulae sancti Benedicti*, PL 197: cols. 1053–66. Joachim of Flora, *Tractatus de vita sancti Benedicti et de officio secundum eius doctrinam*, in C. Baraut, "Un tratado inédito de Joaquín de Fiore: *De vita sancti Benedicti* . . . ," *Analecta sacra tarraconensia* 24 (1951): 33–122. Stephen of Paris, *Expositio super regulam beati Benedicti*, which I have consulted in MS Clm. 3029, fols. 1ʳ–161ʳ. [Commentary on the Benedictine Rule from Pontigny] (late twelfth or early thirteenth century) in MS Auxerre 50, fols. 1ʳ–125ʳ, portions of which have been published in C. H. Talbot, "A Cistercian Commentary on the Benedictine Rule," *Studia Anselmiana* 43, *Analecta monastica* 5 (1958): 102–59, and idem, "The Commentary on the Rule from Pontigny," *Studia monastica* 3 (1961): 77–122; my study of this commentary is based on Mr. Talbot's transcript of the entire work, which he very kindly lent to me.

Commentaries on the Augustinian Rule: [Anonymous, attributed to Hugh of St. Victor and Letbert of St. Rufus], *Expositio in regulam beati Augustini,* PL 176: cols. 881–924. Richard of St. Victor, *De questionibus regule sancti Augustini solutis,* in M. L. Colker, "Richard of St. Victor and the Anonymous of Bridlington," *Traditio* 18 (1962): 181–227. [Bridlington Anonymous or Robert of Bridlington], *The Bridlington Dialogue: An Exposition of the Rule of St. Augustine for the Life of the Clergy . . . ,* ed. A Religious of C.S.V.M. [Sister Penelope] (London, 1960). Adam of Dryburgh [or Adam Scot], *Liber de ordine, habitu et professione canonicorum ordinis praemonstratensis,* PL 198: cols. 439–610. Anonymous, Prologue and Preface *In regulam beati Augustini* (twelfth century), MS Vienna Nationalbibliothek 2207, fols. 8^v–16^v.

Monastic treatises for novices: John of Fruttuaria (†ca. 1050), *Liber de vitae ordine et morum institutione,* PL 184: cols. 559–84, portions of which have been reedited in André Wilmart, *Auteurs spirituels et textes dévots du moyen âge latin: études d'histoire littéraire* (Paris, 1932), pp. 93–98. Anonymous, *De novitiis instruendis* (twelfth or early thirteenth century), MS Douai 827, fols. 60^v–80^r, portions of which have been published in J. Leclercq, "Deux opuscules sur la formation des jeunes moines," RAM 33 (1957): 387–99. Adam of Perseigne, "Letter to Osmond," in *Lettres,* ed. J. Bouvet, 1, SC 66, Sér. mon. 4 (Paris, 1960): 110–29 (see also *Correspondance d'Adam, abbé de Perseigne [1188–1221],* ed. J. Bouvet, *Archives historiques du Maine* 13, fasc. 4 [1955], pp. 62–77 and PL 211: cols. 583–89); and "Letter to G. of Pontigny," PL 211: cols. 614–23 (see also *Correspondance, Archives du Maine* 13, fasc. 9 [1959], 503–23). Anonymous, *Instructio novitiorum secundum consuetudinem ecclesiae cantuariensis* (eleventh, twelfth, or thirteenth century), MS Corpus Christi College, Cambridge, 441, pp. 359b–391a, portions of which have been published in *The Monastic Constitutions of Lanfranc,* ed. D. Knowles (London, 1951), pp. 133–49. Stephen of Salley (or Sawley) (†1252), *Speculum novitii,* in Edmond Mikkers, "Un 'Speculum novitii' inédit d'Étienne de Salley," COCR 8 (1946): 17–68.

Canonical treatises for novices: Hugh of St. Victor, *De institutione novitiorum*, PL 176: cols. 925–52.

Monastic works parallel to commentaries and treatises for novices: Bernard of Clairvaux, *De gradibus humilitatis*, OB 3: 12–59, and Bernard, *De praecepto et dispensatione*, ibid., pp. 243–94. Peter Abelard, *Epistola 8*, in T. P. McLaughlin, "Abelard's Rule for Religious Women," *Mediaeval Studies* 18 (1956): 241–92. Peter the Deacon, *Exortatorium . . . ad monachos . . .*, in *Bibliotheca Casinensis 5, Florilegium*: 61–72. Aelred of Rievaulx, *Speculum caritatis, Opera omnia* 1: *Opera ascetica*, ed. A. Hoste and C.H. Talbot, CCCM 1 (Turnhout, 1971): 3–161. William of St. Thierry, *Epistola ad fratres de Monte Dei, Lettre aux frères du Mont-Dieu*, ed. Jean Déchanet, SC 223, Sér mon. 45 (Paris, 1975), pp. 131–384. Peter of Celle, *Tractatus de disciplina claustrali, L'École du cloître*, ed. Gérard de Martel, SC 240, Sér. mon. 47 (Paris, 1977), pp. 96–324. Guigo II, *Epistola de vita contemplativa (scala claustralium)* and *Meditationes*, in *Lettre sur la vie contemplative . . . et douze méditations*, ed. Edmund Colledge and James Walsh, SC 163, Sér. mon. 29 (Paris, 1970). Arnulf of Bohéries, *Speculum monachorum* (ca. 1200), PL 184: cols. 1175–178.

Canonical treatises parallel to commentaries and treatises for novices: [Anonymous, Compilation of texts relating to regular canons] (late eleventh or early twelfth century), MS Ottoboni Lat. 175 of the Vatican Library, portions of which are published in J. Leclercq, "Un témoignage sur l'influence de Grégoire VII dans la réforme canoniale," *Studi Gregoriani* 6 (1959–1961): 181–223. Peter [of Porto] (?), *Regula clericorum*, PL 163: cols. 703–84. Odo of St. Victor, *Epistolae de observantia canonicae professione recte praestanda*, PL 196: cols. 1399–1418. Hugh of Folieto (or Fouilloy), *De claustro animae*, PL 176: cols. 1017–182. Philip of Harvengt, *De institutione clericorum*, PL 203: cols. 665–1206.

General Index

Index of Secondary Authors